Black Political Organizations
in the Post–Civil Rights Era

Black Political Organizations in the Post–Civil Rights Era

edited by
Ollie A. Johnson III
Karin L. Stanford

Rutgers University Press
New Brunswick, New Jersey, and London

Library of Congress Cataloging-in-Publication Data

Black political organizations in the post-civil rights era / edited by
Ollie A. Johnson III and Karin L. Stanford.
    p.   cm.
    Includes bibliographical references and index.
    ISBN 0–8135–3139–X (alk. paper) — ISBN 0–8135–3140–3 (pbk. : alk. paper)
    1. African Americans—Politics and government—20th century. 2. African
Americans—Societies, etc. 3. African American leadership. 4. African American
political activists. I. Johnson, Ollie A., III 1962– II. Stanford, Karin L., 1961–

E185.615 .B5465 2003
324'.089'96073009046—dc21

                                                                    2002024835

British Cataloging-in-Publication data for this book is available from the British
Library.

Manufactured in the United States of America

To the memory of my mother, Marilyn "Polly" Williams
To my beloved sister, Kelly Ann Johnson
To my beautiful wife, Lori Sasai Robinson
—Ollie A. Johnson III

To those who dared to establish freedom institutions
And to Ashley, my genesis of miracles …
—Karin L. Stanford

Contents

Preface

The idea for this book was the result of a myriad of questions raised by students in American Politics and African American Politics classes. Although the students understood and celebrated the work of African American political organizations during the Civil Rights Movement, they were uncertain about their continued relevance, asking: What is the purpose of these organizations today? Do they really contribute to American society? Is the leadership of African American political organizations out of touch and ineffective? Their questions highlighted the need for serious analysis of African American political organizations in contemporary society.

Karin L. Stanford and F. Carl Walton began this project while they were both professors at the University of Georgia. Eventually, F. Carl Walton's academic and personal commitments required him to turn over coeditorship to Ollie A. Johnson III, who accepted the role enthusiastically. His students at the University of Maryland, College Park, embraced the project and made it their own. Graduate students Todd S. Burroughs, Lynne Gibson, Cedric K. Johnson, Tamelyn Tucker, and Donn C. Worgs provided outstanding research assistance and critical commentary on early versions of all the chapters.

We thank the National Conference of Black Political Scientists (NCOBPS) for its central role in the study of African American politics and for providing a supportive environment for the discussion of various chapters. We received important encouragement from senior NCOBPS scholars, especially Joseph McCormick, K. C. Morrison, Dianne M. Pinderhughes, and Linda F. Williams. We also thank the University of Maryland's African American Leadership Institute and its director, Ronald Walters, for logistical support and intellectual leadership. The institute has sponsored regular workshops, lectures, symposia, and other fora related to Black political organizations. The summer workshops in Washington, D.C., on the National Association for the Advancement of Colored People (NAACP [1996]), the National Urban League (NUL [1997]), and the Southern Christian Leadership Conference (SCLC [1998]) were especially useful in the preparation of this volume.

Finally, we would like to thank the contributors to this volume, whose research and writing have made this an educational and inspirational project. We appreciate your patience and diligence. We also thank professor Taylor Dark whose comments helped to improve the introduction. We extend gratitude to Marlie Wasserman, our editor at Rutgers University Press, for her professionalism and encouragement—and for believing in our project. We also express gratitude to our reviewers, who provided invaluable editorial suggestions.

Acknowledgments

My formal introduction to the study of Black politics, history, and culture occurred in the early 1980s at Brown University. Under the guidance of Professors Barry Beckham, Anani Dzidzienyo, Michael S. Harper, Rhett Jones, and
Wilson Moses, I majored in Afro-American Studies. These outstanding teachers and scholars convinced me that I should major in more than student activism. I thank them for their investment of time and energy in me.

My education in Africana Studies continued under the mentorship of schol-
ars and activists such as Paul Coates, David Covin, Sharon Harley, Charles
Henry, Charles E. Jones, Joseph McCormick, Michael Mitchell, K.C. Morrison,
June Murray, Dianne Pinderhughes, Don Rojas, Robert C. Smith, Ronald
Walters, Linda Williams, the late Rhonda Williams, Francille Wilson, and Ernest
Wilson. These friends have not only a commitment to the liberation of our
people but to peace and social justice for all people. Their personal and pro-
fessional support has been appreciated.

I believe that my initial interest in Black politics resulted from my youth in
Atlantic City, New Jersey. At eight years old I was reading revolutionary Black
Panther poetry on telephone poles around the Stanley Holmes Village. My family facilitated my youth membership in the National Association for the Advancement of Colored People, generally tolerated my growing interest in
fundamental social change, and supported my independent study and travel.
A large and loving family is truly a gift from God.

OLLIE A. JOHNSON III

While working on this volume, I had several tumultuous experiences
that changed the very core of my perspective on life. I was diagnosed with

breast cancer in 1997 and underwent chemotherapy and radiation. Later, I was subjected to the kind of public scrutiny about my private life which caused me to question whether or not I would continue my research, writing, and publishing endeavors. Yet, with the help of God, through sheer perseverance and the belief in the righteousness of my ancestors' struggles, I vowed to continue the work I enjoy—to expose the struggles and rich legacy of African Americans, women, and others who have suffered from oppression. This work is a symbol of my resistance.

I am personally very grateful for the support of my family. The encouragement of my grandparents, parents, siblings, aunts, uncles, and cousins has sustained me. I could not have completed this volume without their support. My personal survival was dependent on the dedication, skill, and compassion of several African American physicians. I extend sincere gratitude to Dr. Robert DeWitty, Dr. Martin Dukes, Dr. John McKnight, and Dr. Pamela Randolph-Bailey. I am also indebted to my colleagues and friends who read and offered suggestions on my Wall Street Project paper. In that regard I would like to thank publicly Lorenzo Morris, Maurice Carney, Simone Green, Joe Davidson, and Valerie Johnson, whose wisdom and insight helped shape the end product. Thanks also to my assistant, Christina Miller, who provided editorial and logistical support, and to Thandisizwe Chimurenga, who provided editorial support, technical assistance, and much-needed laughter. And, finally, I am very appreciative of the friends who have provided balance and unconditional love. Collins Allan, Robyn and Ed Cook, Vanessa and Hassan Hirsi, Stephanie Jones, Kathleen O'Neil, Harry Martin, and James Simmons—you are my heroes and sheroes.

KARIN L. STANFORD

*Black Political Organizations
in the Post–Civil Rights Era*

Ollie A. Johnson III and Karin L. Stanford

Introduction

The Relevance of Black Political Organizations in the Post–Civil Rights Era

Prior to the 1960s most African Americans were denied their basic civil and human rights. The right to vote, the right to protest peacefully, the right to a fair trial, the right to live without fear of state violence, and the rights to live, work, study, and travel were routinely violated by government officials and their allies. The success of the Civil Rights Movement changed that reality and led to important socioeconomic and political changes in the United States. The Civil Rights Act of 1964, the Voting Rights Act of 1965, and related legislation created more opportunities for African Americans to succeed in education, employment, politics, entertainment, and other fields. Blacks gained legal integration and access into American politics. The American political system was further democratized, and Blacks gained rights that had been previously denied.

Despite these positive developments, Black America continues to suffer from discrimination, poverty, and inequality.[1] Moreover, the wealth gap between Blacks and Whites is much greater than racial differences in income, education, and other social indicators.[2] Many substantive aspects of the old racial regime such as discrimination, police brutality, sexism, and unemployment plague the post–Civil Rights era.[3]

More than any other segment of American society, Black political groups have worked to eliminate these problems. Given the multiplicity and variety of challenges facing Blacks, it should not be surprising that historically a myriad of political organizations have addressed distinct and only partially overlapping concerns. While progress has been made on some fronts, the general struggle for Black advancement continues.

1

The post–Civil Rights period of the 1970s, 1980s, and 1990s witnessed un-precedented opportunities for African Americans in education, employment, housing, and politics. As a result, Blacks became more visible in American universities, businesses, suburbs, and political office. Black organizations encouraged their members and communities to take advantage of this new access to previously closed sectors of the American experience. Nonetheless, Black political organizations, particularly those active during the Civil Rights Movement, have come under increasing scrutiny. Questions of accountability, structure, and relevance have surrounded these organizations since the end of the modern Civil Rights Movement. Examples of the validity of such concerns occurred in the 1990s, when Rev. Benjamin Chavis was fired as executive director of the National Association for the Advancement of Colored People (NAACP) over the misuse of organizational funds; Rev. Henry Lyons, former president of the National Baptist Convention (NBC), was convicted of grand theft and racketeering charges; calls were made for a public financial accounting of the Rainbow/PUSH Coalition; and the leadership skills of Martin Luther King III as executive director of the Southern Christian Leadership Coalition were criticized publicly.

Conflicting Views on Black Organizations

Prominent Black political organizations in the post–Civil Rights era have not received sufficient attention from scholars. Discussions of these organizations take place primarily in Black newspapers and magazines, which generally consist of updates on their activities and anecdotal information. The vast literature on American interest groups rarely delves deeply into Black groups. The NAACP, NAACP Legal and Educational Defense Fund, and other majority Black organizations usually are mentioned as a side note to important political events such as the defeat of Supreme Court nominee Judge Robert Bork. Since Black groups generally do not have large staffs, great financial resources, and extensive lobbying operations, they are neglected in most recent texts on American interest groups.[4]

Nevertheless, two recent books focus on Black political organizations and reach divergent conclusions. In *We Have No Leaders* Robert C. Smith argues that Black leaders and their organizations have been ineffective in representing and promoting Black interests in the last three decades. He identifies limited resources, incompetent leaders, and misguided strategies as key factors characterizing African American organizations. Smith strongly criticizes Black groups for being dependent on White philanthropy and passive on the issue of Black poverty. From his perspective Black groups and leaders have lacked innovation and courage. They have failed to pursue the radical and egalitarian public policies necessary to uplift all of Black America.[5]

Dona Cooper Hamilton and Charles V. Hamilton examine the social welfare policies of Civil Rights organizations during this century in *The Dual Agenda*. They emphasize that Civil Rights groups have always fought for Civil Rights and full employment for all Americans. The Hamiltons note that, rather than acting in narrow ways to benefit Blacks exclusively, the leading Black organizations have generally advocated equal economic opportunities for all American citizens and the elimination of poverty. For ideological and pragmatic reasons, Civil Rights groups have consistently (from the 1930s to the 1990s) defended social welfare policies that would incorporate the poor into the regular economy with real jobs provided by the private or public sector. The NAACP, the National Urban League (NUL), and other groups also learned over time that formal race-neutral policies were regularly distorted by the racism of White government officials, employers, and union leaders.[6]

Political organizations can be examined according to numerous criteria.[7] The origins, ideology, internal structure, membership, goals, coalitions, impact, general programs, and decline are some of the aspects discussed in this book. The contributors were not required to examine any specific dimensions of Black organizational life. As a result, the chapters are diverse in their content and style. Robert Smith's essay on the NAACP emphasizes the critical importance of history and ideology, while the essays on Congress of Racial Equality (CORE) and the Nation of Islam accentuate the fundamental role of leadership. This volume acknowledges the diversity of Black organizations and challenges scholars to research more thoroughly the structure, activities, and external environment of existing groups.

Internal Organization

Robert Michels and other proponents of elite theory argue that, regardless of organizational structure, leaders will attempt to increase their power and influence through multiple means.[8] Michels believed in the "Iron Law of Oligarchy," which held that, because organizations required leadership, they inevitably would create or recreate hierarchical and unequal internal structures. According to this view, leaders generally act on psychological and organizational imperatives to enhance and consolidate their positions often at the expense of their organizations. Michels studied European socialist parties, especially the German Social Democratic Party, at the turn of the last century. He reasoned that, if the most democratic and egalitarian political parties reproduced "oligarchical" behaviors and structures, it followed logically that more conservative groups with no principled commitment to democracy and equality would also create many antidemocratic features. The relevance of elite theory can be seen in a parallel between Michels's cases and Black political organizations. Throughout American political history Black groups have often been among those organizations fighting most valiantly for democracy and equality. While Michels exaggerated the universality of his "law," his analysis does assist in understanding Black political organizations.[9]

African American political organizations are generally structured in ways that give high-ranking officials substantial authority and influence. For most leading groups, a chief executive officer has primary responsibility for the day-to-day operations, while a board of directors or trustees has responsibility for selecting the chief executive and ensuring ultimate organizational effectiveness. Board members and chief executives are rarely elected directly by the general members. The boards usually select their own members, and in some cases board members are appointed by the CEO. This type of internal structure has obvious strengths and weaknesses. If leaders are honest, competent, and effective, they can provide many years of dedicated and honorable service. This was the general perception of the period from 1920 to 1977, when the NAACP was led by James Weldon Johnson, Walter White, and Roy Wilkins. For most of those years they led the NAACP with the strong support of the board of directors, mass members, and the Black public.[10]

Organizations with strong leaders often find it difficult to hold leaders accountable to formal guidelines and behavioral standards. As Max Weber noted, religion is often a source of charismatic authority. Charismatic leaders usually provide strong leadership. The Rev. Dr. Martin Luther King Jr., one of America's most charismatic leaders, was able to lead the Southern Christian Leadership Conference (SCLC) to national prominence based upon his strategic vision, his oratorical ability, and his courageous leadership. Charismatic leaders can inspire their members to make great personal sacrifices to achieve desired ends. Yet, when such leaders are misguided, they can severely weaken an organization. Rev. Henry Lyons shook the faith of many members of the Black church by the degree of his criminality. Yet, because of his charisma, the NBC organizational structure, and other factors, Reverend Lyons had the support of the board until he resigned. Newspaper investigative accounts and court proceedings made a persuasive case that Lyons had stolen hundreds of thousands of dollars and lied repeatedly about his illegal behavior. Despite these revelations, Lyons seemed prepared to run for and win reelection to the presidency of the NBC. Many leading ministers initially defended his tenure and minimized his improprieties.[11] During the height of the Civil Rights Movement, however, several activists, including veteran organizer and SCLC member Ella Baker, offered insightful analysis into the pitfalls of charismatic leadership and concentrating too much power in top leaders.[12]

Leadership, Ideology, and Programs

Despite occasional scandals and internal struggles, Black political organizations have been the Black community's strongest advocates and defenders. Following the passage of the 1960s Civil Rights legislation, these groups mobilized their resources to guarantee implementation of the new federal and local laws. Despite the fact that these laws were challenged by most racist and White supremacist officials in the country, Black political groups worked to ensure that Blacks effectively gained their new rights: the right to vote, the right to a decent education, the right to fair housing, and the right to live free from racial discrimination. Where these rights were violated, Civil Rights groups protested and took the violators to court.[13]

While the struggle for Civil Rights united advocacy groups, their achievement contributed to a loosening of the bonds of unity. For example, SCLC's Martin Luther King Jr. came to believe firmly that desegregation and voting rights were not enough. Economic rights and resources were also necessary for Black freedom. King therefore called for a Poor People's Campaign to call the country's attention to poverty and mobilize government and private sector resources to eliminate it. Other Civil Rights organizations such as the NAACP, however, did not share SCLC's commitment to the use of protest, confrontation, and mobilization.[14] Bayard Rustin, a prominent Civil Rights leader, and others advocated a shift "from protest to politics."[15] They believed that the achievement of legal equality required that Blacks begin to pursue jobs, contracts, appointments, and other goals through the traditional means of coalition politics—that is, negotiating, logrolling, and electing sympathetic representatives.

The late 1960s and the early 1970s represented a period of major debate, dispute, and protest within Black America. By 1967 King had become one of the strongest critics of the American war in Vietnam. In his eloquent fashion King described the U.S. government "as the greatest purveyor of violence in the world today." Civil Rights leaders such as the NAACP's Roy Wilkins strongly opposed King's antiwar efforts. Wilkins believed that King, the Student Nonviolent Coordinating Committee (SNCC), and other Black antiwar activists were jeopardizing President Lyndon B. Johnson's support for implementing Civil Rights legislation.[16]

The Vietnam War and the Nixon presidency (1969–1974) widened the gap between public policies supported by the mainstream Civil Rights groups and those advocated by more radical and revolutionary Black activists. After King's assassination in April 1968, angrier Black voices gained more attention. For a few years prominent young leaders such as Stokely Carmichael, Huey P. Newton, and Angela Davis were viewed as formidable foes to the traditional organizations and agenda-setting processes in Black communities. Through local organizing and access to the media, these radical leaders demanded not simply Civil Rights but human rights, Black power, and socialism. They demanded an immediate end to violence against Blacks, a radical restructuring of the American economy, and solidarity with socialist leaders such as Fidel Castro and Ho Chi Minh.[17]

The new Black voices articulated a more fundamental critique of American society and politics. They were supportive of radical solutions. At various times Black Power leaders called for a new constitutional convention, a mass migration of Blacks to Africa, government ownership of the means of production, reparations for Blacks, and the creation of a majority Black country (New Africa) inside the southeastern part of the United States. The NAACP, NUL, SCLC, and other Black organizations disagreed with these demands; indeed, traditional Civil Rights leaders were shocked to see that many of their former youth leaders and members supported these ideas. Many members of SNCC, CORE, and other organizations who had registered voters, integrated facilities, and otherwise participated in the nonviolent Civil Rights Movement in the South were now questioning the basic institutions of the country rather than merely demanding access and reform.[18]

In response to these radical demands, mainstream Black groups defended their work and credentials. They reminded their young critics that they had been involved in the Black struggle for decades, not a few months or years. The tension between advocates of moderate versus radical changes continued throughout the post–Civil Rights era.[19] As the Black Power Movement declined, by the late 1970s, the mainstream organizations regained prominence and visibility. Now, however, Black organizations had to share public leadership with a new and growing group: Black elected officials.

In the last several decades Black political organizations and politicians have struggled together to make governmental institutions more responsive to Black interests. In terms of public policy, Black leaders have been generally more liberal than their colleagues. They have advocated more governmental intervention in the economy to produce jobs and reduce poverty. They are also outspoken critics of police brutality, racial discrimination and profiling, and limited educational and professional opportunities.[20] While representatives of the Congressional Black Caucus, Black church, and national Civil Rights organizations were generally the most visible Black leaders in the 1980s and 1990s, conservative Black groups emerged to characterize their activities as outdated and counterproductive. Black conservative intellectuals and politicians such as Thomas Sowell, Clarence Thomas, and J. C. Watts have criticized traditional Civil

Rights leaders for supporting special "quotas" for Blacks in jobs, college admissions, and government contracts. Black conservatives have also accused Black liberals of abandoning the Civil Rights dream of a "color-blind" America and contributing to racial tension and conflict by their continued racial advocacy.

In sum, Black Civil Rights groups have developed various programs and supported diverse policies to improve the socioeconomic and political situation of Blacks. From their perspective government can and must play a positive role in creating social change. Black radicals were highly critical of U.S. domestic and foreign policies and skeptical of the new group of Black elected officials. Black conservatives argued that, by supporting affirmative action and other alleged divisive policies after the Civil Rights Movement had ended, traditional Black leaders became more self-interested and misguided.

External Context of Black Political Activity

Blacks are a numerical minority in the United States. Since the 1960s Blacks have represented approximately 12 percent of the population. Given the country's history of race relations and Black minority status, developments outside the Black community have always had major consequences for African Americans. In the post–Civil Rights era several trends have influenced the context within which Black groups operate.

First, in many respects there has been a conservative drift in American politics. Since 1968 the Republican Party has elected four of the last six presidents. In addition, the presidency of Ronald Reagan from 1981 to 1989 promoted conservative values and policies opposed by most national Black leaders. President Reagan emphasized a strong military, appointed conservative judges and justices, and criticized many social service programs as fostering citizen dependence on government. Vice President George Bush followed Reagan as president. During this twelve-year period of Republican control of the White House, Black conservatives gained increasing visibility and prominence as administration officials and appointees. For example, Clarence Thomas held several political and judicial positions and was eventually appointed to the Supreme Court in 1991. In 1994 the Republicans gained control of the House of Representatives for the first time in more than forty years. Led by Representative Newt Gingrich, the Republicans were seen as hostile by most Black national leaders and members of Congress. Even with the election of Democrat Bill Clinton to the White House in 1992, many Black leaders were disappointed that Clinton supported many policies on welfare, crime, and foreign affairs favored by the centrist Democratic Leadership Council.[21]

Second, formal and legal White racism has declined. Survey research confirms that Whites have become less racist than they were four decades ago.[22] Whites are less hostile to the idea of living near Blacks, less supportive of discrimination against Blacks, and more supportive of equal rights and opportunities for Blacks. These attitudinal changes have accompanied the dismantling of the worst features of racial segregation in the country. The formal and separate facilities that were targets of the Civil Rights Movement no longer exist. In the South the schools, restaurants, hotels, bathrooms, and neighborhoods that denied access to Blacks no longer discriminate in the same way. Outside the South Blacks have also gained impressive access to leading universities and professions. There are currently more Black physicians, lawyers, engineers, university professors, and elected officials than in any point in American history.[23]

Third, despite the decline in formal White racism and important Black group progress in the economic, political, and cultural arenas, Blacks still experience daily racism, discrimination, and violence. In this respect African Americans continue to confront their main historical and contemporary problem: de facto White supremacy. In his important comparative research historian George Fredrickson has defined White supremacy as "the attitudes, ideologies, and policies associated with the rise of blatant forms of white or European dominance over 'nonwhite' populations. In other words, it involves making invidious distinctions of a socially crucial kind that are based primarily, if not exclusively, on physical characteristics and ancestry."[24] While formal White racism has been made illegal, the informal and substantive dimensions of racism have persisted in various guises. Joe R. Feagin and Hernan Vera define *White racism* as "the socially organized set of attitudes, ideas, and practices that deny African Americans and other people of color the dignity, opportunities, freedom, and rewards that this nation offers white Americans."[25]

Several incidents occurred in the 1990s which illustrate the most recent public face of White supremacy and White racism—for instance, the case of Susan Smith, a young White woman who falsely accused a Black man of kidnapping her two sons. This report quickly gained national coverage and the American people's sympathy. Nine days after her initial report, however, Smith admitted that she had drowned her own kids in a lake and fabricated the abduction story.[26] In June 1998 three White supremacists kidnapped, tortured, and murdered James Byrd, a local Black man in Jasper, Texas. And in February 1999 four White undercover police officers in New York City shot Amadou Diallo, an unarmed West African immigrant, to death as he stood on his doorstep. The officers claimed that it was a case of mistaken identity. During that time New York mayor Rudolph Giuliani and police commissioner Howard Safir refused to criticize the police officers. Black leaders and political groups, led by the

Rev. Al Sharpton, president of the National Action Network, organized rallies to protest police brutality, excessive use of lethal force, and government insensitivity to Black citizens. After a change of venue the four police officers were tried and acquitted of murdering Diallo.

Unfortunately, there is also the widespread practice of racism by mainstream institutions and professionals in such areas as education, housing, health care, and financing.[27] As a result, Blacks suffer a racial tax. They often pay more for homes, apartments, cars, and medical treatment. In fact, in the areas of consumption and commerce which have variable pricing, Blacks are often charged more than Whites for equivalent goods and services. In addition, Blacks have faced great obstacles in entering the most elite arenas of American business, politics, and culture. Blacks are conspicuous by their absence in the top rungs of major corporations.[28]

Finally, Blacks live in a country that is more racially and ethnically diverse than it was three decades ago. The Latino and Asian populations have increased throughout the country but particularly in the West, Southwest, and some major cities. These population dynamics have created opportunities for political cooperation and conflict. Advocacy groups from the Black, Latino, and Asian communities often unite in support of antidiscrimination laws as members from all groups tend to be victims of racial violence. On the other hand, attempts at "people of color" multiracial and multiethnic electoral campaigns have not always been successful. For example, in the recent mayoral election in Los Angeles most Black leaders supported the centrist White candidate James Hahn over the more progressive Latino candidate Antonio Villaraigosa. Issues related to immigration, language, and access to public services continue to be challenges to coalition building for urban and suburban communities.

Purpose and Overview

This book provides an analysis of the goals, strategies, and activities of Black political organizations and leaders in contemporary America. The volume focuses on the organizations active in the Civil Rights Movement such as the NAACP, NUL, National Council of Negro Women (NCNW), CORE, and SCLC as well as more recent groups such as the Rainbow/PUSH Coalition. The contributors examine how important organizations and institutions have responded to the new political, economic, and social realities of the post–Civil Rights era (1970s–1990s). The authors address ideological, strategic, and policy shifts within Black political organizations. They also explore the nature of organizational membership, leadership, goals, resources, and coalitions. As a result, the chapters examine the historical significance as well as the contemporary relevance of each group. This book attempts to contribute to a better understanding of specific Black organizations and leaders and emphasize the need for much additional research.

Black religious organizations have often served as the backbone of the Black political struggle. Allison Calhoun-Brown offers an analytical overview of the Black church, one of the Black community's most important institutions. Calhoun-Brown reviews how scholars have explained the church's political involvement based on the existing social environment, available political resources, and prominent theological frameworks. The Black church continues to play a fundamental institutional role in the lives of Black people in the United States. Calhoun-Brown argues, however, that in the post–Civil Rights era, because of limited capacity, the church has not maintained its vanguard role in the contemporary Black freedom struggle.

Robert C. Smith analyzes the constraints facing the NAACP in the twenty-first century. Smith reminds us that White racism is alive and well, although it now often assumes a more informal, sophisticated, and disguised form compared to its widespread, explicit, and institutional manifestations in the pre–1960s era. In addition, Smith notes that the Republican majority in Congress as well as a more conservative federal judiciary have not been supportive of NAACP concerns. Finally, Smith argues that the NAACP does not have the financial resources and professional lobbyists that other national interest groups have to pursue their interests in Washington, D.C., and around the country.

The National Urban League has helped Blacks adjust to city life for almost a century. The organization recognized early that Blacks faced multiple problems as they migrated from the rural South to the major urban centers of the North. Jennifer A. Wade and Brian N. Williams emphasize that the NUL has always focused on the social and economic concerns of Blacks. This focus on social services, job training, employment, and education has often prompted criticism that the League was not committed to Civil Rights protest. Wade and Williams show how Whitney Young in the 1960s was able to combine the traditional mission of the NUL with a more visible concern for Civil Rights. The authors recommend Young's servant leadership style as a guide for the NUL as it looks to increase its effectiveness in the twenty-first century.

Women have not received enough attention as leaders and members of Black political organizations. Erika L. Gordon contributes to filling this gap in her chapter on Black women's community work. This chapter is a rare scholarly study of one of the oldest Civil Rights organizations in the country. Her investigation documents the many community development programs that Black women have engaged in and continue to sustain in Washington, D.C., and around the country. The numerous tutoring, mentoring, education, health care, social networking, and economic support programs of organizations such as the NCNW have generally gone unacknowledged by scholars. Gordon conceptualizes these programs as "political" and contextualizes them as an integral part of the African American struggle for freedom and equality.

Charles E. Jones documents the dramatic decline of the Congress of Racial Equality. A former leader in the Civil Rights Movement, CORE is now a shadow of its former self. Jones argues that CORE was unable to maintain its effectiveness during the transition from the Civil Rights era to the post–Civil Rights era. Internal power struggles, financial difficulties, and questionable leadership decisions reduced the organization's visibility and activity. When the dust settled, Roy Innis had gained supreme control of the group and combined Black power rhetoric with neoconservative policy positions. CORE now operates a small office in New York City and is identified with conservative politicians in the Republican Party.

The Nation of Islam is one of the most controversial Black organizations of the post–Civil Rights era. Claude A. Clegg III illuminates the secretive organization through a penetrating study of its current leader, Minister Louis Farrakhan. Clegg focuses on Farrakhan's visibility in national American politics since the early 1980s. In 1984 Farrakhan supported the Rev. Jesse Jackson's candidacy for the presidential nomination of the Democratic Party. Farrakhan could not have fully anticipated the sustained and bitter attacks that he would receive from the mainstream media, diverse Jewish groups, and even some Black politicians as a result of his formal participation in the American political process. Clegg's analysis is especially enlightening about Farrakhan's evolving relationship with major Black political leaders and his performative style of leadership.

The Southern Christian Leadership Conference has been linked inextricably to its most famous founder and leader, the Rev. Dr. Martin Luther King Jr. Since King's death in 1968, the organization has continued the struggle for Civil Rights and equality. F. Carl Walton examines the SCLC's activity since the late 1960s. He maintains that the group has lacked a clear focus and agenda, which has reduced its effectiveness in the post–Civil Rights era.

Karin L. Stanford examines the economic strategies and programs of the Rev. Jesse L. Jackson within SCLC, Operation PUSH, Rainbow Coalition, and the Rainbow/PUSH Coalition. Stanford finds the roots of Jackson's economic thinking in the Civil Rights Movement, especially SCLC's "Operation Breadbasket" program. Her analysis suggests that Jackson has been more dynamic and successful than other leaders in adapting to changes resulting from the demise of formal Jim Crow segregation. Jackson and his various organizations have consistently emphasized that African Americans and other people of color do not receive their fair share of the opportunities, income, and wealth generated by the American economy. In this time of unprecedented prosperity the Rainbow/PUSH Coalition has opened an office on Wall Street, the financial capital of the country, to call attention to the need for American corporations and businesses to diversify their ownership, management, and boards of directors.

Todd C. Shaw also highlights the unsung roles of Black women in political struggles of the last thirty years. Shaw shows that welfare rights and antipoverty activism has persisted in various organizational forms. The National Welfare Rights Organization and the National Welfare Rights Union, among other groups, consist of a dedicated group of working-class women and men who maintain that no American should live and work in poverty. Through local and national protests these activists have attempted to influence government social policy. Hostile public opinion and growing support for concepts such as "workfare" have made it increasingly difficult for activists to achieve their goals of more generous welfare payments, education programs, adequate job training, and decent jobs.

Most chapters in this volume examine specific Black political organizations. Yet Akwasi B. Assensoh and Yvette Alex-Assensoh offer a brief review of Black political leadership. The Assensohs argue that Black leaders generally underestimate the social diversity within the Black community. According to the authors, if Black leaders direct more attention to the concerns of Blacks who are foreign-born, homosexuals, Republicans, women, and non-Protestants, they would be more effective in addressing and solving some of the socioeconomic and political problems plaguing African Americans. These "minority groups" within Black America have resources and skills that Black leaders should draw upon more directly in the fight against poverty, inequality, discrimination, and other issues.

Valerie Johnson concludes the book with an analysis of Black issue articulation in the post–Civil Rights era by contrasting the strategies of mainstream Black political organizations with those of Black nationalist and radical organizations. Johnson's chapter also offers suggestions on how Black political organizations can revive their commitment to eliminating racial and economic inequality.

Overall, the authors in this volume make a solid contribution to our understanding of Black political organizations, institutions, and leadership in the post–Civil Rights era. The chapters demonstrate that over the past three decades Black political activists have continued their centuries-old struggle to improve the political, social, and economic situation of Black people. Why does this struggle persist? In short, because racial discrimination, inequality, and oppression persist despite the valiant efforts of many Americans to move beyond the hard legacy of racial slavery, segregation, and prejudice. Although this book focuses on the neglected topic of Black political organizations, it must be kept in mind that most of these organizations have, or at least are open to, participation from members of other racial and ethnic groups. For example, Whites, Latinos, Asian Americans, Native Americans, and others attend Black churches, are members of the NAACP, and contribute to the NUL's programs.

Among themselves and with external forces, Black political organizations and activists have debated the question of how best to define and advance the interests of their community in the post–Civil Rights period. Given the complexity of American culture and the American political system, readers should not be surprised that many different types of Black organizations have flourished. Even though opportunities for participation in the American political system have expanded dramatically since the 1960s, both subtle and explicit challenges to Black progress remain. Sexism, poverty, intolerance, homophobia, violence, and the unfortunate concentration of political and economic power are some of the historic and contemporary obstacles to collective Black advancement. As long as these problems exist, Black political organizations will remain relevant.

One

Allison Calhoun-Brown

Will the Circle Be Unbroken?

The Political Involvement of Black Churches since the 1960s

The Black church is unique among Civil Rights organizations in that it is not a single organization, nor was it founded with the express purpose of addressing racism and discrimination. *Black church* is a term that aggregates all predominantly Black Christian congregations whose primary purpose is to meet the spiritual needs of their parishioners. Yet perhaps no institution has been more central to the Black community or done more to uplift the race. The fact that thousands of disparate groupings can be referenced with meaning as a single unit is a testament to the integral role that the church has played.

Chronicling the origins of the Civil Rights Movement, Aldon Morris concluded that the Black church functioned as the "organizational hub of Black life" and as the "institutional center" of the Civil Rights Movement.[1] This was not a new role. In large part due to the exigencies and indignities of slavery, for many people the Black church antedated even the Black home and family. This fact alone bears witness to the special place that the Black church has had in its community. W. E. B. Du Bois noted that "this institution peculiarly is the expression of the inner life of a people in a sense seldom true elsewhere."[2] E. Franklin Frazier contended that the enslavement of African people, because of the organization of labor and the extreme forms of social control, destroyed the possibility of social cohesion based on traditional African kinship or any system (e.g., common language) which may have emerged on plantations but for slavery. According to Frazier, the Christian religion provided a new basis for social cohesion.[3]

While other scholars such as Gayraud Wilmore have rejected the degree

14

to which Frazier believes slavery destroyed social cohesion and African culture, few dispute the pivotal role the church has played in the very survival of African American people. Indeed, Benjamin E. Mays and Joseph Nicholson identified the Christian religion as a technique that the slaves developed to mitigate the dehumanization that they were forced to endure. This function continued long after slavery had ended, with the church providing a wide array of educational, social, business, and political opportunities.[4] The church became the center of community life, and the preacher became the leader of the community. Writing in the 1940s, Gunnar Myrdal observed that "the chief function of the Negro church has been to buoy up the hopes of its members in the face of adversity and to give them a sense of community."[5] He asserted that this role was unique to Black churches because so many other channels of activity outside the church were closed. In the colder and more critical words of Mays and Nicholson, "It is not too much to say that if the Negro had experienced a wide range of freedom in the social and economic spheres, there would have been . . . fewer Negro churches."[6]

Nonetheless, the reality is that for the vast majority of African Americans opportunities were severely constricted. As the result of the elimination of Black people from the political life of the American mainstream, the Black church became the main arena of their political and social activities. According to Eric C. Lincoln and Lawrence Mamiya, "It has no challenger as the cultural womb of the Black community."[7] Most forms of musical, artistic, and dramatic expression as well as colleges, banks, insurance companies, low-income housing, and political leadership find their genesis in the Black church. Writing in 1964, E. Franklin Frazier asserted that "for the Negro masses in their social and moral isolation in American society the Negro church community has been a nation within a nation."[8] And, when the subnation called for integration, it was the Black church that "provided the ideological framework through which passive attitudes were transformed into a collective consciousness supportive of collective action."[9]

This collective action resulted in significant changes for the Black community and for American society, culminating in the passage of the Civil Rights Act of 1964 and the Voting Rights Act of 1965, both of which substantially ended the codification of racism in the United States. These laws, at least formally, laid the basis for the full integration of African Americans into mainstream society. As Robert C. Smith observed in this new legal framework, protest politics began to decline and institutionalized political behavior became the dominant form of Black politics.[10]

But what has been the role of the Black church in sociopolitical movements with the institutionalization of political behavior since the 1970s? How has the church adapted to this new context and to the different dynamic of mobilization which accompanies it? Does it still serve as the organizational hub of Black life or as the institutional center of sociopolitical movement in the African American community? Are new organizations, new leadership, different tactics, and novel ideas needed to bring about the contemporary changes that African Americans seek? The major thesis of this chapter is that the role that African American churches play in politics has diminished since the 1960s not because churches are unwilling to participate but because declines in important political resources over the last thirty years have diminished their capacity.

Models of Black Church Influence

While the centrality of the Black church to the Black community is widely accepted, a debate exists within the literature on two questions. The first question is whether or not the parallel nature of Black church society has been a positive or negative development. The second question is whether the church has always been a willing and effective representative of the social and political desires of the Black community. Several models of Black church influence reflect the diversity of perspective with regard to the secular role of the African American church.

The assimilation-isolation model sees the Black church as a hindrance to the assimilation of Blacks into the larger American society. While the church has offered opportunities denied by the larger society, its undemocratic patterns of control and organization, otherworldly orientation, and the apathy often associated with lower socioeconomic groups impede social action and political participation, and thus the church is rendered "involuntarily isolated" from the kind of power that brings about change.[11]

Hart Nelsen and Anne K. Nelsen see the Black church in a markedly better light. Their "ethnic community prophetic" model highlights the capacity of Black churches to increase group consciousness in the African American community. Recent research by Allison Calhoun-Brown and Fredrick Harris has further defined the nature of this relationship. Group consciousness has been found to be a basis for collective action and increased political participation.[12] From this perspective the church builds community and in the process supports the fight for racial justice by providing not only its institutional resources but a psychological base for action as well.

In proposing the "dialectic model," Lincoln and Mamiya attempt to reconcile these perspectives. They assert that the error of previous schemes is that they have not appreciated the dynamic nature of the orientation of the African American church toward social action. A dialectic holds polar opposites in tension, constantly shifting between the polarities over time. They identify six dialectics in which the church is involved for which no synthesis exists: priestly versus prophetic functions; otherworldly versus this-worldly orientation; the universalism versus particularism of the Christian message; the communal versus privatistic nature of church involvement in the affairs of parishioners; charismatic versus bureaucratic organizational styles; and resistance versus accommodation to the larger society. The balance that the church adopts on these dialectics determines its willingness to be involved in social action at any given point in time.[13]

The dialectic model is helpful in understanding Wilmore's paradoxical comment that the Black church has been simultaneously "the 'most conservative' and the 'most radical' institution. The dialectic model offers a context for scholars such as Gary Marx who found an inverse relationship between the intensity of religious belief and practice and degree of political activism. The dialectic aids in the comprehension of Adolph Reed Jr.'s chapter "The Mythology of the Church in Contemporary Afro-American Politics," in which he asserts that the connection of the church with the development of politics in the Black community is almost a complete invention.[14] This model is useful because it suggests that different people will come to different conclusions about the level of sociopolitical involvement by the Black church depending on the time and focus of their analysis.

The attractiveness of the dialectic model is that it recognizes that the relationship between religion and society is not static. The central question then becomes, however, what holds the polarities in dynamic tension? What leads the church to more activist stances? Is the balance an act of institutional will, or are there other factors that structure these choices? Many assert that since the Civil Rights Movement the sociopolitical role of African American churches has changed. What are the determinants of this new positioning?

Determinants of Black Church Involvement

The 1950s and 1960s represent the apex of Black church involvement in social and political action. Leading explanations for why the Black church was so influential during this time period do not emphasize the will of the church to act but, instead, highlight its capacity to act. Anthony Oberschall's resource mobilization explanation, Douglas McAdam's political process model, and Aldon Morris's indigenous perspective all focus on the conditions that promote an activist church.[15] Taken together, these theories suggest three basic determinants of capacity: a conducive political environment, resources with which to exploit opportunities, and a theology aimed at alleviating social ills. By evaluating the state of these factors in the 1990s, one can come to a better understanding of the contemporary sociopolitical role of the African American church.

Political Environment

The role that any institution comes to play does not emerge in a vacuum. As Robert Putnam has observed, historical circumstances help to determine if institutions will act as resources for political engagement. Tracing the history of the Black church's sociopolitical involvement, Harris notes the importance of different opportunity structures to the development of the resources most identified with the church and political mobilization.[16] Indeed, Lincoln and Mamiya assert that churches move "back and forth [on the dialectic continuum] in response to certain issues or social conditions."[17] And, according to Eisinger, "Protest is a sign that the opportunity structure is flexible and vulnerable to the political assaults of excluded groups."[18] McAdam has suggested that "any event or broad social process that serves to undermine the calculations and assumptions on which the political establishment is structured occasions a shift in political opportunities." As he sees it, "increased political power serves to encourage collective action by diminishing the risks associated with movement participation."[19] Regardless of the causes of expanded "political opportunities" such shifts can facilitate increased political activism on the part of excluded groups.

There can be no doubt that political opportunities shifted considerably between the 1960s and the 1990s. Executive and judicial support of the Civil Rights and Voting Rights Acts basically ended legal overt discrimination in public life. Protest politics declined, and institutionalized political behavior became the dominant form of Black politics. In fact, the "new Black politics" was characterized as a means to achieve Black political and social empowerment.[20] Nelson defined it as "an effort by Black political leaders to capitalize on the increasing size of the Black electorate; the strategic position of Black voters in many cities, counties, and congressional districts; and the growing consciousness of the Black community."[21] Initially at least, the new Black politics was conceived as a way to translate the energy of the Civil Rights Movement into electoral strength. Indeed, moving from protest to politics was seen as necessary for perpetuating the movement's goals. As Robert Smith observed, the vast majority of those who study social movements "tend to argue that protest is not enough, that if the causes represented by mass movements are to be sustained and advanced it must be through institutionalized structures and processes or not at all."[22]

Although opportunities for institutionalized electoral inputs have greatly increased, it is not clear that this process has sustained and advanced the causes represented by the movement or that institutionalization has produced an environment that is conducive to social and political action. Smith suggests that neither protest nor politics is enough to produce systemic responsiveness at the national level.[23] Marcus Pohlman contends that the structure of the political system precludes it: "In the United States, both the election process and the political party process are inherently biased against fundamental redistributive change."[24] Even though the number of Black elected officials has more than quadrupled since 1970, they still constitute less than 1.5 percent of all officeholders in the country. This percent is considerably less than the 12 percent that Blacks represent in the population. Although descriptive representation is no guarantee of substantive representation, the degree of discrepancy is an indicator of the challenges Blacks face in being incorporated into electoral offices. Smith finds that Blacks face a similar challenge among appointed officials. Moreover, as Frances Fox Piven and Richard Cloward assert, electoral politics undermines group politics.[25] The inherent individualism of "one person, one vote" encourages the primacy of individual interests over group-based assessments. This can make race-based mobilization difficult. Individualism runs counter to the racial solidarity that was displayed during the Civil Rights Movement.

Katherine Tate has examined the question of whether or not this shift toward electoral politics constitutes a "second stage" of the Civil Rights Movement. She notes that favorable political conditions are among the factors necessary for social movements but that these conditions do not presently exist. While the Million Man and Million Woman Marches indicate that some segments of the African American community are interested in noninstitutional modes of societal transformation, according to Tate, "the political environment that helped make possible Black's efforts to organize for and to realize political and social change is today far less open to such efforts."[26] In shifting from calls for legal to economic rights, or what Tate calls "equal opportunity to equality of fact," White support of Black Civil Rights initiatives has diminished, the Republican Party has strengthened its influence in politics, the Supreme Court now leans rightward, tensions have emerged between Blacks and their liberal allies, Section 5 of the Voting Rights Act has increasingly come under attack, political divisions have been exacerbated within the Black leadership community, and class distinctions have grown sharper within the community at large. This has all occurred within the context of the "opportunities" of electoral politics, which have often left Blacks suggesting, paradoxically, that deracialized political strategies are the best means of gaining political power and of addressing the problems that face the Black community.[27] Given the complexity of this political environment, the expectation that Black churches would be inclined toward activism may be somewhat optimistic.

Resources

A conducive political environment only affords the aggrieved population the opportunity for successful insurgent action. It is the resources of the minority community which enable insurgent groups to exploit these opportunities. In the absence of those resources, the aggrieved population is likely to lack the capacity to act even when granted the opportunity to do so.[28]

The mobilization of resources lies at the heart of any successful social movement. Without it there is no capacity for action. A central concern of most accounts of the Civil Rights Movement is how the resources of the Black community were marshaled to accomplish political ends. In fact, resource mobilization theory holds that this linkage is paramount; without institutions that can coordinate and articulate grievances, no mass political action will result.[29] Placing the church at center stage in explaining the connection between the Black church and the Civil Rights Movement, Morris described the church as "an institutional setting where oppression could be openly discussed and resources could be developed to organize collective resistance."[30] As the "institutional center" of the Civil Rights Movement, the Black church provided the movement with autonomy, communication networks, facilities, a membership base, leadership, and a tradition of protest.

Today many of these resources continue to exist. The autonomy of the Black church is maintained by the fact that more than 80 percent of all Black Protestants are in Black denominations.[31] These Black denominations are administered independently from White denominations. Thus, the Black church remains an indigenous institution wholly owned and controlled by African American themselves. The finances of the Black church are also intact. Emmett Carson records that more than 90 percent of all Black giving is channeled through the church.[32] This could easily constitute more than two billion dollars in offerings every year.[33] This resource makes the Black church one of the few institutions in low-income communities with the ability to secure major credit. Among the most enduring resources of Black churches are their facilities. Lincoln and Mamiya confirm the economic independence of Black churches by finding that more than 90 percent of the Black churches they surveyed owned their own buildings, and close to 60 percent of those reported that the property had no mortgage on it.[34] Not only do buildings represent an economic resource, but they represent a social resource as well. Although the degree to which Blacks are denied access in society has diminished considerably, the church continues to provide a forum for social, political, and artistic expression. Finally, the tradition of protest is the heritage and legacy of the Black church. In many ways its very establishment was "the first Black freedom movement," and its existence is a testimony to the spirit and will of Black people to be recognized as equal before God and equals in society.

Two important resources of the Black church have declined, however, over the last thirty years. The nature of its membership base and its leadership has changed significantly, which has resulted in a diminished capacity for effective social and political action. Whereas a generation ago as many as 80 percent of Blacks went to church, today some contend that number is down as low as 40 percent. Although this figure is probably low, the feeling that the Black church is in trouble persists. As Wilmore has said: "The Black church is in a serious crisis. At stake is whether it will remain a viable institution in the African American community in the twenty-first century or whether it will become irrelevant."[35] Much of the basis for this concern emerges from the fact that the unchurched come disproportionately from the young, men, and the underclass. These are precisely the communities toward which much contemporary social action has been focused.

Robert Franklin, president of the Interdenominational Theology Center in Atlanta, contends that, while many upwardly mobile Black congregations are experiencing surges in membership, there has been a mass exodus of the urban poor from the church, particularly young men. He estimates that 60 percent of young men and boys have virtually no contact whatsoever with Christianity.[36] The appeal of Islam, the association of the Black church with the pacifism of the Civil Rights Movement, the image of a White Jesus, as well as the temptations of popular culture all distract from the spiritual and moral life of the inner city. Studying the relationship between churchgoing and the socioeconomic performance of Black inner-city males, Richard B. Freeman has found that churchgoing behavior is one of the most accurate indicators of success or failure.[37] Cheryl Sanders of the Howard School of Divinity believes that the patriarchy of most Black churches is a hindrance to Black male participation. "You have a male pastor at the top of a heap and mass of women frying chicken," she explains.[38] Lincoln and Mamiya note that the church has the most difficulty in recruiting and maintaining young adults ages seventeen to thirty-four. They attempt to attract this "post–Civil Rights" generation by rallies, revivals, and youth group activities.[39] But, as Henry Duvall observed in the *Crisis* more than ten years ago a new generation of young socially conscious Blacks have come to expect an increased social responsibility for the church. In that article Lawrence Jones of the Howard Divinity School contends that Blacks are asking for social relevance from the Black church. Those churches that are not in such a growth pattern will likely have problems attracting and retaining young Blacks.[40]

The young are not the only ones who feel somewhat alienated from the Black church. More than fifteen years ago Dr. Jones observed that the generalized economic deprivation of the African American underclass and the social isolation created by the social advancement of the African American middle class have contributed to the continued fragmentation of the Black religious community.[41] Jack Bloom contends that even in the Civil Rights Movement the church was used by middle-class Blacks to achieve their limited objectives. The middle class did not call for the type of radical economic and political transformations which may have benefited the underclass. They simply sought integration into society.[42] When the Civil Rights Bill of 1964 was signed, the overt and collective oppression of Black people ceased. This benefited all Blacks. Within the African American community, however, the social and economic cleavages that had been suppressed by this racial oppression were then free to manifest themselves. Ida R. Mukenge records that over time there has been decreasing uniformity in the needs and resources of the Black urban population. She asserts that differentiation among the urban Black population precipitated the church's movement from "undifferentiated race consciousness to class consciousness."[43]

Economic prosperity has led to some "Black flight" from the inner cities. In Atlanta, for instance, almost 50 percent of the Black population has moved to suburbia.[44] Today the neighborhood church is often populated by those who commute to it. According to Andres Tapia: "Middle class Blacks still feel a cultural tie to the urban Black community and want to maintain that connection through Sunday visits. They seem less willing to cast their lot with a struggling community as opportunities open up for them to provide a better education and safer lifestyle for their children."[45] This presents Black pastors with a real dilemma. Do they solidify the demographic trend, move to the suburbs, and service their primary constituency, or do they remain in the inner city and continue to attempt to transcend class barriers by reaching out to the poor? This class gap also affects the church's standing within the community. As William Turner of the Duke University Divinity School has observed, when all Black folks lived in the same place there was an overlap among educators, business people, and church leaders. This arrangement set the tone and values for the community. With Black middle-class flight, the bonds that used to be there are gone. For the first time there is a large portion of a generation for whom church has not been a part of their lives. People nurtured within the church do not know what to say or do without a shared worldview.[46]

The other resource that has changed significantly since the 1960s is the leadership of the Black church. Throughout most of African American history, key political leaders have come out of the Black church. The decline and loss of the Christian church's authority was demonstrated, however, by the emergence of the Black Power Movement under the leadership of charismatic figures such as Malcolm X and Huey P. Newton. The Black Power Movement encouraged African Americans to adopt a more combative posture, which resulted in a series of riots, rebellions, and civil disturbances around the nation in the late 1960s. Because government responded quickly to these "extralegal" forms of political participation, the hegemony of traditional African American clergy and African American churches in the movement for social and political power was significantly undermined. The Black Power Movement represented dissatisfaction with the limited progress of the Civil Rights Movement under the leadership of mainline clergy. Ironically, to a certain extent, the leaders of the movement became victims of their own success. As more and more avenues of opportunity were opened to African Americans, largely as a result of the movement, the parallel society that the church had provided for centuries was needed less and less. As James Q. Wilson has observed, with professional training, administrative skills, and political sophistication, experts emerged and assumed some of the political and social responsibilities that had previously been the exclusive domain of ministers.[47]

Du Bois predicted in 1903 that there would be a supersession of clerically grounded leadership and that the development of and access to other institutions would replace the centrality of the church vis-à-vis political activity. Reed contends that the "institutional logics and functions" of the Black church are incompatible with political action. According to him, the projection that the Black church is a source of authenticating leadership is particularly problematic because it assigns the responsibility for political legitimation to an intrinsically antipolitical agency.[48]

The challenge to the Black church's leadership hegemony was most graphically demonstrated by the controversy over the Million Man March, held in Washington, D.C., in October 1995. The march was planned by Nation of Islam leader Louis Farrakhan. Many of the leading Black ministers, including Henry Lyons, of the National Baptist Convention USA, and Bennett Smith Sr., of the Progressive Baptist Convention, distanced themselves from the demonstration. Reverend Smith was quoted as saying: "To participate would give an erroneous message to the world that Mr. Farrakhan is a bona fide leader of Black people. I don't want to be a part of that."[49] It is an indication of the primacy that Black Protestant ministers have maintained for so long that Reverend Smith would infer that his participation or lack thereof would have any effect on Farrakhan's status as a leader. Despite the opposition of most of the major Black denominations, hundreds of thousands of Black men attended the march. It is worth noting that Benjamin Chavis, the ousted NAACP executive director who played such a vital role in helping Farrakhan organize the demonstration, recently joined the Nation of Islam, having formerly been an ordained minister in the United Church of Christ. His conversion highlights the declining priority within the African American community of association with traditional Protestant churches for attaining leadership roles within social movements.

The authority of the traditional Black church is also challenged by the charismatic leadership and organizational styles of many of its ministers and major denominations. In particular, the million-member National Baptist Convention USA has been plagued with continuing revelations of financial mismanagement and personal indiscretion on the part of its president, Rev. Henry Lyons. While allegations of extramarital affairs may indicate moral failings, the allegations of misappropriation of funds may indicate organizational challenges in the degree of access, discretion, and accountability which the president had concerning convention funds. In fact, a convention commission appointed to investigate these financial irregularities found that Lyons had violated no rules, although some of the commission members raised serious questions about the nature and propriety of the transactions, and the commission called for sweeping changes in its rules. Meanwhile, on February 27, 1999, a jury convicted Lyons of grand theft and racketeering in Largo, Florida. Three weeks after his conviction on these state charges, Lyons pled guilty to five counts of a fifty-four-count federal indictment. He admitted to making false statements to authorities, bank fraud, and tax evasion. Following these embarrassing developments and anticipating spending the next few years in prison, Lyons finally resigned from the presidency of the National Baptist Convention.[50] This type of scandal only fuels the misperception that Black ministers lead merely on the force of their personality, lack moral authority, and seek little more than personal aggrandizement. This misimpression hinders the ability of Black ministers to speak with legitimacy and alienates many in the Black community.

Commenting on the Civil Rights Movement, Morris observes that "the principal resource of the church was its organized mass base. The church not only organized the Black masses, but also commanded their allegiance."[51] In the 1990s the base is shrinking, and allegiance is undermined from within and without. Given this situation, one expects churches to be inclined toward the less activist poles of the dialectic.

Theology

The final resource that enhanced the capacity of the Black church to be inclined toward activism was a theology aimed at curing social ills. During the 1960s many Black churches preached that oppression was sinful and that

God sanctions protest aimed at eradicating social evils. This development was important because, as McAdam stresses, "one of the central problematics of insurgency is whether favorable shifts in political opportunities will be defined as such by a large enough group of people to facilitate action." "Before collective protest can get under way," he explains, "people must collectively define their situation as unjust and subject to change through group action."[52] He calls this process "cognitive liberation," an important component of group consciousness. Miller and his colleagues note that the way in which people perceive and evaluate their position is an important link between the experience of certain social situations and political participation to address them. If the experience is politicized through consciousness and assessments of social justice, it can indirectly motivate social action. One of the major agents responsible for this type of socialization in the Black community has been the Black church.[53]

In their comprehensive work Lincoln and Mamiya conducted the first systematic, empirical attempt at charting the influence of Black consciousness on the clergy since the Civil Rights period. They found that since that time the majority of the Black clergy have placed more pride in their racial and denominational heritage, have come to appreciate the need for Black role models in Sunday School literature, and have a greater understanding of the uniqueness of the mission of the Black church in its community. Generally, however, they have not accepted liberation theology as a social gospel of reform and revolution based on Black nationalism and liberation stories from the biblical tradition. Lincoln and Mamiya observed that most of the Black clergy "have not been influenced by the new movement of Black liberation theology."[54]

The theology itself has developed greatly since James Cone first published his groundbreaking book *Black Theology and Black Power* in 1969. Cone, the most influential Black American theologian at that time, took an affirmative stand on Black Power. He viewed it as a means of challenging White racism and of speaking with a prophetic voice in the current generation. For Cone, Black Power was an expression of Jesus's identification with the oppressed. Patrick Bascio has observed that from this perspective a community that fails to produce a theology of the oppressed is not a Christian community. According to this view, the fact that Christ is the Liberator is the key to understanding Scripture and the Black struggle, God is on the side of the oppressed, and it is a "religious" act to fight for one's rights. Problems exist only because the Black church has not clearly embraced this theology. Thirteen years later, in *My Soul Looks Back,* Cone explained that his severe criticism of the Black church arose out of his observation that Black denominations were not interested in relating the politics of Black liberation. "It [the church] had failed to remain faithful to its heritage of freedom," he argued.[55] Because the Black church is one of the major proponents of social and political integration, it has difficulty embracing the more nationalistic principles that undergird liberation theologies.

This reluctancy is compounded by the fact that, in moving from what Charles Hamilton has characterized as the politics of rights to the politics of resources, theological justifications for political action are not so straightforward. There is a general hesitancy to believe that economically and socially based problems can be changed through social action. Even Bernice King, Rev. Martin Luther King Jr.'s daughter, commenting on what makes for a relevant church, has argued, "We need to understand the nature of the problems that we are seeking to solve. Ephesians 6:12 reminds us that 'we wrestle not against flesh and blood, but against principalities, against powers, against the rulers of the darkness, against spiritual wickedness in high places.' In other words, many of the problems we confront are spiritual in nature."[56] It is difficult to fight spiritual warfare with either protest or politics.

Moreover, Blacks are overwhelmingly evangelical in orientation. They are substantially more likely than Whites to say they believe in the inerrancy of Scripture, the divinity of Christ, his physical resurrection from the dead, and the necessity of having a "born again" experience. This evangelical tradition tends to be highly correlated with conservative political positions, especially with regard to the social issues.[57] Blacks continue to be more liberal than Whites on economic issues and racial issues and on questions involving the governmental role in society, but on many contemporary "civil rights" issues, such as abortion, sexual preference, and women's role in society, political leaders are left scrambling for support in Black churches. Many within the Black Protestant community believe that theology provides a justification for opposing liberal civil rights positions on these contemporary issues.[58] Thus, it can be difficult to mobilize African Americans about these issues. This lack of enthusiasm by Blacks has the potential to alienate gays, women, and other liberal political coalition partners. Part of the reason for this lack of involvement is that, instead of cultivating a theology that is directed at social action—by providing the cognitive liberation that is needed for such action—the theology of the Black church is often opposed to supporting much contemporary social activity.

Conclusion

Given this level of resources in the contemporary Black churches, it is not difficult to understand why it tends to steer away from sociopolitical activism. It is not a lack of willingness on the part of the church which prevents it from playing a role similar to that of the 1950s and 1960s. Capacity structures these choices, and capacity is determined by the environment, resources, and theology that exist over time. Perhaps the greatest irony is that, while much has changed relative to the African American church, the expectation that it should be at the forefront of helping Black people has not changed. The long tradition of its involvement, its strength relative to other institutions within the community, and the withdrawal of government support for the social welfare agenda over the last few decades makes this expectation reasonable. There is considerable evidence that Black churches continue to service the communities to which they belong. For example, the Antioch Baptist Church in Atlanta dedicated itself to remaining in the urban area by erecting a five million–dollar sanctuary across from a public housing project. The church expanded its outreach into the community by offering everything from soulfood suppers to ministry for people with AIDS. The Greater Christ Baptist Church in Detroit provides members with opportunities to work in a church-owned fast food franchise. The Full Gospel African Methodist Episcopal Zion Church in Temple Hill, Maryland, draws as many as five hundred people to its drug rehabilitation program.[59] Rev. George Stallings of Imani Temple in Washington, D.C., has been at the forefront of bringing Afrocentricity to Catholicism.

Moreover, although this chapter has identified general trends in Protestant churches, it is important to remember that different denominations have varying levels of resources and differing theological traditions on which to draw. The congregations of the Progressive Baptists as well as the African Methodist Episcopals and African Methodist Episcopal Zionists have traditionally been more oriented toward activism than many other Black denominations.[60]

Today, however, Black churches are individually producing individual change, rather than serving as the vanguard of any particular movement. Of course, historically, the Black church has not always been the vanguard of movement, but the church has always been somehow different. The church was either engaged in protest, or it was offering an effective escape. Today, to some extent, it can do neither, and this leaves the African American community uneasy about the future of its most established and beloved institution.

Two

Robert C. Smith

The NAACP in the Twenty-first Century

In recent years a number of Black scholars have questioned both the effectiveness and the relevance of the National Association for the Advancement of Colored People (NAACP) in the continuing struggle for racial justice in the United States, arguing that in its organizational structure, programs, and strategies the group is out of touch with the complex realities of race in the post–Civil Rights era.[1] Criticism of the NAACP by African American scholars is of course not a new phenomenon; see, for example, Ralph Bunche's critique during the New Deal era and Louis Lomax's critique during the Civil Rights era.[2]

W. E. B. Du Bois, one of the association's founders and early leaders, contended that, while the "crusade waged by the National Association for the Advancement of Colored People from 1910 to 1930 [was] one of the finest efforts of liberalism to achieve human emancipation; and much was accomplished," by the 1930s "I realized that too much in later years the Association had attracted the higher income of colored people, who regarded it as a 'weapon to attack the sort of social discrimination which especially irked them; rather than an organization to improve the status and power of the whole Negro group.'"[3] And, as the Civil Rights era approached its end, Kenneth Clark worried whether the NAACP would be capable of dealing with the post–Civil Rights era problems of concentrated poverty and increased "social pathologies" of the urban ghettos. Clark wrote: "The disturbing question which must be faced is whether or not the present Civil Rights organizations are equipped in terms of perspective, staff and organizational structure to deal effectively with the present level of Civil Rights problems. And, if not, whether they are flexible enough in order to become relevant."[4] Twenty years later Clark woefully concluded that the NAACP had not been flexible enough, titling his 1985 *New York Times* essay "The NAACP: Verging on Irrelevance."

While in general I tend to agree with Clark and the other critics of the NAACP, in this chapter I want to focus on some of the constraints facing the association and other Black advocacy organizations as they enter a new century of freedom struggle.[5] I will also suggest some modest reforms and new directions for the organization at the national and local levels but especially the latter.

Constraints on the Twenty-first Century NAACP

Historically, the NAACP has avoided direct action approaches such as mass demonstrations in favor of conventional political approaches of antidefamation, litigation and lobbying. At the present time and for the near-term future the association faces severe constraints in using these approaches. Its anti-defamation work and lobbying in the Congress are hampered by four factors: first, the changed climate of post–Civil Rights era opinion on race among the White majority; second, the ambiguous "now you see it, now you don't" quality of contemporary racism; third, control of the Congress and the Supreme Court by the Republican Party; and, fourth, severe resource constraints.

A Hostile Climate of Race Opinion

Opinion studies in the last thirty years show a steady, and for the most part consistent, decline in expressions of racist and White supremacist attitudes among White Americans.[6] For example, in 1963, 31 percent of Whites agreed with the statement that Blacks were an inferior people; by 1978, 15 percent agreed.[7] Studies also show that White Americans by large margins now embrace the principle of racial equality.[8] Yet, while White Americans in general are less openly racist in their attitudes, this does not mean that hostility toward Blacks has disappeared or even markedly declined. Instead, it has become less obvious and more subtle.

This new form of defamation has been labeled the "new racism," "symbolic racism," "modern racism," "racial resentment," or "laissez-faire racism."[9] What this research purports to show is that, because of their commitment to basic or core American values, especially individualism, White Americans resent or are hostile to Blacks. Paul Sniderman summarizes the research: "White Americans resist equality in the name of self reliance, achievement, individual initiative, and they do so not merely because the value of individualism provides a socially acceptable pretext but because it provides an integral component of the new racism."[10] As a function of individualism, modern or symbolic racism is a product of the "finest and proudest of American values."[11] It is as American as the flag, baseball, the Fourth of July, and apple pie.

Blacks, of course disagree, viewing racism and racial discrimination as primary causes of continuing inequalities between the races.[12] Donald Kinder and Lynn Sanders summarize this chasm in race opinion: "Whites tend to think that racial discrimination is no longer a problem—that prejudice has withered away; that the real worry these days is reverse discrimination, penalizing innocent whites for the sins of the distant past. Meanwhile, Blacks see racial discrimination as ubiquitous; they think of prejudice as a plague; they say that racial discrimination not affirmative action is still the rule in American society."[13]

This climate of racial hostility and resentment cloaked in the ethos of individualism makes the antidefamation work of the NAACP very difficult. For example, the new racism is much more difficult to combat than the old-fashioned racism that Du Bois so effectively challenged in the early pages of the *Crisis*.[14] This inhibits the effectiveness of electioneering and lobbying, as, for example, against passage in 1996 of the anti–affirmative action proposition 209 in California (and its legislative equivalent in Congress when or if it comes to a vote) or the punitive 1996 welfare reform bill.

The recent welfare reform legislation is the most telling example of the impact of this climate of modern racism. A principal line of argument of proponents (in Congress, the media, and the academy) of the welfare reform bill was that welfare dependency reflects a lack of individual responsibility, initiative, and "family values" on the part of the recipients, who themselves are disproportionately Black and who are thought to be a majority by most Whites. By the time President Clinton ran for president this modern racist view was dominant in Washington, D.C., political, policy, and media circles. Thus, Clinton campaigned on the theme of "personal responsibility" (implicitly implying that poor Blacks lack such values) and a promise to "end welfare as we know it." Then, in the midst of the 1996 reelection campaign, Clinton signed (at the urging of his political advisors but over the objections of all his welfare policy advisors, three of whom resigned in protest) a Republican-crafted reform bill that indeed ended the sixty-year-old federal guarantee of income support for poor women and their children.[15]

This radical legislation was opposed by the NAACP and virtually the entire Black leadership establishment. Yet a democratic president felt free to sign it without fear of sanctions by that establishment or Black voters, even during an election year. This is partly because of the influence of modern racism on national discussions of race-related issues.

The Ambiguity of Modern Racism

The second constraint on the NAACP's antiracist work is the ambiguous "now you see it, now you don't" quality of modern institutional racism.[16] When I was growing up in the rural South in the early 1960s racism was relatively easy to see; even in the North it was relatively easy to see. The Civil Rights revolution changed all of this, making virtually all forms of racism illegal and therefore less visible and more intractable. Yet in housing, education, employment, and health, and even such things as how drug use is punished and how automobiles are purchased, there is evidence, albeit ambiguous, of ongoing patterns of institutional racism.[17] To take one example, low-income Whites have an equal or better chance of getting a home mortgage loan than middle-income Blacks, yet this seemingly clear-cut case of racism is rejected by leaders of the banking industry. As Barney Becksma, the head of the U.S. League of Savings Institution put it: "As for people being discriminated against because they are a minority, I've never heard of that. I admit I probably don't have a good answer."[18] This is the dilemma confronting the NAACP and other Black organizations in fighting the institutional form of modern racism. As I have written in my book on the problem, "How can one propose specific policies or programs to deal with what cannot be seen or what one refuses to see or what one refuses to acknowledge even when it is seen?"[19]

The Republican Congressional Majority

Another constraint facing the NAACP and its lobbying in Washington has to do with control of the Congress—especially the House—by the Republican Party. Throughout the post–Civil Rights era, beginning with the Nixon Administration, the NAACP prevailed on every major Civil Rights issue that came to a vote in the Congress, more than a dozen major votes over a twenty-five-year period, ranging from busing to affirmative action; from South African sanctions to the Martin Luther King holiday act; from voting rights to Supreme Court nominees.[20]

Frequently, these legislative victories were achieved against the will of determined presidents. The key to these victories was Democratic control of Congress for most of this period which was lost in 1994 and is not likely to be regained in its entrenched form for some time to come, if ever. Blacks' leverage in Congress is "notably exposed," to use Matthew Holden's phrase, when Republicans control the Congress.[21] This is because the Republican Party oscillates between indifference and hostility to Civil Rights. For example, the Leadership Conference on Civil Rights rates congressional support for Civil Rights on a scale of 0 to 100 (with 100 representing total support). In 1989 northern Democrats scored 90, southern Democrats 73, northern Republicans 43, and southern Republicans 13. (It is also worth noting that most of the Republican leadership in both houses of Congress is in the hands of southerners.)

A Conservative Judiciary

Apart from lobbying and antidefamation work, litigation has been a key part of the NAACP's struggle for freedom and justice.[22] Yet, because of the symbiotic relationship between the Supreme Court and the climate of public opinion generally and race opinion specifically, the association's litigation strategy is as constrained as its lobbying strategy.[23] As Harold Cruse bluntly puts it, "Civil Rights justice, for all intents and purposes, has been won, there are no more frontiers to conquer, no horizons in view that are not mirages over the hill of the next Supreme Court decision on the meaning of equal protection."[24]

In its 1987 annual report the NAACP reported that the lion's share of the work of its Washington Bureau was devoted in the 1980s to blocking confirmation of conservative judicial nominees at all levels, the districts, the circuits, and the Supreme Court. By 1989, however, conservatives had achieved a narrow five-person conservative majority on the Supreme Court insofar as race matters are concerned as well as substantial influence on the circuit and district courts.

While the NAACP and the Civil Rights coalition lost the battle to prevent conservative dominance of the Supreme Court, it was not an easy or quick victory for the Right. Rather, it took more than twenty years, four presidents, and thirteen nominees before conservatives could claim a narrow working majority. President Nixon was able to place only one strong ideological conservative, Rehnquist, on the Court, in part because of the efforts of the Civil Rights lobby. The rejection early in the Nixon Administration of Judges Haynsworth and Carswell led Nixon, and later President Ford, to choose more moderate nominees—Blackmun, Stevens, and Powell—who could more easily win Senate approval.

Reagan came to office with a more determined ideological agenda than Nixon or Ford and was more successful in appointing right-wing conservatives—O'Connor, Scalia, and Kennedy—and Bush's nomination of Clarence Thomas to succeed Justice Marshall reinforced the conservative tendency. But, as a consequence of the battle leading to the defeat of Robert Bork, Reagan and Bush were able to get their choices through only by selecting "stealth" nominees, persons without any clear record on the major legal and constitutional conflicts of the time, especially on Civil Rights.[25] Judge Bork's defeat had made it clear that nominees with clear records of opposition to Civil Rights, broadly construed, or to affirmative action specifically could not win the approval of the Democratic Senate. This is further testimony to the influence of the NAACP and the Civil Rights lobby in the post–Civil Rights era. Yet with Republican control of the Senate (especially with the shrinking of its moderate-liberal bloc) this influence is a thing of the past.

Once the conservatives got their fifth vote on the Court, they immediately began to undermine the entire structure of post–Civil Rights era jurisprudence. First, in its 1988–1989 term, in six decisions, rendered one after another, the Court significantly narrowed the structural basis for enforcing employment discrimination law. These decisions led Justice Marshall to state bluntly in a speech after the close of the 1988–1989 term, "It is difficult to characterize the term's decisions as anything other than a deliberate retrenching of the Civil Rights agenda."[26] Although the decisions were to some extent reversed by the Civil Rights Act of 1991, the Court nevertheless continued to ignore the intent of Congress in this area by interpreting laws in ways that undermined long-established precedents.[27]

The Court has also undermined the post–Civil Rights era structure of minority set-asides in government contracting (policies that grant, or "set aside," a proportion of government contracts to businesses owned by minorities or women). First, in *J. A. Croson v. City of Richmond* the Court in a 5-to-4 decision declared Richmond, Virginia's set-aside program unconstitutional. Writing for the Court, Justice O'Connor declared that, while Congress as a co-equal branch of government might have the authority to establish remedial set-aside programs, the states and localities were prohibited by the Fourteenth Amendment's equal protection clause from doing so unless the plans were "narrowly tailored" to meet identified discriminatory practices. In one of his many angry dissents during his last years on the Court, Justice Marshall described his colleagues decision in *Croson* as a "deliberate and giant step backward in this Court's affirmative action jurisprudence," which assumes "racial discrimination is largely a phenomenon of the past, and that government bodies need no longer preoccupy themselves with rectifying racial injustice."[28]

In *Croson* Justice O'Connor implied that Congress had the authority to do what cities and states could not do in remedying racial discrimination in the way government contracts are allocated. Six years later in *Adarand Contractors v. Pena* she rejected this view and ruled that Congress had to follow the same strict standards as the states.[29] In this decision the Court, again by 5-to-4, overturned two long-established precedents in this area of the law of affirmative action.[30] As a result of *Croson,* there has been a dramatic decline in minority access to contracts in Richmond and other states and localities.[31] A similar result may follow *Adarand.*

After eviscerating the laws of employment discrimination and minority set-asides, the Court next turned its attention to voting rights. In a series of 5-to-4 decisions beginning with *Shaw v. Reno* the Court radically altered its approach to race and redistricting, making it much more difficult for state legislatures and the federal courts to create districts with Black majorities.[32] The implications of these decisions might reduce the size of the Black congressional delegation by as much as a third, with similar consequences for state and local legislative and judicial districts. Thus, as in the post-Reconstruction era, in the post–Civil Rights era the NAACP's use of the strategy of litigation to advance the cause of freedom may be at a dead end.[33] While future Democratic presidents may be able to break the conservatives' narrow hold on the Court, the precedents established by the current Court in the area of civil rights may be too recent for a liberal majority to overturn without risking the Court's legitimacy.

Resource Constraints

The final constraint on the NAACP's effectiveness in the new century is a long-standing one: it has a broad, multiple-issue agenda but, compared to other Washington, D.C., interest groups, relatively few resources. Dianne Pinderhughes writes that "the subordinate, dependent status of the Black population limits the capacity of Black interests to create well-funded and supported groups capable of the consistent monitoring required in the administration and implementation of law. This same status multiplies the number of potential issue areas of importance to Black constituencies, but their resource difficulties limit the number of issues they can address, and weaken their likelihood of being taken seriously within any of these areas."[34]

Table 2.1 displays data on the membership and financial resources of selected Washington, D.C., interest groups, including the NAACP, the National Urban League, and the Congressional Black Caucus, the three most important Black groups. With the exception of the gay and lesbian lobby, the trial lawyers' association, and the lobby group for Israel, all of the non-Black associations have greater resources in terms of membership or local chapters than do the three major Black groups. And, with the exception of the National Abortion Rights Action League (which has a membership comparable to the NAACP) and the National Gay and Lesbian Task Force, all of the non-Black groups have larger budgets than the NAACP, the National Urban League, or the Congressional Black Caucus. Also, with the exception of the Conference

_____ Table 2.1 _____

A Comparison of the Resources of the Three Major African American Interest Organizations with Selected Nonblack Organizations in 1995

Organization	Estimated Membership	Annual Budget (Dollars)
NAACP	450,000 members, 2,200 local chapters	12[1]
National Urban League	118 local affiliates	24
Congressional Black Caucus	40 members of Congress	550,000[2]
AFL-CIO	14 million	63
National Association of Manufacturers	2,800 local chapters	17
National Abortion Rights Action League	400,000	9
Mothers against Drunk Driving	2.9 million	43
Tobacco Institute	13 companies	38
National Rifle Association	2.6 million	89
Sierra Club	600,000	39
American-Israeli Public Affairs Committee	50,000	2
Conference of Catholic Bishops	300 bishops	31
National Gay and Lesbian Task Force	15,000	1

Notes:
1. Unless otherwise noted, the budget figure is in millions of dollars for the year 1995.
2. The budget for the Congressional Black Caucus is for the Congressional Black Caucus Foundation, a separate, tax-exempt organization organized in 1982 to raise funds to support the group. Until 1995 the caucus itself raised four thousand dollars from each of its members in order to support its operations. The Republican congressional majority under House Speaker Newt Gingrich discontinued this form of member support.
Source: Adapted from Hanes Walton Jr. and Robert C. Smith, *American Politics and the African American Quest for Universal Freedom* (New York: Addison Wesley Longman, 2000), 120.

of Catholic Bishops and the AFL-CIO, most of the non-Black groups are narrow, single-issue groups, focusing their lobbying on one issue such as gun ownership, abortion rights, drunk driving, or United States foreign policy toward Israel. And most of these single-issue lobbies, unlike the multiple-issue Black groups, have larger budgets. The budget, for example, of Mothers against Drunk Driving (MADD) is larger than the budgets of the three Black groups combined, and the budget of the National Rifle Association (NRA) is three times greater than the budgets of the three Black groups combined.

The size of an interest group's membership and budget are important resources. A large membership permits grassroots mobilization in terms of letters and phone calls to the media and members of Congress as well as voter mobilization on Election Day. Money is, as former California House Speaker Jesse Unruh once said, "the mother's milk of politics." It can be employed in a wide range of activities, such as grassroots organizing, voter mobilization, polling, radio, and television ads and litigation. Critically important, a large financial base permits interest groups to form political action committees (PACs) to raise and give campaign contributions to candidates for office. Since the passage of campaign finance reform laws in the 1970s, PACs have become very important in the lobbying-election process, contributing nearly half of the money raised by incumbent congressional candidates (federal law limits PAC contributors to organizations to $5,000 and to $1,000 for individuals). Several of the non-Black groups (the NRA, the trial lawyers' association, the AFL-CIO) have large PACs that contribute millions of dollars to congressional candidates. None of the Black interest groups have PACs, although several unsuccessful efforts were made in the 1970s by a number of Black groups to form one.

In the last decade lobbying in Washington has become increasingly well financed and sophisticated, involving e-mail, the World Wide Web, talk radio, sophisticated polling, as well as campaigns and cable television. Black groups, in part because of a lack of resources, have been slow to take advantage of these techniques, which in fact conservative groups employed as early as 1993 in the campaign to defeat President Clinton's nomination of Lani Guinier, a former attorney for the NAACP, to be assistant attorney general for Civil Rights. African American interest groups did not employ such techniques; indeed, most were unaware that those opposing the nomination were using such techniques until a week or so before President Clinton withdrew the nomination.[35]

Given its multiple-issue agenda and its relative lack of resources compared to other Washington, D.C., interest groups, the NAACP and other Washington-based Black interest groups are at a considerable disadvantage. Indeed, given these resource constraints, the successes of the NAACP and the Washington, D.C., Civil Rights lobby in the last two decades are rather remarkable. These successes were in large measure, however, products of a somewhat less hostile climate of public opinion and Democratic control of the Congress. In the new century, therefore, it will be useful to consider how the association might rethink its traditional reliance on litigation and lobbying at the federal level while strengthening the capabilities of its local chapters—which are perhaps its principal resource. In the final parts of this chapter I turn to this process of rethinking, focusing on the roles of the national office and a revitalization of the local chapters.

The NAACP in the Twenty-first Century:
The National Perspective

In the face of a hostile or indifferent climate of public opinion, a hostile or indifferent Congress and judiciary, and, very likely, hostile or obsequious presidents, the NAACP should consider devoting less of its limited resources to traditional lobbying and litigating at the federal level.

Litigation might be undertaken by the specialized Legal Defense Fund, the ACLU, or other Civil Rights litigant groups, rather than NAACP counsel. In any event it is probably not a prudent investment of scarce resources to spend a great deal of time and money trying to change Justice O'Connor's mind on Civil Rights, voting rights, and affirmative action because, as Cruse puts it, there are (for the foreseeable future) no more frontiers or horizons that are not mirages that will vanish with the next Court opinion or nominee.

If the NAACP national office is to de-emphasize its traditional lobbying and litigation roles, what should its responsibilities be in the new century? First, it should continue its traditional antidefamation work as well as its "fair share" arrangements with corporate America in the areas of employment and contracting. Second, and critically important, the association should revitalize its publication, *Crisis*. In his prospectus for the *Crisis* Du Bois said first and foremost the journal would record "very important happenings and movements in the world which bear on the great problem of interracial relations and especially those which affect the Negro-American; second as a comprehensive review of 'opinion and literature' pertinent to the race problem; third as a forum for a 'few terse' articles"; and, finally, "editorially standing for the rights of men, irrespective of color or race, for the highest ideals of the American democracy."[36] Du Bois used the pages of the *Crisis* to "hammer at the truth" about White supremacy, racism, race, and the distortion of the American democracy, making it, as David Lewis writes, "the very embodiment of the NAACP's struggle for racial integration."[37] In recent years, however, the magazine has become almost trivial, focusing on celebrities, consumerism, and entertainment rather than as a vehicle for hard news and critical analysis and commentary. Meanwhile, news and commentary on race in the United States is dominated by conservative, neoconservative, and neoliberal journals. A revitalized *Crisis* requires a considerable investment of resources, but such an investment would be worthwhile if it could contribute to reshaping the debate and the climate of opinion on race in the new century.

The final responsibility of the national office should be to inspire, revitalize, coordinate, and serve as a clearinghouse for the local chapters, providing them with resources and models for effective community action and local political mobilization. Local leaders and organizations were critically important in the mobilization of resources during the Civil Rights Movement, laying the foundations and establishing base camps that facilitated the successes of national leaders and organizations.[38]

The NAACP in the Twenty-first Century: "All Politics Is Local"

Perhaps the NAACP's greatest resource is its near half-million mass base and its more than two thousand local chapters. Former House Speaker Thomas "Tip" O'Neill's famous refrain that "all politics is local" might be applied with equal force to the work of the NAACP, especially in an era when federal programs and responsibilities are being "devolved" to the state and local levels. Political scientists and political activists constantly call for "grassroots" community leadership and organization while ignoring their local NAACP chapters, which could serve as organizational vehicles for local community organizing, political participation, social mobilization, and pragmatic problem solving in the areas of community development, crime, drugs, and especially the education of the children. Generally, local chapters in most cities and towns are recognized as a dominant voice on issues of Civil Rights and Black community interests and usually have at least nominal access to local economic and political elites. The NAACP locals therefore are potentially important fora for leadership development and democratic discussion and organization.

The NAACP Special Project Studies

The African American social science research community knows very little about the local chapters in terms of their leadership, organizational structures, and political and programmatic effectiveness.[39] To remedy these deficiencies in our knowledge, the National Conference of Black Political Scientists (NCOBPS), in collaboration with the Academy of Leadership at the University of Maryland, plan to study local NAACP chapters.[40]

This undertaking is envisioned as a multiyear project that will study at least fifty chapters in all parts of the country, including rural and small towns, suburban and urban as well as those organized on a countrywide basis.[41] The papers will initially be prepared for presentation at the annual NCOBPS meetings then evaluated, assembled, and edited in a volume for presentation to the national office for purposes of strategic planning and reform.

Perhaps on the basis of these and related studies, the national office will establish a number of "Model NAACP Chapters" with respect to effective leadership, staffing, and programs. These model chapters (perhaps twenty-five in urban and rural areas and five suburban chapters) could be given an infusion of resources so they might develop as democratic forums for open debate and discussion of the continuing dilemmas of race; develop fresh approaches to dealing with local economic and political elites; encourage innovative leadership recruitment and nurturing processes; and propose fresh remedies for dealing with community problems, again especially the education of the children. What works in these model chapters could then be diffused to other chapters around the country through the pages of the *Crisis,* at regional and national meetings, and electronically through the World Wide Web.

To come to grips with the exceedingly complex problems that African Americans face in the new century will require a revitalized and aggressive NAACP, working in concert with other elements of Black civil society, especially the churches and schools. While I cannot present a detailed plan or blueprint for revitalizing the NAACP, I will suggest that a bottom-up approach would be a good starting place.

Three

Jennifer A. Wade and Brian N. Williams

The National Urban League

Reinventing Service for the
Twenty-first Century

The National Urban League (NUL) defines itself "as the premier so-cial service and civil rights organization in America."[1] Headquartered in New York City, this nonprofit, community-based agency has an organizational struc-ture of over one hundred affiliates in thirty-four states and the District of Co-lumbia and is known for its signature programs in the areas of employment, job training, housing, youth services, education, and social welfare. Current scholarly literature reveals little attention to the contributions made by this or-ganization, its leadership, and its affiliates during the post–Civil Rights era. The following chapter provides a normative examination of the goals and strate-gies of the National Urban League since the end of the Civil Rights movement and of the ways in which the organization attempts to cultivate its mission in order to remain relevant and address the needs of its constituency. Additional-ly, the chapter addresses key organizational concerns and problems that may threaten the National Urban League's efforts to remain a viable organization well into the twenty-first century.

The League's Mission

Unlike more protest-oriented groups such as the National Association for the Advancement of Colored People (NAACP) and the Southern Christian Leadership Conference (SCLC), the "true nature" of the National Urban League and its affiliates is one of direct action through social services. Since its incep-tion in 1910, the leadership has emphasized the League's mission as a way to distinguish it from other "civil rights" organizations.

In fact, the current president and chief executive officer of the NUL, Hugh B. Price, has begun the process of modernizing the League's mission statement for the twenty-first century, asserting the importance of shaping the mission according to what the League "concentrates on most of the time and [is] best at, instead of continually being known as the second oldest and second largest civil rights organization after the NAACP." "In truth, we aren't a civil rights organization," Price explains. "That isn't what we do [twenty-four hours a day, seven days a week] and the new mission statement makes that clear:"[2] "The mission of the Urban League movement is to enable African-Americans to secure economic self-reliance, parity and power and civil rights. The Urban League movement carries out its mission at the local, state and national levels through direct services, advocacy, research, policy analysis, community mobilization, collaboration and communications."[3] This chapter will discuss the Urban League's evolution from an organization founded to provide direct social services to one with an expanded mission of extending civil rights and economic power. It will include a historical analysis and a discussion of Urban League leadership and internal organization.

The Founding of the National Urban League

Guichard Parris and Lester Brooks write that more than 90 percent of all African Americans lived in the rural South until 1900. Over the next ten-year period more than one-fifth of southern African Americans, fleeing the South's discriminatory laws, migrated to the northern cities of New York, Philadelphia, and Baltimore and the midwestern cities of Columbus, Cincinnati, and Chicago in search of a better life. Their hope of finding new opportunities was met with the harsh reality, however, that without marketable skills it would be impossible to have a better life. This reality was especially difficult for many African American women, some of whom eventually turned to prostitution or other illicit means in an effort to provide for their families.

After the turn of the twentieth century, life for African Americans became even more arduous, for they found themselves living in restricted areas that were populated with saloons, brothels, and gambling places. In cities such as Philadelphia and Harlem it was not uncommon to find African American populations estimated at close to thirty-five thousand crammed into eighteen city blocks. With the arrival of European immigrants to the United States, employment opportunities for African Americans became extremely limited. Soon many found themselves expelled from the job market because employers preferred to hire White male immigrants. This placed further pressure upon the African American female to work harder. In fact, by 1905, 59 percent of all African American women in New York City were employed (mostly as domestics), compared to 27 percent of immigrant women. Furthermore, African American women were often forced to leave their children largely unsupervised. Such factors contributed to a death rate for all African Americans which was one and a half times greater than that for Whites; a high African American infant mortality rate; an African American illiteracy rate that was twelve times that of Whites; and, in New York City, the lowest rate of home ownership of any urban city with a population of more than twenty-five hundred.[4] This bleak picture of the northern lifestyle and experience led to the birth of an organization whose primary mission would be to combat the societal ills plaguing African Americans.

By October 1911 three key groups had come together to work on the urban conditions of African Americans: Francis Kellor's National League for the Protection of Colored Women (NLPCW); the Committee for Improving the Industrial Conditions for Negroes (CIIN), and George Edmund Haynes and Ruth Standish-Baldwin's Committee on Urban Conditions Amongst Negroes (CUCAN). The newly formed organization was known as the National League on Urban Conditions Among Negroes (NLUCAN); later the name would be shortened to the National Urban League. With Haynes leading the charge, the racially integrated organization challenged the urban White elite to help alleviate the plight of urban African Americans by working with and supporting African American–based organizations. The prevailing ideology was that Whites were to work with Blacks for their mutual advantage and advancement rather than view them as a problem. Additionally, this urban White elite began to fund the educational activities of individuals entering into the social work profession. Upon graduation these individuals were placed in jobs within the Black community in which they provided direct services.[5]

The cornerstone of the League agenda has been its goal of impacting the community by delivering direct social services. Nonetheless, questions regarding the organization's focus and methods have emerged, especially during the height of the Civil Rights movement. In particular, many have asked how the organization compares with that of mainstream civil rights organizations.

Overcoming the Myth: Moving Away from Apologies

Through their attempts to overcome racial barriers, organizations such as the NAACP, the SCLC, and the Congress on Racial Equality (CORE) received enormous public attention during the Civil Rights movement. These organizations were committed to the idea of active nonviolent political protest through the use of marches, sit-ins, and other nonviolent demonstrations, which would later become the symbolic hallmark of the Civil Rights movement.

While this was occurring, various factions within the African American community vilified the NUL of the late 1950s and early 1960s. Leaders of numerous Black Nationalist and militant organizations denigrated the League's strategy of promoting social service and polite protest; they viewed the NUL as being controlled by the contributions of private White citizens and corporations, directed by an assimilationist and integrated board of directors, while being administered by apologetic Blacks.[6] Consequently, Whitney M. Young Jr. the League's executive director at the time, embarked upon a campaign to gain the kind of trust and respect of Black America which was needed to ratify his leadership and the leadership of the NUL.

In 1961 Young began repairing, reconstructing, redirecting, and reengineering the organization via "strategic planning" techniques. He consulted with various academics in the hopes of finding the appropriate role for the organization by creating a new vision and direction for it for the 1960s and beyond. He developed an agenda that centered upon building coalitions with civil rights organizations, major corporations, and foundations; increasing minority employment; and ultimately gaining the trust and respect of the African American community by engaging in more direct protest activity (e.g., participation in the March on Washington in 1963). Additionally, Young wanted to maintain support for the organization's integrated board of directors.

The organizational philosophy of the League changed to one that advocated engaging in peaceful protest and demonstrations. According to the League, this new agenda "constituted an expression of broad community concern in which the League should be represented."[7] Young recognized the need to align the organization with the Civil Rights movement. "To divorce ourselves from this would be an expression of irresponsibility," he explained. "To isolate our organization from this activity would be to deny corporations, foundations and community funds a unique opportunity for representation and participation in a new era of social planning. The Urban League will be valueless to responsible institutions in our society if it does not maintain communication and respect of other responsible Negro organizations and the respect of the masses of Negro citizens."[8]

The NUL attempted to support the mainstream Civil Rights organizations without compromising the integrity, mission, and historical foundation of the League. Consequently, Young became a "Washington insider" and served as an advisor to the presidential administrations of John Kennedy, Lyndon Johnson, and Richard Nixon. Facing the reality of a changing political climate within the African American community, the NUL, under Young's leadership, was able to project a new vision that animated, inspired, and transformed internal and external actors involved with the organization. As a result, the NUL was able to build lasting relationships and coalitions with other Civil Rights organizations and select industries to benefit the African American community. Young's attempt to pursue social service as well as engage in mainstream Civil Rights activism has indeed been embodied in the leadership of the League in the post–Civil Rights era.

The National Urban League in the Post–Civil Rights Era

The challenges faced by NUL presidents Vernon E. Jordan Jr. (1971–1981) and John E. Jacob (1982–1994) were similar to those Young encountered. Young's death (a drowning incident off the coast of Lagos, Nigeria) in 1971 brought forth new leadership. Vernon E. Jordan Jr., former executive director of the United Negro College Fund and a close friend of Whitney Young, was appointed to the post. For the first time in the organization's history, the League would no longer have a professional social worker running the agency. Instead, the organization gained a skilled lawyer who also had considerable fund-raising skills. Under his leadership Jordan oversaw the expansion of the organization's social service efforts.

Unanimously selected by the board of directors, Jordan used his knowledge of politics to help the Urban League gain government grant money to fund job training programs, early childhood education, and poverty programs. Additionally, under his guidance Jordan continued the League's tradition of infusing the organization with corporate support. Under Jordan the League grew to have an average annual budget of over one hundred million dollars (much of it was from federal government dollars).

During this time period the League once again was plagued by criticisms from Black activists. Playwright Amiri Baraka stated in *People* magazine, for example, that the Urban League was nothing more than a "vehicle for allowing the interests and thinking of White racist monopoly capital to penetrate the Black movement." Jordan responded in *Ebony* magazine that "Black people are not the only beneficiary; so is the country. The country has a vested interest in Black people doing well. It is really true that the chain is as strong as its weakest link."[9]

Jordan's accomplishments included overseeing the expansion of the League with the opening of seventeen new affiliates and the development of a partnership with the federal government which enabled the Urban League to establish programs and deliver services to urban communities in the areas of housing, health, education, and minority business development. He also instituted a citizenship education program that not only helped to increase the vote among African Americans but also bought new programs in the area of energy, the environment, and nontraditional jobs for women of color. In the areas of research and policy Jordan established *The State of Black America* report. This annual publication provides a forum to discuss the current status and conditions of African America.

Jordan served a ten-year tenure as executive director before being wounded in 1980 by a sniper in Fort Wayne, Indiana. He asserted, however, that the shooting did not factor into his decision to retire from his League post and enter the practice of law in Washington, D.C. Instead, he believed the time had come to move in a different direction. Unfortunately, Jordan's departure came during the administration of Ronald Reagan and his new policy on federalism. Under Reagan nonprofit organizations experienced severe cutbacks in government funding. In fact, approximately 80 percent of the NUL's budget was lost. Jordan's tenure was followed by that of John E. Jacob, a former chief executive officer of the Washington, D.C., and San Diego Urban League affiliates who at the time was serving as deputy director of the NUL.

Jacob assumed the presidency in 1982, bringing with him to the national office his knowledge of affiliates and an appreciation for the work done in the field. Jacob's leadership was set against the background of an era of rising political conservatism and Reaganomics. Self-destructive elements plagued the African American community unlike at any other time in history—homicides of Black men, gang violence, and increased drug use being among the more salient. Additionally, the disparity between African American and White unemployment rates widened; the gap between the average incomes of Black and White families increased; and the gap between Black-White business development and wealth also grew.

Under Jacob's leadership the League brought attention to these matters by emphasizing issues relating to youth and family. He established youth development programs and placed more attention on existing programs to reduce teenage pregnancy, assisting single female heads of households, combating crime in Black communities and increasing voter registration. He also used his tenure to criticize the federal government's agenda publicly and to issue the NUL's "Marshall Plan for America."

The plan recognized the mutual dependency between the needs of the African American community and the interests of the United States. Characterized as an economic investment program, the Marshall Plan consisted of three areas: investment initiatives, human resource development, and physical infrastructure. Investment initiatives "addressed both long-term economic productivity goals and short-term improvements in social well-being that concentrated on the areas of greatest need; involved sustained, programmed collaborations on the part of government, the private sector, and nonprofit organizations; and rigorous accountability systems for monitoring and assessment." In the area of human resource development the plan called for the combination of proven programs with investment initiatives (with heavy emphasis on youth), including "providing disadvantaged children with quality preschool education; supporting disadvantaged elementary and secondary students with sound basic education in public schools; and expanding the nation's employment and training system to deliver more relevant and viable job skills." Lastly, with respect to physical infrastructure the plan called for the nation to "invest in the development of a world-class transportation system; improve the nation's water supply and treatment facilities; and pursue more aggressively the development and application of advanced telecommunications technology."[10] Jacob used the plan to not only bring attention to the problems facing African Americans but also to engage external actors (e.g., the federal government or other nonprofit organizations) in a dialogue for finding programmatic solutions.

Jacob also paid careful attention to strengthening the internal dynamics of the NUL and its affiliates. He created the Permanent Development Fund, which was designed to increase the organization's financial stamina. In honor of former NUL chief Whitney Young, he also established several programs to aid the development of those who work for and with the League. These include the Whitney M. Young Jr. Training Center, which provides training and leadership development opportunities for both staff and volunteers; the Whitney M. Young Jr. Race Relations Program, which recognizes affiliates doing exemplary work in race relations; and the Whitney M. Young Jr. Commemoration Ceremony, which honors and pays tribute to long-term staff and volunteers who have made extraordinary contributions to the Urban League Movement.

Jacob also revisited the League's mission for the first time in over eighty years. By May 1990 the NUL communicated its newly defined mission in a document entitled *A Refocused National Urban League,* which called for the identification of a target population, methodical approach, and desired end result. According to a July 1991 report prepared by the NUL's National Planning and Evaluation Department, the decision to review the mission statement was a "result of questions raised in numerous circles regarding exactly what the [NUL] movement does."[11] The League recognized that for the first seventy-nine years of its existence they had been driven by a mission statement that had no end result. In a report issued at the 1992 Western Regional Assembly of the League, Executive Vice President Frank Lomax III stated:

> Equal opportunity was always looked at as a means and not an end result. While the movement historically worked for equal opportunity for African-Americans, it did not seek equality in the way of end results. After eight decades of service, the national organization realized that an equal chance at success was not the same as an equal success rate. . . . The management of

the National Urban League decided to shift the focus of the mission state-ment to social and economic equality and the primary target population back to the African-American community. . . . The designation of the African-American community as its primary service population meant that the League could more effectively target its available resources.[12]

The new mission statement incorporated key phrases such as *African American and other minorities* and *social and economic equality,* replacing the terms *Black* and *equal opportunity.*

Breaking from its past, the Urban League began to target a specific popula-tion and set forth requirements for effective service. The purpose was to reaf-firm the organization's "commitment to its foundation population and help allay fears amongst some elements within and outside of this community that the League lacks relevance and clarity."[13] Therefore, the Urban League sought to position itself as a leading advocate, informational source, and service provider for African Americans.

After twelve years at the helm, Jacob retired. He had led the Urban League during a time when Reagan-style conservatism predominated American poli-tics. This environment led to the Urban League's quest for increased economic development initiatives and programs under Jacob's leadership.

A New Crossroads: The Development Revolution

The challenges that civil rights and social service organizations are facing today are a direct result of the changing societal values. Ideas of indi-vidual responsibility and accountability supersede those of social responsibil-ity. Contemporary urban America is also facing dire circumstances. Problems remain, such as the erosion of local government tax bases (a consequence of White, Black, and industrial flight from urban cities), the lack of affordable housing, crumbling public school systems, crime, unemployment and limited job opportunities, drug abuse, and the breakdown of the family structure. Moreover, the legal foundation of affirmative action and other equal opportu-nity programs and policies in higher education and employment are eroding, even during an era associated with unprecedented racial and ethnic diversity.

In this new era the cohesive African American community of the 1960s has passed. The days when children attended the same schools and were taught by the same educators who had provided instruction and guidance to their par-ents, their aunts and uncles, and their cousins are practically nonexistent. The cohesion of family and community which used to exist (e.g., the one that focused and agreed upon a "Black Agenda") has also passed. African Ameri-can and other communities of the new millennium are more diversified and stratified than before. No longer sharing a common agenda as a guiding moral and political compass, African Americans and other disadvantaged citizens find themselves wandering amid a vast and hostile jungle. The United States has lost its great "social conscience," which was its guiding force during the Civil Rights era.

To this end the NUL and its affiliates face challenges similar to other civil rights organizations in the new millennium—in particular, how to best serve their constituencies while enduring the political and social dynamics of the post–Civil Rights era and how to develop a vision that guides the organization and an agenda that resounds and reverberates within contemporary American society. Understanding the pressures being brought to bear on the traditionally conservative organization, Hugh B. Price has sought to promote a more aggressive agenda. A former senior officer of the Rockefeller Foundation and frequent commentator on social issues, Price became the League's seventh president and CEO in 1994.

Known for his coalition-building experience and extensive administrative capabilities, Price dedicated himself to transforming the NUL into an organization of the twenty-first century. In order to better serve the League's constituents, a new agenda was proposed, this one with a primary focus of positioning African Americans and other disadvantaged populations for greater economic and social gains. In a 1995 speech entitled "Public Discourse: Our Very Fate as a Civil Society Is at Stake," Price envisioned "three areas of concentration for the National Urban League: education and the development of children; enabling their parents to become economically self-sufficient; and encouraging racial inclusion so that African-Americans can participate fully in the mainstream economy."[14] Similar to Jacob's mission to improve the economic plight of African Americans, the NUL developed a multifaceted plan under the theme "Economic Power: The Next Civil Rights Frontier." The goal of this agenda is to shape the economic future of African Americans. Specific objectives include the following: (1) increasing the number of Black entrepreneurs; (2) increasing access to capital for minority entrepreneurs; (3) focusing on urban revitalization by building and attracting businesses in inner-city neighborhoods; (4) producing more minority corporate executives; (5) increasing home ownership; (6) convincing youth that academic excellence is the key to success; and (7) partnering with large companies to bring about self-sufficiency and wealth building in the African American community.[15]

The new agenda of the NUL places heavy emphasis on restoring individual responsibility and, to a lesser degree, group responsibility. As such, the African American community must play an active and proactive role in child rearing, education, and encouraging self-reliance by stressing entrepreneurship and economic development. Additionally, in keeping with the League's long-standing tradition of involving and partnering with private enterprise, corporate America is given a role within this vision. Price encourages the business community to recommit to providing opportunities to the historically disadvantaged in inner cities. This community-building strategy parallels the previous strategy under-taken by Young by shifting more responsibility toward corporations and away from government. The NUL issued a challenge: "We who care must recapture America's heart before the nation's minorities and poor entirely lose theirs. Our very fate as a civil society is at stake. We must each extend a hand so that all of America's children, regardless of their station in life can march onward and upward."[16]

The NUL entered the twenty-first century—or an era it calls the "Develop-ment Revolution," a phrase coined by T. Willard Fair of the Urban League of Greater Miami—calling for a new revolution based upon activism and taking responsibility. According to Price, the nineteenth century is known as the Free-dom Revolution, during which slavery was eradicated, while the twentieth cen-tury is known as the Equality Revolution because civil rights were gained. Although, the work of the Civil Rights era continues into the twenty-first cen-tury, there needs to be further attention toward reducing economic gaps.

Becoming a Model Organization of the Twenty-first Century: Meeting Internal Challenges

A promising agenda is not enough to ensure that the legacy of the NUL will endure during the twenty-first century. Success is also dependent upon its ability to recognize and provide adequate solutions to internal organi-zational problems. In particular, three challenges face the organization in the coming years: funding, staffing, and leadership. These challenges are common problems that afflict most social service nonprofit organizations. Price and Ur-ban League affiliate presidents have developed strategies, however, which seek to minimize threats to the League's internal organization. Price has voiced his commitment to making sure that the "affiliates are shipshape organizationally for the 21st century," and he plans to "continue growing the League's endow-ment so [the organization is] resilient and resourceful well into the future."[17]

The first challenge facing the NUL is that of declining funding opportuni-ties. Typically, the Urban League and its affiliates receive funding from a vari-ety of sources, including grants (e.g., governmental and foundation), donations (e.g., corporate and individual), fees for service, nonprofit funding agencies (e.g., the United Way), fund-raising events, and service delivery contracts (e.g., local government contracts). Since the Reagan-Bush Administration, the Ur-ban League, especially on the affiliate level, was forced to begin finding more entrepreneurial ways to fund its programs of service as government grant money decreased. Affiliates such as the Atlanta and Los Angeles Urban Leagues created innovative fee-for-service partnerships with corporations in the area of employment training to fuse their budgets.

Another example of fiscal stress was evidenced by the decrease in the endowment of the NUL over this time period. Price relates that by the time he joined the League in 1994, the organization was running an "annual operating deficit in excess of $1 million against a general support budget of $7.5 million or so."[18] The operating deficit was also draining the League's endowment. Understanding the significance of such a deficit, Price downsized the staff by 40 percent and in 1996 began running balanced budgets with surpluses every year. He also launched an endowment drive in 1999. In the year 2001, counting cash and pledges, the endowment had increased to approximately 28 million dollars.[19]

The NUL must continue to work within its financial framework. The organization will also have to work with its affiliate organizations on building alternative income streams and procedures for financial planning if it is to survive as a movement. For example, affiliate Urban Leagues (e.g., Los Angeles, Detroit, and Denver) are utilizing alternative techniques for revenue generation; specifically, they are using social entrepreneurial activities (i.e., the incorporation of for-profit business techniques and language within a nonprofit context). The NUL must become increasingly proactive in helping affiliates find mechanisms for adopting such techniques and helping affiliate organizations to share their lessons and techniques with one another. Additionally, the national headquarters should encourage affiliate staff to continue their ongoing professional development by attending conferences and workshops outside of those offered by the NUL.

The second challenge facing the League has to do with staffing. Finding skilled personnel who are administrators and activists is difficult considering the myriad of skills involved in both pursuits. In addition, because of its affiliate structure, the staff must be personally involved in the process of systems change in their respective cities by being members of boards, commissions, study groups, and professional organizations. Furthermore, league staff must recognize that it is through the delivery of quality, individual human services that the NUL has gained the legitimacy and the right to participate in larger issues of advocacy and social change. They must develop the necessary training and skills that will allow them to be seen as "instruments" of change.

It has become important that the staffing policies of the Urban League include ways to allow the most proficient and highly skilled people to be employed. Prior to the 1960s and the infusion of project grant monies, most Urban League staffers were "generalists"—meaning they did it all: community organization, employment interviewing, rehabilitation, industrial relations, public relations, fund raising, research, and advocacy. Because of its corporate structure and desire to attract administrators, the NUL, like most nonprofits, must offer compensation and benefit packages (e.g., retirement benefits, medical and dental insurance) and flexible working environments (e.g., hours during which parents can attend to the needs of their children) which are attractive and comparable to those of for-profit agencies.

The last challenge facing the NUL concerns its leadership. In the twenty-first century the League leadership (i.e., the national and affiliate boards of directors and staff) faces a tremendous challenge as the organization transforms itself to serve the eclectic urban masses of the United States. Urban League leadership must sustain and invigorate the vision and agenda of economic empowerment which guides the organization.

Perhaps the Urban League's greatest leadership challenge is building a new coalition of businesses, government institutions, and the community which is uniquely suited for political, social, and economic dynamics of contemporary American society. This challenge also represents the repeated challenge the League has faced time after time with regards to using a board of directors that is not only integrated racially but one that is strongly represented by the corporate sector. Additionally, due to the societal dynamics associated with the post–Civil Rights era, Urban League leadership must build coalitions not only between African Americans and Caucasians but also Latino, Asian, and other ethnic and racial communities that make up the fabric of the new urban American landscape. This emphasis differs significantly from that of the coalition-building and mediation exercises of the Civil Rights era.

The leadership challenge also includes possessing a strong board of directors. The Urban League, like other Civil Rights organizations, has been criticized for having large, ineffective boards whose members rubberstamp the decisions of the CEO. Price transformed the board to one that was strong and activist. Price stated that he "inherited a huge board with trustees who believed passionately in the League. [Yet] many had served on the board for 10 to 20 years or more and were past their prime time in terms of their clout and their ability to contribute."[20] Consequently, Price and members of the national board of the Urban League imposed term limits and reconstituted the board.

Another challenge for the Urban League has been to counter the perception that it is dominated by corporate elites. The NUL board certainly includes CEOs and senior managers of major American corporations. The concerns range from the level of corporate influence on internal Urban League policies to whether or not League programs reflect corporate interest and not those of the African American community. In response to such challenges Price states:

Yes, we have plenty of corporate [executives] on our board, but our board are mostly made up of people who are either involved in the Urban League movement or who have a long history of concern about [the issues the League addresses]. The National Urban League and our affiliates are professionally run, staff driven organizations. As staff, we formulate the strategies and implement the programs associated with the League. Of course, our board must approve our strategic directions and plans, select [chief executive officers] who lead our organizations and [fulfill the roles and responsibilities associated with being a board member of a nonprofit organization]. But that is what boards of all well-run organizations do, be they nonprofit or for-profit.[21]

On the local level League affiliates are experiencing changes in leadership as executive directors with more then twenty years of experience with the organization retire. The changing of the guard may result in an overall loss of institutional memory if mechanisms are not put into place to retain this history. Yet the retirement of this generation also provides affiliate organizations with the opportunity to reconstitute itself along the lines of Price's agenda. As new blood infuses itself into the organization, the creation of what could be a new and more dynamic Urban League is possible. The impact of new leadership has yet to be felt, however, and is worthy of future study.

Conclusion

An examination of the NUL reveals several unique factors that have allowed the organization to endure in the post–Civil Rights era. Despite skepticism and criticism pertaining to its characterization as a nonprotest organization in comparison with other Civil Rights organizations, the league has survived. The organization has been successful in reinventing itself in times of crisis to meet the changing demands of American society.

Consequently, the NUL need not waste any time or energy debating its "essence" as an organization. Debates over whether it should be like the NAACP or the SCLC will only contribute to what can be characterized as a schizoid identity. With careful examination of the NUL's history, mission, objectives, and programs of service, there should be no confusion about its purpose and role during the post–Civil Rights era and in the twenty-first century:

The Urban League history is rooted in social work, namely in direct service. Indeed the Black social work movement emerged from the Urban League [the first executive director of the Urban League, George Edmund Haynes, was the first Black American to receive a doctorate in social work from Columbia University], and many of the early deans of the legendary Atlanta University School of Social Work were Urban Leaguers. That school is now named after Whitney Young, by the way. Our affiliates operate programs that help real people with needs get ahead day-in and day-out. We engage heavily in direct service aimed at improving the lives and life prospects of everyday people. In a companion effort to change the systems that serve our people, [the League engages] in policy analysis, research, advocacy, community mobilization and bridge building. Unlike the predominant pattern with the NAACP and SCLC, our local affiliates are professionally staffed operating agencies. Our largest affiliates have annual budgets of $5 to 15 million. I don't want to characterize the other groups. This is who we are.[22]

The twenty-first century brings new challenges to the NUL movement. Yet, with a new agenda designed not only to tackle the issues facing its constituency but also to perpetuate its development, the organization is well positioned to handle these challenges.

Four

Erika L. Gordon

A Layin' On of Hands

Black Women's Community Work

At its core this study is about the linkages between African American women, the political community work they perform in gender-specific organizations, and the development of a distinctive race- and gender-informed style of politics produced from these locations. It seeks to examine the significance of race, gender, and socioeconomic context in shaping African American women's organizational politics in the post–Civil Rights era. Many critics and scholars of African American politics have observed that the post–Civil Rights era has been characterized by a lack of popularly recognized African American leadership and clearly defined and communicated objectives for group economic, political, and social demands. This chapter seeks to broaden this debate by focusing on the organizational activity of African American women. In particular, this study seeks to draw some distinctions and parallels between middle-class Black women's involvement in organizational politics at a community level contemporarily and historically. A new body of scholarship on African American leadership, particularly as it relates to the development and sustenance of the Civil Rights Movement, points to the critical role that women played as organizational leaders, albeit ones that were not acknowledged for a variety of reasons.[1] This chapter draws on the conclusions provided from this scholarship and applies them to discussion of the so-called lack of African American leadership in the post–Civil Rights era by considering the ramifications of race, gender, and socioeconomic contexts on the processes of acknowledging and defining leadership practices within organizations. Like their sisters during the movement, the role these women, who are the subject of this study, play within their communities typically go unnoticed.

The main research question this study addresses is the role of African American middle-class women's community work in the production or maintenance of contemporary organizations involved in articulating and defining public policy agendas, defining community-building practices, and engaging in the "micromobilization" of African American communities. I argue that Black women's community work in the post–Civil Rights era plays an important and often neglected role in developing a wide range of important political resources, including: (1) local African American female support for a social policy agenda; (2) an organizational basis for African American political demands; and (3) responses, both at the mass and individual levels, to social policies that affect the African American community.

In the post–Civil Rights era these organizations have become even more critical to the development of a political practice that gives African American women a leading role in responding to the specific gendered ways that racial discrimination, economic marginalization, and leadership are experienced. Black women's community work should be viewed as an important and distinctive way for Black women to claim full citizenship rights. It not only serves as a way of analyzing how Black women have taken on the mantle of public leadership but also reflects on the activities and psychological characteristics that may differentiate Black women's leadership styles. Perhaps most important, an examination of community work as performed by Black women identifies the successes and failures involved in creating local institutions and political behaviors that contribute to community building through micromobilization.[2]

Micromobilization, as this chapter defines it, refers to the process of building institutions, and relationships and identifying political goals. It is a process of preparing the community for political activity by synthesizing political goals, strategies, and identities. A closer examination of Black women's community organizations highlights the challenges faced in creating a Black women's politics that is simultaneously derived from and representative of a distinct geographic and ideological setting. This chapter will present a theoretical framework for examining African American women's community work, political identity, and leadership; provide detailed insights into the strategies and political culture of African American women's community organizations; and suggest a relationship between African American women's self-perceptions as political actors, their organizational efforts, and the policy areas that their activities target.

One of the most widely used paradigms for understanding the organizational political motivations of Black women has been a perspective that tends to view race and gender as additive. The additive approach assumes that the underlying factors influencing the political and economic motivations of Black women can be understood by using methods that do not contextualize the potential effects of power systems based on race and gender. Additive approaches to understanding the implications of race, gender, and even class assume that there is a single direct independent effect that can be easily attributed to one of these systems when examining the political and economic experiences of Black women.[3]

The double disadvantage, or double jeopardy paradigm, formulated by scholars such as Marianne Githens and Jewel Prestige and Sandra Baxter and Marjorie Lansing presents a challenge to the additive perspective by highlighting the interconnection of race and gender in contextualizing Black women's experiences and political choices. Black women cannot simply disassemble their status to support race or gender concerns; rather, Black women operationalize their political motivations from a perspective that holds race and gender are inseparable. In order to understand the behavior of African American women, these two forces must be considered collectively in an analysis of African American women's political behavior. The political preferences, motivations, and levels of political engagement of African American women cannot be understood or predicted from what is known about White women or Blacks in general. Rather, since Blacks and women are politically disadvantaged, African American women are doubly so.[4] Race and gender combine in ways to create and limit the political aspirations and behavior of African American women. As a result, African American women are characterized as possessing a double consciousness and faced with the difficult political choice of selecting or prioritizing their dual political identities, often choosing political strategies that mutually address these needs.

In contrast, a third paradigm, the matrix of oppression perspective, proposes that the political and social motivations of Black women can be best understood by contextualizing Black women's experiences using an interactive model that identifies multiples sources of oppression. Multiple sources of oppression—or a matrix of race, class, and gender—suggests that Black women are subjected to several simultaneous oppressions that have interconnecting multiplicative linkages among them. A consequence of the multiplicative nature of systems of oppression like race, gender, or class is that the relative importance of one factor in explaining the problems and reactions of Black women varies depending on the particular dynamic being examined.[5] Black women's lives are constructed through their experiences in a matrix of systems of oppression. More specifically to this chapter, Black women's political responses, motivations, and experiences have been profoundly constructed by their location within this matrix of domination. The matrix of oppression paradigm provides needed explanatory power for situations in which it appears that Black women have supported or pursued causes that seem on the surface to focus exclusively on their race versus their gender. Additionally, this matrix of oppression perspective supports the use of race and gender as analytic categories. Treating these statuses as analytic categories, which this chapter will do, argues that Black women's organizational practices and political lives cannot be fully understood unless both race and gender are used as analytic categories within the investigation of such phenomena. Gender and race are not only parts of political institutions and processes but are constitutive of these very institutions and processes.[6] *Race* and *gender* are not merely identities or categories that result from political processes and institutions. Instead, they have specific meanings that become embedded in the very formation and operationalization of political practices.

Over the last decade a growing body of literature has examined the implications of women's collective action strategies and their impacts on social policy initiatives. Research within this genre has its roots in the sociological, political, and historical frameworks. Within these frameworks scholars have considered the relationship between gender and the state. This literature has often centered on the lives of middle-class White women or the tension between White women and working-class White immigrants. Research on African American women often focuses on race in prohibiting the formation of multiracial coalitions for policies sensitive to the needs of women as mothers, or it has focused on the ways in which African American women as clients of the state have been negatively characterized and stereotyped as a justification for directing resources away from welfare policies in general.[7]

The case study of African American women's organizational activity which this chapter presents is therefore highly important. African American women's organizational power is an indicator of the daily effects of race, class, and gender in shaping responses to political and economic challenges. This research contributes to the political science scholarship that discusses African American women as political strategists, intellectuals, or leaders, either within or outside of traditional political processes. It also provides supporting evidence for the perspective that African American women's political socialization takes a much different path than that of African American men or White women due to the impacts of race and gender. The ways in which these differences structure political activity organized and promoted exclusively by African American women have not been documented. African American women's political activity within community organizations and the linkages to processes of social change highlight the ways in which gender, race, and socioeconomic context may alter the dynamics of collective action strategies. The ways in which these women activists and community leaders experience race, gender, and economic reality may critically affect the motivations for organization, strategies, and incentives used to initiate and maintain activity.

Defining African American Women's Community Work

As this chapter defines it, community work entails the construction of integrative informal and formal networks that redistribute resources, challenge access to power, construct strategies to address policy problems, and create political meaning for events within the African American community. This chapter builds on an understanding of community work based on Gilkes's model, which characterizes community work as a process of articulating and confronting power relationships. The objective of community work is building the institutions that form the political culture of African American communities.[8] The practices of community work organizations are the persistent effort across time to close the gap between Black and White life chances, with the effects of activity developing in a cumulative fashion over time. Community work is conceptualized as a specific labor that takes place outside of the labor force, home, and family: it is labor that has as its objective the generation of an alternative set of commitments and ideological understanding of Black community. As a practice, community work is not inherently focused on addressing the specific needs of African American women and children. Rather the specific focus of community work activities and organizations is produced in part by the dynamics of internal analysis of structural arrangement, power, and needs that Black women involved in community work come to express as a common viewpoint.

According to Gilkes's model, community work is an interactive process that develops through three phases: discovery, challenge, and development. The discovery phase of community work entails the process by which Black women come to make connections between their quality of life and the oppressive institutional frameworks that structure their interactions. The actual relationships, ideas, and resources that Black women manufacture or collect in order to change their relationship to the power structure defines the challenge phase of community work. The development phase of action occurs when women disseminate the benefits of their collective action to the community and in the process forge important connections to institutions of the community.[9] In the conceptualization of community work which this chapter employs, these processes are not necessarily linear. Participants in community work may be engaged in a combination of phases. For example, while the discovery phase of community work is the one that begins the process of analyzing structures and quality of life and oppressive institutions, it is the case that, even while challenging or disseminating benefits, women may once again be engaged in the process of making and reevaluating the connections between their quality of life and oppressive conditions.

This study builds on Gilkes's model by focusing on those activities that are specifically designed to confront power relationships, promote attention to specific policy issues, and mobilize other sectors of the community for action. Examples of the community work activity that this chapter focuses on will include coalition building with other women's organizations; traditional Civil Rights organizations or organizations that cross color and class lines; creating initiatives to address the lack of government resources for problems such as daycare or tutoring; strategizing responses to local officials' interpretations of access to school computers or other resources; and challenging the ideology underlying welfare-to-work programs as they relate to Black women. Community work organizations are also understood as those groups that have as an explicit part of their mission an understanding of the importance of volunteerism as a means of addressing political, economic, or social community needs. They are by definition nonpartisan, are typically organized to convey benefits to the broader community, and, most important, may interact with various levels of government or none at all in order to accomplish their objectives. This emphasis differentiates these groups from traditional political interest groups, which are organized with the intention to win benefits for their members exclusively through the public sector and typically are engaged with a smaller range of issues and a limited range of government officials or agencies.

Perhaps most important, the concept of a Black woman's standpoint is essential to understanding the motivations behind Black women's community work. As Patricia Hill Collins suggests, Black women's community work and the underlying political content of these efforts are informed by Black women's particular positioning as an oppressed group within a distinctive political and economic hierarchy. In this hierarchy race and gender identities significantly constrain the political and economic choices of Black women. This status at the lowest end of the power hierarchy results in the development of a Black woman's standpoint, a perspective on the sources of oppression and its remedies. From this perspective the content of Black women's lives informs the types of analysis which are produced about the power networks linking their material conditions and the identification of possible means of subverting and challenging these conditions.[10] This specialized knowledge influences African American women's political activism by supporting the development of spheres of influence in which protest activity can take root. It also supports the objectives of organizational activity, that is, the struggle for institutional transformation. This standpoint influences the development and structure of institutions that can respond to community needs as well as those institutions that have direct control over the resources of African American communities.

The Historical Legacy of African American Women's Community Work

Investigations into the community activity and organizational practices of Black women have been developed from both historical and sociological perspectives. This literature suggests that Black women have long-standing traditions of creating both local and national organizations to address the distribution of resources to and within Black communities and that the major areas of concern have historically been education, equal rights, wage and employment issues, and social welfare.[11] From the very earliest struggles against slavery, Black women have played critical roles in promoting economic and political freedom for themselves, their families, and their larger communities. Relationships to the community, both the immediate community and to the entire race, have been historically significant in determining the way Black women conceptualize politics. These community-based strategies have been generated from Black women's concerns as mothers and often as the primary economic providers for their family.[12] The goal of improving the quality of life experienced by family, friends, and the immediate community has provided the organizational foundation for Black women's political activity as well as a basis for theorizing and developing a Black female political identity.

African American women's involvement in community work and community organizing is not merely an outgrowth of the Civil Rights Movement of the 1950s and 1960s or of the women's movement of the 1970s. African American women's involvement in community work as political activists has a long historical precedent. Their involvement in community work organizations began in the late nineteenth century with the founding organizations that constituted the basis of society for newly emancipated Blacks. Within these communities of former Black slaves, Black women were participants in creating new mechanisms for marshaling resources to their communities. The frontrunners to nineteenth-century community work organizations were sewing circles, mutual aid societies, and women's church auxiliaries, all of which provided economic assistance and molded the cultural and political identities of Black women, men, and children.[13] As Black communities faced challenges in gaining access to education, public services, employment, and citizenship rights, these fledgling women's organizations developed strategies to address these needs. Community work organizations or clubs were founded by Black women of all economic backgrounds in cities across the nation. Smaller Black women's voluntary associations or clubs were unified under regional and eventually national institutions, starting in 1896 with the founding of the National Association of Colored Women (NACW). Black women who were involved in founding these initial formal clubs were responding to the particularly gendered way in which Black women were experiencing the consequences of racism as well as existing cultural and societal norms about female involvement in public life.[14] These organizations, which grew steadily in number and size from the late 1870s through the 1920s, were primarily started by middle-class women to address problems of community and identity. They were invested in improving the lives of African American people and, in particular, the lives of women and girls. This was accomplished through activities such as the creation of schools and day care for young children, protests against city officials for equal access to public facilities, demands for equal access to public services, and the formation of protection and employment agencies to safeguard the wages of working Black women.

Community work organizations were faced with new challenges in response to the changing relationships between Black women, labor markets, and Black popular culture during the 1920s. In the 1930s and 1940s Black women faced new challenges in addressing community problems due to the combined effects of federal government evolution, World War II, and the changing national economy. New national organizations were founded such as the National Council of Negro Women, created in 1935. The early 1950s and 1960s brought a new period of activism for Black women's community work organizations, whose grassroots affiliates provided the initial financial resources and support for Civil Rights activity. While Aldon D. Morris's work acknowledges the critical role women's organizations played as incubators and "halfway houses" of the movement, others document the critical role that women's community work organizations played in developing political strategies aimed at creating social change.[15]

The significance of gender, race, and socioeconomic context in formulating strategies to address social problems of education, citizenship rights, and poverty within the context of struggle against racism becomes clearer in examining the origins of protest strategies and agenda setting within the Black community during this period of political activity. For example, the institutional relationships and agenda setting of organizations such as the Women's Political Council of Montgomery illustrate the significance of race and gender identities in examining the politics of community work as well as the relevancy of Black women's relative socioeconomic status. The Women's Political Council, organized in 1946 by Mary Fair Burks, was composed of concerned community women, many of them professional women with occupations such as community workers, teachers, educators, social workers, and supervisors. The community work of the Women's Political Council was organized around a three-tier strategy: political action, including voter registration and interviewing candidates for office; protest about abuses on buses and the use of taxpayers' money to operate segregated parks; and the education of high school students on how democracy was intended to operate, as well as the operation of literacy schools so that adults could pass the requirements for registration.[16]

In the post–Civil Rights era Black women's voluntary organizations have been involved in struggles for better education for children, remedies against poverty, welfare rights, and the battle for better wages. Middle-class Black women's community work organizations, on a local and national level, have been forced to confront the difficulties of addressing the continued political economic problems facing Black women in the midst of crumbling inner cities, massive unemployment, and a reconfiguration of the politics of racism in the recent attacks on affirmative action.

While community work as a practice has not historically been isolated to middle-class Black women, middle-class Black women have been in a unique position to found and encourage the development of such organizational spaces for themselves. Black middle-class women in the late nineteenth century became particularly invested in community work because it served multiple purposes in advancing their own political and social agendas.

First, community work practice represented a clear way that Black women could address the issues facing their communities in concrete ways, using solutions tailored from their own experiences. Additionally, Black middle-class women were inspired by middle-class intellectuals such as Ida B. Wells Barnett, Mary Church Terrell, and Anna Julia Cooper to conceptualize their own progress as women as critical to the progress of the race. Black middle-class women understood that their own relative economic privilege did not shield them from critiques about the oversexualized, savage, and unworthy nature of Black women. These prevailing stereotypes did not protect middle-class women from sexual violence or from systematically being taken advantage of by their employers.[17] In the post–Civil Rights era the so-called pathology of the Black family and, more specifically, the so-called pathology of Black women, described in documents such as the Moynihan report and public policy arguments revolving around the culture of poverty thesis, have provided a shifting foreground for Black women's grassroots activism in the midst of changing race and gender relations and economic opportunities.

Several critical aspects of the organization and structure of the Black community speak to the ways in which race and gender have become embedded within Black institutions and political culture and are relevant in examining Black middle-class women's community work practices. This study recognizes that racism and discrimination are contextual, reflecting the political, economic, and cultural dimensions of geographic regions throughout the United States. The concept of "Black community" is used to signify the reduced economic and political opportunities that African Americans as a collective have experienced. Systems of racism and segregation have historically had a dramatic effect on the construction of gender relationships as well as access to resources within the Black community. A relatively small body of research documents the ways in which slavery separated families and constructed a specific gender ideology that was applied to Black women. It suggests that the relative privileges accorded to White women as a function of gender were not applicable to Black women.[18]

During Reconstruction patterns of segregation and Black economic dependence contributed to the development of separate spheres of influence for Black men and women within the community. The development of such spheres placed Black women in positions of performing economic labor to sustain the family unit as well as needing to create networks to obtain necessary goods and services across community lines. Research also documents the practices of enforced labor whereby Black men, under the pretext of law enforcement, were separated from their families and communities and sent to work camps or to prison as a cheap and easily exploitable labor force. Their labor was then utilized by both public and private interests in order to construct roads, build factories, and cultivate farms.[19] These brutal practices placed Black women in the vulnerable position of having to hold together not only their families but their entire communities.

The end of Reconstruction also encouraged the specific division of public and private political space within the Black community. As Black men were increasingly disenfranchised from public life at the end of Reconstruction, Black middle-class women and Black working-class men and women were in turn disenfranchised. Without the public outlets for Black males to participate fully in political life, Black men and women were forced into developing community institutions that would take the place of the franchise and help fulfill their rights as citizens. These citizenship rights were addressed through the creation of Black organizations that were divided by gender in order to satisfy male needs for full citizenship rights in a climate that was being increasingly defined by a masculine-defined political culture.[20]

In the contemporary era the differential economic situations of African American men and women continue to impact African American communities.

While the Black population faces increasingly difficult chances in obtaining quality education and higher-paying jobs, access to the resources of financial institutions, and limited city services, economic disparity has gender dimensions. The economic circumstances of Black men and women are structured such that gender and race ideologies create different realities for the two sexes within American society.[21] These realities reflect differences in access to employment, higher education, and opportunities for promotion or advancement and in treatment by law officials. The use of community work, such as that of the NCNW, has been a significant method for addressing the ramifications of these differences.

Methodology

My theoretical approach examines the relationship between gender and race ideologies and the structure of social change. Like a majority of feminist and womanist political investigations, this framework also utilizes the understanding that to capture fully the economic and cultural behaviors that structure contemporary political practices, the definitions or boundaries around activities that are considered to be political in nature must be expanded.[22] For this investigation political activity includes any struggle to gain control over definitions of self and community, to create alternative political processes and institutions, and to increase the resources and power of the community. The theoretical framework also suggests a model of politics which accounts for the significance of the nature and location of power while also examining the structural societal relationships that support or challenge group attempts at creating political agency. The model of politics advocated here suggests that power circulates in smaller localized networks at both the community and electoral level and that this circulation is relevant to explaining how people interface and interact with political phenomena.

My theoretical approach suggests that micromobilization and community work are interrelated because they both embrace a particular understanding of politics. *Politics* is understood to be a process that reflects the significance of race, gender, and socioeconomic context in access to resources and the ability to influence institutions and others. Politics is a process that crosses the boundaries between public and private life. Within this definition of *politics,* race and gender are critical concepts in specifying and identifying modes of resistance. Power is not only understood as something that individuals have but also as a social and political relationship that determines access to the basic material resources of society.[23]

The framework used in this chapter for examining community work and the development of African American women's responses to social policy initiatives also makes a distinction between African American women's organizational efforts and successes. The full range of practices, climate, and strategies can be considered separately from the question of whether or not they were successful. This case study of a local field section of the NCNW focuses on the efforts of African American women's community work. In this context *efforts* refers to the NCNW's practices, strategies, organizational formats, political cultures, and range of coalition building and networking.

In order to investigate the linkages between African American women, the political community work they perform in gender-specific organizations, and the development of a distinctive race- and gender-informed style of politics produced from these locations, a targeted in-depth qualitative case study was developed. The case study included participant observation of the selected community work organization, document analysis of records and minutes, and semistructured interviews with fifteen respondents. This approach had three benefits: it allowed the development of a detailed description of organizational activity from those most engaged in it; it illustrated the specific patterns of interrelationships between events; and it preserved the chronology of activity in distinguishing between efforts and results. In the case of investigating women's community activism, qualitative methods are often the best way of chronicling activity while also developing a perspective on how participants themselves perceive their actions. This is due in part to the fact that the nature of political activity requires special attention to discussions, meetings, and activities that may not appear to be politically significant upon initial observation. The case study approach also assists in the development of theory. Within the feminist research tradition, personal narratives and interviews represent a significant way in which women are able to express their own understanding of their political environment and their abilities to impact it.[24]

The local chapter featured in this case study was identified from a directory of known local field sections in the Washington, D.C., area provided by the national headquarters of NCNW. The directory or listing of area organizations was obtained through telephone calls and correspondence with the national headquarters of each organization. The interviews were primarily conducted via telephone, with a few participants opting for a face-to-face interview. All of the interviews took place between March and May 2000. The participant observation period lasted from February to October 2000. With the permission of the respondent, all of the interviews were recorded and professionally transcribed. The personal interviews allowed for detailed descriptions of political beliefs and stressed the participant's definition of the problem, encouraged her to structure her account of the problem, and enabled her to communicate her notion of relevance.[25]

Interview contacts were solicited using snowball sampling interview techniques through two starting points of contact. One starting point consisted of interviewing the president of the chapter; the president was asked to consent to a personal interview. After this initial interview the president recommended another person, either an officer or rank-and-file member, to be interviewed. This next interviewee was also asked to recommend a person or persons who would be interested in being interviewed. Additionally, interview contacts were also solicited through an introductory letter and sign-up form distributed at the monthly meeting during the period of participant observation for this case study. Interested respondents were provided with a postage-paid envelope to submit their responses. The respondent was asked to provide a contact address, telephone number, and e-mail address, along with the time of day most convenient for an interview. During the interview these respondents were also asked to recommend another person who might consent to an interview.

The interview protocol consisted of six multiple-choice questions and thirty open-ended questions. The multiple-choice questions asked respondents to provide key demographic information about themselves, such as their marital status, whether or not they were a parent, the highest level of education attained, their income earned in 1998, and what economic class they belong to. The thirty open-ended questions covered areas such as how individuals became members of their organization; what personal and professional contacts were significant; their level of previous information about the organization; the leadership styles used by their chapter; the organization's sensitivity to both race and gender concerns, differences between Black women's community work organizations and other organizations, and an understanding of what activities constitute politics. The interview questionnaire was pretested with a Washington, D.C., area chapter of NCNW. The interviews were analyzed using content analysis techniques identifying repeated themes, concepts and perspectives. Careful attention was also given to potential distinctions in perspectives among the interviewees. In conducting the participant observation, I attended the local section's monthly meetings, programmed activities, and executive board meetings, and I observed the interaction with other organizations. Detailed field notes were taken to capture the focus of the activity, method of participation, number of participants, types of participants, and target audience for the activism or advocacy.

National Council of Negro Women: 1935–2000

The great need for uniting the effort of our women kept weighing upon my mind. I could not free myself from the sense of loss—of wasted strength—sustained by the national

> *community through failure to harness the great power of*
> *women into a force for constructive action. I could not rest*
> *until our women had met this challenge of the times.*
> —Mary McLeod Bethune

The National Council of Negro Women (NCNW) was founded in 1935 by Mary McLeod Bethune, an active participant and former national president of the NACW. In December 1935 she convened a meeting of African American women representing a wide array of Black women's organizations. Bethune firmly believed in the need for Black women to present a united front in addressing the multifaceted challenges confronting the Black community and to open the many doors that were closed to African Americans. At that meeting Bethune proposed the establishment of a united organization of Black women which through force of numbers could make its voice heard.

According to Bethune's vision, the NCNW was to serve as a national organization with the primary purpose of unifying all of the diverse women's organizations within the Black community in order to harness the leadership, interests, and potential political and economic power of all Black women.[26] Specifically, Bethune envisioned that the organization would serve as a clearinghouse for placing Black women in the spotlight for national leadership and political opportunities while also drawing attention to their special concerns. Bethune envisioned NCNW as a grassroots, forceful, inclusive group with roots solidly in the ground to sustain African American women's growth, broaden their vision, and extend their service. According to Bethune's vision, the organizational philosophy argued that Black America's needs were served when Black women's needs were addressed. The mission of the organization was to demonstrate a commitment to race and gender sensitivity. NCNW defined itself as reaching out to Black women and their families to advance the quality of life through service and advocacy. Its primary goal was to have Black women fully represented in national public affairs.[27] The NCNW constitution defined the specific purpose of the organization as a powerful group of united Black women's organizations which could function as an instrument for information distribution, leadership, and economic opportunity. The organization's historical institutional legacy focuses on Black women's economic empowerment and entrepreneurship. The organizational ideology favored community work that strengthened these opportunities for Black women.

The NCNW's founding coincided with a changing national economic structure for African Americans as well as with developing tensions within existing Black women's organizations. NCNW was founded after the second wave of mass Black migration to the North and in the wake of the Great Depression.

Black women's organizations were also struggling with declining resources for community work and a shifting sense of expectation in terms of addressing the problems of race and gender faced by Black women. The NCNW was founded during a time period when the NACW in particular was losing its ability to draw on the support of Black women to define and support their issues using previous organizational methods. From her experience as a past NACW president, Bethune noted that Black women did not seem as ready to devote their time and resources to the NACW as they had before. It was perceived as being out of touch with the current dilemmas facing Black women of all economic backgrounds.[28]

Initially, the NCNW approach to community work was defined by networking. This strategy involved NCNW national and local representatives corresponding, attending, and coordinating at other organizations' policy meetings. These other organizations included Black women's organizations, national and local women's organizations, and policy-specific organizations. The objective was to establish a physical presence and idea exchange that would foster the inclusion of Black women in policy developments. Over time NCNW developed a second tier to its approach to community work which emphasized identifying the particular concerns of Black women in terms of both race and gender at the local level. To this extent NCNW supported the development of leadership training for its local-level membership. Black women's middle-class status became paramount to operationalizing community work within NCNW at the national and local levels. Both the institutional philosophies and strategies used to carry out the organization's local community work reflected the interests and aspirations of Black middle-class women. Having Black professional women serve as conduits for resources and ideas to their local communities in its networking strategy reflected the significance of class to the organization.[29] Its original emphasis on incorporating Black women into the nation's economy also took shape through NCNW's campaigning for Black professional women to be included in the leadership of federal and state agencies. Such strategies were not necessarily a radical challenge to the way federal government functioned or a radical challenge to capitalist exploitation of Black working- or middle-class communities.

In 1937 the organization moved to create its own metropolitan councils to function in local African American communities. NCNW's early activities focused on increasing Black female employment and economic opportunity. To this end it launched campaigns to support the elimination of photographs from civil service applications, nondiscriminatory public housing, fair and equal inclusion of all Blacks in New Deal welfare and job programs, and social security coverage for domestic workers and farm laborers.[30] Additionally, its members were taught how legislation and government policy affected them then were advised to give or withhold their support. From 1935 to 1949 the national NCNW program was administered through thirteen committees. During this period NCNW early activities included collaborations with the YMCA and labor unions to collect, analyze, and distribute data regarding the employment of African Americans, especially women in federal jobs. In 1945 Black women's organizations affiliated with the NCNW on a national level included the Black Greek letter sororities, Black women's professional organizations, and missionary associations. During the late 1930s the NCNW represented 500,000 Black women through its affiliates. By the end of the 1940s the number of women NCNW members increased to one million.[31]

During the 1960s the organization also established two national programs for recruiting and training African American women for local community service. In 1964 NCNW participated in registering voters and setting up freedom schools. More specifically, NCNW was involved in a national project to build alliances between Black and White southern women in order to challenge racism and discrimination. To encourage women of different faiths and races to work together, NCNW initiated the Women in Community Service (WICS) program. The project brought together NCNW members, the National Council of Catholic Women, the National Council of Jewish Women, and Church Women United to work on community projects such as Head Start, low-income housing, desegregation, and voter registration. The NCNW's Wednesdays in Mississippi project sent integrated teams of women out once a week to different towns in Mississippi to work in freedom schools that had been created in the wake of school closings brought on by the threat of desegregation. In 1967 these projects were established in Danville, Virginia; Paterson, New Jersey; and Boston, Massachusetts.[32]

From 1965 to 1980 NCNW sponsored at least forty national projects. Typically, national projects are operationalized through a dual-prong strategy involving the organization's national resources and local community chapters. These projects have primarily been targeted to youth and women in the areas of unemployment, teenage pregnancy, health care, and affirmative action.[33] In 2000 the NCNW consists of 38 affiliated national organizations, 250 community-based sections chartered in forty-two states, 20 college-based sections, and 60,000 individual members. NCNW is governed by a board of directors made up of the heads of each of its affiliated national organizations and an executive committee of 20, elected by the membership at the biennial national convention. A chairman of the board is selected by members to lead the organization. The NCNW organizational structure features a top-down relationship that privileges the national level, specifically the CEO, in designating organizational objectives.[34] The core membership of the NCNW consists of professional Black women ranging in age from thirty-five to fifty-five. NCNW's programs are based on the concepts of commitment, unity, self-reliance, and community empowerment. NCNW community work has been directed to create programs providing food for the hungry, educational opportunities, job training, HIV / sexually transmitted disease (STD) awareness programs, and child care for disadvantaged and working mothers.[35] The work of the NCNW has taken on new significance in recent years with the dramatic reductions in and the elimination of numerous government programs, a retrenchment that only increases the burdens borne by the poor and Black communities.

The NCNW is an organization that is not without difficulties. Like many long-time Civil Rights organizations, it faces the challenge of attracting new, younger members. The median age of NCNW members is fifty. In order to draw more women in their twenties and thirties, the organization is redefining itself to offer more local-level opportunities to younger women. Part of this process is the establishment of new local "millennium" sections in large metropolitan cities such as Washington, D.C., and Atlanta. These sections are comprised exclusively of women in the twenty-one to thirty-five age range.

The Washington, D.C., metropolitan area has been the home of many metropolitan field sections of the NCNW.[36] Currently, the Washington metropolitan area is home to six field sections, some of which have been tailored to involve special demographic groups of women in community work. For example, one of two currently existing millennium sections, is located in the region, while other sections exist on university campuses, such as the Howard and American University Sections. The Potomac Valley Section (PVS), which is the focus of this chapter, was organized in 1997. The section was organized as a response to the declining community work performed by the demographically older existing Montgomery County NCNW Section. The great majority of the PVS community work has been focused on meeting the needs of children and younger women.[37] The section as a whole consists of college-educated women who identify themselves as middle class. The section has members who range in age from the early thirties to mid-sixties. A majority of the chapter's members are in the twenty-six to thirty-five age range (36.7 percent) and the forty-six to fifty-five age range (38.8 percent). At the time of this study the chapter had ninety members who had paid local dues to the section and to the national NCNW. The dues served as seed money to maintain the national headquarters and to supply local members with the organization's membership materials. The dues amount was twenty dollars. All of the ninety members were not active: about half of the members attended regular meetings and participated in planning and carrying out the section's activism and advocacy.

A majority of its community work is performed with the Tobytown and Scotland communities, two historically Black and poorer communities located in Montgomery County. From time to time, the section partners with the People's Community Baptist Church, a Black Baptist church located in lower Montgomery County, which typically provides free space, desks, and chairs for this community work. Since its inception the section has developed a partnership with the Montgomery County executive office in seeking solutions to problems that disproportionately affect African American teens. The section supports a public policy committee, with the sole purpose of researching policy issues of interest to Black women. Additionally, it partners with the African American Heath Initiative to work on issues of infant and fetal mortality, diabetes, and AIDS. It has also sponsored community initiatives concerning economic opportunities.

African American Middle-Class Women's Community Work Practices: The Potomac Valley Section of the NCNW

The NCNW is an organization that reflects a particular understanding of African American women's identity as political actors. The women of the Potomac Valley Section of the NCNW identify the organization as specifically focused and organized around gender and race concerns. According to the members interviewed, the organization is a place of empowerment for African American women who might otherwise be left out entirely or not as engaged with political and social change. Members of the PVS indicated that their membership possesses an understanding of the relationship between African American women's quality of life and political and economic circumstances surrounding them. The interviewees indicated that in their view African American women face a type of oppression that is substantively different from that experienced by the African American male. The interviewees were asked a series of questions on the relationship between their perceptions of the relative importance of their race, gender, and socioeconomic status and the rationale underlying their community work activities. All of the respondents indicated that they personally felt that race and gender together translated into differential economic and political circumstances for Black women versus Black men. Most often, respondents indicated that the implications of both race and gender on African American women resulted in limited attention to the unique problems faced by Black women. These problems were described in terms of issues that disproportionately affect Black women across a variety of socioeconomic categories, such as references to inadequate healthcare, lower wages, and the implications of crime against Black women as well as the process of identifying concerns as important in setting an agenda. The experiences of

Black women due to the effects of both race and gender on politics and economics were described by all of the respondents as giving them a sense of invisibility or a sense of constantly having their knowledge challenged.

> *R1:* Racism for Black men and women is very different and it plays itself out different. They [White men and women] see us in a different way. It's like "I don't know how to identify her" so Black women are ignored, not paid attention to. And for me that's another very frustrating part in terms of not having my presence recognized. This scenario can really hurt Black women. It means our concerns or issues are never validated.

> *R2:* I feel as Black women, our burden is more than any other race or gender combined. Because as you know, we receive the least amount of pay, when you look at White men, White women, Black men. We also receive the least amount of respect. I find that constantly on a day to day basis, I am facing individual men and women who are challenging my ability, so I'm not being taken seriously. I am also not really getting support from other Black men in these situations. Often times they are just as bad or worse. I don't know whether it is age, race, or gender, but you are constantly on the defensive in fighting back.

> *R3:* I think we're in a unique position being both female and Black. Because of our experiences with racism and discrimination and sort of day-to-day life that we have a different perspective on what community problems might be or have a different way of identifying solutions to them.

Interviewees also expressed the belief that Black women's community work organizations identify different issues and strategies because of the relative impact of both race and gender on the quality of Black women's lives. All of the respondents identified their local organization as one that uses both race and gender to identify concerns and strategies. This distinction was based in the differential impact of racism and sexism on Black women's life opportunities.

> *R5:* I definitely think as a Black woman's organization, concerns with race and gender affect the type of issues that we are interested in. As well it should. And also the manner in which this is to be addressed. The types of issues we choose and the manner in which we try to address them are definitely affected by our status as both women and African Americans.

> *R7:* I think it's important for Black women to be in an environment where it's safe for them to voice their concerns. I'm talking about the race and gen-

der issue, but they're not necessarily going to be able to share in their normal every day, probably male dominated world. NCNW does address issues from a race and gender perspective. Locally, our goals are to address concerns faced by a wide variety of Black women in our community.

Many interviewees developed this point further to indicate a distinction between the selection of agenda issues based on identifying them as Black women's concerns and their ability to develop strategies that incorporated a race and gender perspective. These interviewees indicated a distinction between the support of issues that disproportionately affect Black women and the ability to operationalize community work activities based on a perspective that incorporates a Black women's standpoint or understanding of the interactions between race, gender, and socioeconomic status. For example, the following respondent highlights the section's attention to the way race and gender impact African American women's feelings of personal empowerment.

R4: I feel that the section is sensitive to the specific race and gender concerns. We are about giving women and children and choice, giving the tools to feel empowered. As African American women, we have so much pride. No matter how much money we have or don't have, we have a tremendous sense of pride and it has been like this through history. And a lot of people don't understand this like African American women. We understand each other no matter which economic place we are from. Also, health issues, we understand the reticence of our men to go to the doctor. We understand that HIV/AIDS, breast cancer, are things that we have not wanted to talk about. One because we have often felt or been made to feel that we can't talk about them intelligently. Rather then risk sounding unintelligent, we just don't discuss these issues. We understand this and it's clear when we are just dealing with us (African Americans). But it is not so clear when other folks are dealing with us, they think "Well what is wrong with these people, don't they understand that HIV/AIDS is killing more of them?" One of the other things that we understand better than most about us as African American women is we have things that are faith based, we have a tremendous faith. So a lot of things that are unexplainable to us, we will readily give it to faith, and that doesn't happen in other situations. We understand this about each other.

When asked why they were members of this particular organization as opposed to other Civil Rights organizations, the interview participants indicated that they believed that African American women were the only ones capable of defining and addressing the social and political issues facing their communities. All of the respondents indicated that traditional Civil Rights organi-

zations and elected officials, both Black and White, were either unable or unwilling to consider fully the ways in which race and gender impact the political and social problems faced by African American women. Most of those
interviewed (80 percent) indicated that they had been or currently were members of the NAACP. Yet all of them indicated that they believed organizations
such as the NAACP were less effective than the NCNW in addressing African
American women's problems. The interviewees believed that African American men had been the focus of organizational efforts, both in terms of identifying problems and directing efforts, for so long that the issues affecting African
American women had been neglected. Furthermore, the effects of racism on
African American men had created conditions in which African American
women were left to pick up the pieces of family life.

R2: We (Black women in community work organizations) have a tendency
to try to do it all, and while it is great to be able to do a great many things, I
feel that we have this feeling because we are not getting the support from
Black males, other Black organizations in the community to address the issues that we as women are facing. And definitely not the government. I think
NCNW is important in today's society for keeping a support structure, an
organization that can work on the grassroots level to advocate on behalf of
Black women. I think we need even more activism. I really believe that we
need to be more vocally active in advocating our issues. Like African American women are on the bottom of the food chain when it comes to advancing
cures, research aimed at addressing the specific illnesses that we suffer from.
We can't change this unless we are involved in a two-pronged approach, working in the community and making our voices heard with our (government)
representatives. We have to ask ourselves, what are we going to actively do
to advance our issues?

R6: When we see and we look at, look on TV and look at Congress, the Senate, the House, etc., and we're looking at the decision makers, I think we
see that our race and gender perspective is such that, well, our issues aren't
being heard. So we need to do something to get those issues heard. And
through community work you are also interacting with women who may be
in less fortunate positions and you're trying to assess their needs. I think
that might be our main motivation—just very seldom are our issues being
heard and that we have to step up and do something about that.

The interviewees indicated that they believed that their local section and
the national organization are important players in defining the political agendas of African American communities. In referring to their efforts in the local

grassroots section, the study participants indicated that, while these efforts may not be well known, they are important because they address the everyday needs of individuals while preparing African American citizens for politics. This is accomplished by making everyday problems into full-blown concerns for the larger community.

> *R4:* I would say that people in the community for the most part do not know us by name. This is because we are not as visible as some of the other Black organizations, because we do our thing at the grassroots level, working behind the scenes. However, we (the PVS) do get called on to be involved in a range of issues and in a lot of different places within the community. We have a reputation at the local level for being trustworthy and fair. Therefore, we are always being asked to become involved in some issues or to mediate some dispute. I receive these letters all of the time for the Section's leadership.

At the time of these interviews all of the respondents indicated that the PVS's community work focused on making everyday problems into broader concerns in two major policy areas: education and welfare. In the area of education the PVS objective was to ensure that African American students of all economic backgrounds received equal access to educational opportunities, particularly as they related to the areas of science, math, and technology, and devising methods to address the lack of educational inputs or resources in the lives of poorer students. To this end the PVS operationalized two major programs for youth in the two local communities with which the section works, Tobytown and Scotland. These initiatives were the "Right Turns Only" and "Rites of Passage" programs.

The first program was a series of efforts designed to provide support for low-income African American youth and their parents in the form of mentorship, exposure to a range of different educational opportunities, including science and technology, and building networks with local schools to support the concerns of parents and provide additional resources for local youth. Perhaps most important, the monthly sessions were designed to provide youth with a set of decision-making tools to assist them in their academic and home life. The Rights of Passage program was designed specifically to target African American teenage females. The program was designed to provide a set of life skills to lower-income teenage girls which would promote educational success but also provide basic survival skills for future employment opportunities and leadership within the community. For this type of advocacy the PVS section worked with the participants' parents as well as with local schools to ensure that participants had the necessary resources for success. At the same time the section was involved in providing these resources to the local community, it was also utilizing a networking approach, which placed it in the position of being able to broaden the attention to the specific issues facing the youth in the broader community. For example, over the course of the year 2000, members of the Potomac Valley Section's executive council have also been involved in mediating a school dispute between Black and White parents and the school principal at Kennedy High School concerning Black students' access to computer technology, advanced curricula, and other classes.

In the area of welfare the PVS is working with the aftereffects of the Personal Responsibility and Work Opportunity Reconciliation Act of 1996 on the African American community. This legislation ended over thirty years of federal government support for social welfare programs by mandating that welfare relief would end after a two-year period and by shifting the responsibilities for the creation and execution of welfare programs from the federal government to the states, which now receive federal funding in block grants.[38] One of the issues of greatest concern to the PVS is the potential fallout or response of those welfare recipients who are not as successful at developing job skills and finding a job that provides family wages when welfare time limits expire. This issue had a particular resonance with the section because of the ways that race and gender mediate employment opportunities for the section members themselves. PVS efforts in the area of welfare are primarily directed at providing the community and societal networks needed by African American women transitioning from welfare to employment. The section has a firm commitment, however, to creating initiatives that both provide a sense of empowerment as well as a range of life skills to mothers leaving welfare. These life skills include having a checking account, balancing a budget, developing literacy, and attending to healthcare. These initiatives occur in a more targeted fashion over the course of the section's program year. According to several respondents, the empowerment aspects are incorporated into activities "by consciously thinking about what it feels like to be on the receiving end of someone else's efforts" and by involving the beneficiaries of the activity in the planning stages.

> *R4:* The Potomac Valley Section sat down and figured out for example, how does it feel to be on the receiving end of a handout? And we said you know that doesn't really feel too good. Well, on one level, it feels good, because without the organization, mothers would have fewer resources for their children, but it doesn't feel good from the standpoint of decisions being taken away from the mother. So what we did was talk to the welfare mothers. Black women, we are very particular about who we get help from. It goes back to our pride. Which means, "How dare you feel sorry for me. Whether it's smart

or not, I'm not going to take the help because I don't trust your motives."
Understanding this aspect of ourselves (as Black women) helps us to develop
the trust we need to be effective advocates in the community and not perceived as outsiders.

The section then brings this type of input to its work as a partner in the Montgomery County Welfare Reform Leadership Group, which tackles issues involving women and families leaving welfare.

Identifying the Linkages and Outcomes of African American Women's Community Work in the Post–Civil Rights Era

From this case study one of the central functions of the organization's
community work is to identify main issues of concern to African American communities and to communicate the importance of ongoing policy debates to the
African American community. These activities play a critical role in expanding
the scope of conflict by getting residents involved in the political processes
affecting their lives and by providing a framing context for their responses.
An important function fulfilled by African American women's community work
is the selection of policy issues to pursue, combined with mechanisms designed
to influence community opinion and reaction to the selected policy areas. African American women's political community work also functions as a creative
process in which potential remedies to the social problems of African American communities can be created, strategized, and tested. These community-
based initiatives represent a concrete method of organizing a political response
to public policy problems which is informed by both gender and race. The existence of a gender- and race-informed framing context for the selection of
policy issues and its use in strategizing solutions is highly significant for de-
tecting the amount of political power African American women have in their
own communities, particularly given the degree to which sexism has influenced
their ability to play recognized and acknowledged leadership roles in Civil
Rights struggles of the past.

In relation to the second theme, the PVS's method of activism and advocacy employed a strategy that paired the section-developed Black female identification of political and social problems with internally generated strategies
for ameliorating the effects. The strategies developed focused on finding solutions to community problems which could be embraced and sustained by the
affected communities while bringing Black women's perspectives on these issues to larger political forums in which decision making occurred. This community work activity was directed toward taking advantage of existing political
opportunity structures while creating new ones.

The examples discussed in this chapter indicate that the catalysts for African American women's community action are the disparate effects of race and gender on African American women's political and economic opportunities. Based on the fifteen respondents' self-perceptions of their activity and the types of problems they identified, as well as observational data, it is evident that African American women's community work is a direct result of their economic positioning within the network of social reproduction. African American women's experiences in professional and personal settings informed the analysis of the types of problems most relevant to African American women as well as the specific consequences of the impact of race and gender on Black women's political and social problems. Respondents also indicated the belief that their relative socioeconomic position also affected their approach to strategizing and identifying problems to address, along with the methods used to address issues. African American women's roles as caregivers and economic providers influenced the resources used for activities as well as the degree of mobilization around particular issues.

Given the wide range of social problems facing African American communities, sections such as the PVS could select a myriad of issues to address, but the targeting of education and welfare reform is especially significant given the interviewees' identification with the potential consequences of these policy areas. The women interviewed expressed their concern as educators of African American youth as a main motivating factor in targeting education issues. In regards to the implications of changing social welfare policies, the respondents expressed outrage at the potential additional burdens being placed on African American mothers while also acknowledging their own economic vulnerability to the realities of postindustrial capitalism. The strategies selected for problem solving, ranging from creating substitute programs to coalition building and community forums, are indicative of the types of resources available to these communities.

The ways in which African American women view their own political activity in relation to other sources of political influence is also communicated through the responses of the PVS members. The local field section views its activities, and those of other local field sections and the NCNW more broadly, as holding the community together in the absence of adequate support from local, state, or national government, as well as little support from other organizations within the African American community. Interestingly, the interview participants suggested that their attention to the political issues facing African Americans, particularly women and children, was critically important given the decline in the ability of African American churches and traditional Civil Rights organizations to address social and political issues or to generate social protest activity as in the past. Perhaps even more significant is the expression of the belief that, due to the particular implications of living in a society with racism and sexism, Black women perceived themselves to be in a unique position to identify core issues of concern to themselves and the broader community. Respondents overwhelmingly indicated the absolute need for gender-specific community-based organizations such as the Potomac Valley Section of NCNW due to the need for a place in which they can fully develop a perspective on political and social problems which acknowledges Black women's similarities and differences. Community work was considered an important part of the respondents' political identity and a significant source of community-informed leadership by Black women on behalf of their communities.

Five

Charles E. Jones

From Protest to Black Conservatism

The Demise of the Congress of Racial Equality

The tribute in honor of the late James Farmer held in Washington, D.C., on September 10, 1999, underscored the Congress of Racial Equality's (CORE) historic role in the struggle for African American equality.[1] CORE, co-founded by Farmer in 1942, was a forerunner to the nonviolent, direct-action Civil Rights Movement that successfully dismantled de jure segregation in the 1960s. A decade before the 1955 Martin Luther King Jr.–led Montgomery bus boycott, CORE activists systematically employed an array of protest tactics challenging racial discrimination in the nation's northern cities. In May 1961 CORE launched the legendary Freedom Rides, which confronted Jim Crowism in the cradle of the old Confederacy. Indeed, the vicious beatings of CORE activists and the fire bombing of their bus by a mob of White racists in Anniston, Alabama, remains one of the more horrific images of the modern Civil Rights Movement. Similarly, the disappearance and brutal murder of three CORE members—James Chaney, Andrew Goodman, and Michael Schwerner—finally awakened the nation to southern White terrorism. As a prominent member of the civil rights coalition, CORE helped to secure the passage of significant Civil Rights legislation. In short, as August Meier and Elliot Rudwick have concluded, "CORE's contribution to the Black protest movement and to racial advancement had, in fact, been enormous."[2]

During the mid–1960s CORE underwent a dramatic ideological transformation. It evolved from a biracial, pacifist, integrationist organization into one with an allegiance to Black nationalism. During the Black nationalism period (1966–1979) CORE activists refocused their early efforts on grassroots community organizing, particularly in the urban northern setting. Instead of interracialism, CORE now advocated Black self-determination, economic development, racial pride, and the eradication of police brutality. In the final years of its Black nationalist stage, a host of maladies afflicted CORE. Fund-raising scandals, questionable policy ventures, and the personal aggrandizement of leadership left the organization in disarray. Beginning in 1980, CORE drifted to the ideological Right. By 1983 Manning Marable observed that "CORE has retreated from the vanguard of progressive struggle into the open arms of reaganism, racism and economic reaction from 'Black Power' of the 1960s. CORE and its leader Roy Innis have abandoned their militant history for acceptance into the posh corridors of the ruling military industrial complex."[3]

CORE's current conservative orientation is an important yet neglected post–Civil Rights era development. This chapter seeks to explain CORE's conservative metamorphosis, which has resulted in the ignoble demise of the once illustrious Civil Rights organization. Informed by the client-relation construct, a salient dynamic of African American politics, CORE's organizational permutations are examined by highlighting the leadership, goals, tactics, and major activities of the three respective phases. The analysis asserts that CORE shifted to the political right in order to resurrect the organization. It further posits that CORE's waning status led to the adoption of political objectives that paralleled the interest of powerful conservative elites in order to reinvigorate the impotent organization. A discussion of the theoretical lens initiates the following analysis of CORE's ideological transformation. In order to demarcate CORE's evolution into a Black conservative interest group, a brief historical synopsis of the organization's integrationist phase (1942–1965) is given. Afterwards, the chapter moves to an examination of the organization's Black nationalist period (1966–1979). CORE's conservative organizational dynamics (1980–1999) are analyzed in the subsequent section, and the chapter concludes with an assessment of the role of CORE in contemporary African American politics.

Client Relation Politics: A Theoretical Explanation

How does one account for CORE's vast ideological fluctuations, which transformed the once militant protest group into a Black conservative political organization? Students of social movements offer a host of theoretical explanations for the transformation and demise of social movement organizations. Scholars stress the importance of broader external forces as evident in the political process model formulated by Doug McAdam. Conversely, other theorists emphasize the role of internal factors such as the psychological makeup of the membership (collective behavior model), organization capacity (resource mobilization theory), and charismatic leadership (theory of charismatic movements).[4] While each of these theoretical perspectives contributes to our understanding of the organization's evolution into a Black conservative interest group, this essay demonstrates that CORE's ideological oscillation is best understood and explained by the parameters of the client relation leadership construct.

According to this theoretical notion, an essential feature of African American politics is the linkage between African American leaders and powerful external benefactors. Adolph Reed Jr., political scientist and social critic, has suggested that "Afro-American politics has been structured persistently around a client relation that binds Black elites individually and primarily to external sources of patronage while they simultaneously require legitimization internally among Blacks."[5] Outside elites provide African American leaders with critical resources needed to enhance and fortify their respective leadership positions. Nonetheless, African American leadership authority also depends on the support of its primary constituents. One is reminded of the Black protestors in Miami, Florida, who rejected attempts by prominent Black leaders—including Benjamin Hooks, executive director of the National Association for the Advancement of Colored People (NAACP), Andrew Young, and Jesse Jackson—to quell the rebellion in the city.[6] These national leaders came to Miami at the behest of the mayor, who requested their assistance as spokesmen of the Black community to help end the civil unrest that engulfed the city. Thus, African American leaders are confronted with dual and oftentimes conflicting sources of accountability. They must navigate between Black constituent demands, which undergird their internal legitimacy, and the expectations of powerful non-Black benefactors who dictate the parameters of external legitimacy. In order to navigate between the dual accountability constraints of the client relation dynamic of Black politics, African American leaders employ three major strategies.

Matthew Holden has identified three primary political approaches—opposition, withdrawal, and clientage—utilized by African American leaders. The strategy of opposition entails the use of nonconventional political tactics within the prescribed rules of the polity in order to enhance White commitment to the democratic norms and constitutional principles of the American political system. Conversely, the withdrawal strategy emphasizes autonomous Black political action. Holden observed, "It is more likely to activate the symbols of 'independence' and very open and explicit defiance of almost all 'white values.'"[7] The priority placed on independent Black political action by advocates of the withdrawal approach undoubtedly enhances the internal legitimacy of African American leaders. On the other hand, the clientage political strategy accepts and recognizes an inherent interdependence between Black and White Americans. Therefore, the proponents of the clientage approach "find a basis for coexistence by choosing objectives which the more influential outsiders (in this case whites) will support."[8] In return for selecting compatible policy preferences, African American leaders receive vital resources from powerful external (White) elites. The accommodationist orientation of the clientage strategy fosters external legitimacy at the expense of Black internal leadership. The following analysis demonstrates that the client linkage dynamic, a salient feature of African American leadership, explicates CORE's conservative metamorphosis in the post–Civil Rights era.

CORE and Interracialism: 1942–1965

Founded in the spring of 1942, CORE was an offshoot of the Fellowship of Reconciliation (FOR), a pacifist organization formed during the end of World War I. James Farmer originated the concept, which led to the formation of the Civil Rights organization. According to Marvin Rich, a CORE activist who later assumed the community relations director's position, Farmer formulated the strategy undergirding CORE after visiting his family in the South, where he and his friends were obligated to view a movie from the "colored section" of the town's movie theater. Farmer's firsthand experience with the indignity of Jim Crowism after his extended hiatus from the South crystallized the need for a militant, biracial, mass-based organization dedicated to abolishing de jure segregation. In a February 1942 memorandum entitled "Provisional Plans for Brotherhood Mobilization" prepared for A. J. Muste, the executive director of the Fellowship of Reconciliation, Farmer wrote:

> Above all, the Brotherhood Mobilization must present a distinctive and radical approach. It must strive, for example, not to make housing in ghettos more tolerable, but to destroy residential segregation; not to make Jim Crow facilities the equal of others, but to abolish Jim Crow; not to make racial discrimination more bearable, but to wipe it out. In the words of the Twenty-Sixth Annual Conference of the FOR, we must "effectively repudiate every form of racism. . . ." We must forge the instrumentalities through which that nationwide repudiation can be effected. We must not stop until racial brotherhood is established in the United States as a fact as well as an ideal. Ironically enough, the present unfortunate circumstances brought on by the war afford an excellent setting for immediate spadework in this direction.[9]

After deliberations by the national Council Reconciliation, Farmer received authorization to create an organization modeled on his "Brotherhood" proposal in Chicago. Four White and two Black pacifists comprised the original CORE unit—the Chicago Committee of Racial Equality. All of the six founding members were well educated and, like Farmer, who held a divinity degree from Howard University, possessed deep religious ties. The primary objective of the inaugural CORE delegation was the abolishment of racial discrimination in the Chicago metropolitan area. Although the group enjoyed only limited success, several traits of the embryonic Chicago unit defined CORE's integrationist phase (1942–1965). During its formative stage, "Gandhian nonviolence and internal action were the twin ideological beliefs underpinning CORE's organizational structure."[10]

Early CORE activists employed nonviolent direct action tactics to eliminate all forms of racial discrimination. Gandhian principles of nonviolence resonated with the pacifism of the founding members. Moreover, the biracial character of the original CORE members exemplified the organization's commitment to interracialism during this period. Elliott Rudwick observed that "as late as the spring of 1963 nearly two-thirds of the members were white."[11] Furthermore, the pacifist orientation of the first contingent of CORE activists created antibureaucratic biases within the organization. In contrast to the NAACP's hierarchical structure, the organizational arrangement of CORE favored decentralization. Strong affiliates often meant local CORE chapters pursued their individual respective policies. CORE affiliates also frequently failed to pay organizational dues or provide financial assistance to the national office.[12]

Finally, throughout its integrationist phase CORE remained primarily a northern-based organization. It did not appoint a full-time representative to the South until 1957, nor did the civil rights organization have an affiliated chapter in the South prior to this appointment.[13] During its first two decades CORE largely concentrated on targets of racial discrimination in nonsouthern cities. Under the leadership of James Farmer, the principal founder and national director of the organization from 1961 to 1965, CORE utilized nonviolent unconventional political tactics to abolish discriminatory racial practices. During the 1940s CORE activists preceded the student sit-ins with a sit-down to protest the "white only" policy of the segregated roller rink. CORE members challenged the system of racial covenants in Chicago. Biracial teams would rent apartments by sending a scout group comprised of White CORE members who first rented the apartment before disclosing their Black roommates. CORE activists also initiated a campaign against the segregated policy enforced by some of the city's restaurants. In March 1943, six months after protracted protests including sit-ins, CORE activists successfully integrated Stoner's restaurant, a downtown Chicago eatery.

Although CORE experienced some limited success during its embryonic stage, in the 1940s, the burgeoning Civil Rights organization was largely ineffectual and lacked a national base.[14] CORE's first major national effort was the Journey of Reconciliation, a predecessor to the Freedom Rides of the early 1960s. The protest group launched the national campaign to test a 1946 Supreme Court ruling, *Morgan v. Virginia,* prohibiting segregation in interstate transportation. James Farmer recalled that: "FOR and CORE were jointly sponsoring a most imaginative project to be called the Journey of Reconciliation testing the enforcement of that decision. A small group of Whites and Blacks were going to ride regularly scheduled buses through the upper south—Virginia, North Carolina, West Virginia, and Kentucky—Blacks sitting in the front and Whites in the back refusing to move when ordered and responding to violence and arrest with nonviolence."[15] On April 9, 1947, a biracial delegation of sixteen members left Washington, D.C., on the two-week direct-action venture throughout the upper South. Members of the CORE sojourn were frequently arrested as they traveled farther South. The group only experienced one incident of violence, however, which occurred in a small mill town near Chapel Hill, North Carolina. While the Journey of Reconciliation certainly did not eliminate segregation in interstate transportation, Meier and Rudwick noted that the innovative direct-action tactic "functioned as a dramatic high point, a source of inspiration to CORE for years to come."[16]

Notwithstanding the infusion of morale emanating from the Journey of Reconciliation, CORE languished from the late 1940s to the eve of the Black student movement of the early 1960s. The Civil Rights organization sponsored annual interracial workshops from 1947 to 1954. These biracial seminars offered leadership training and instruction in the theory of nonviolence. During this period CORE was hampered by a weak relationship between the national office and affiliate units. With the exception of the interracial workshops, CORE found it difficult to galvanize a national program. The decentralization often resulted in the precedence of local activities over those sponsored by national headquarters. During this period the approximately thirty CORE affiliates focused on selective targets of segregation such as department stores, hotels, restaurants, and recreation centers.[17] These CORE chapters varied with respect to activism and success. CORE affiliates in St. Louis and Omaha, Nebraska, were exemplary chapters, while others, such as Berkeley and Cleveland, remained hampered by organizational problems. Herbert Haines argued that by 1954 CORE "was in a state of organizational and financial disarray owing to its loose structure. A convincing argument can be made, however, that the decline of CORE was also due to its being ahead of its time."[18]

The Montgomery, Alabama, boycott of 1955 proved pivotal in reducing the gap between the vanguard direct-action tactic of CORE and the prevailing strategy of litigation championed by the NAACP. The success of the one-year bus boycott in Montgomery validated the efficacy of direct-action tactics. Moreover, the boycott significantly increased CORE's fund-raising efforts as well as providing the organization with an inroad to the South. In 1957 CORE appointed Jim McCain as its first full-time field secretary responsible for organizing the South. Between 1957 and 1959 McCain successfully organized nine CORE affiliates in South Carolina.[19] This groundwork assisted in positioning CORE at the forefront of the Black student protest movement, which erupted in the early 1960s. In May 1961 CORE initiated a second round of Freedom Rides in response to *Boynton v. Virginia,* the Supreme Court ruling that prohibited segregation in the terminal accommodations of interstate transportation. Modeled on its earlier predecessor, the Journey of Reconciliation, the new Freedom Rides would test the enforcement of the Boynton ruling. The 1961 Freedom Rides differed dramatically from CORE's early efforts, however, in that the CORE activists traveled to the Deep South. This geographical difference meant that the participants of the second Freedom Rides were met with intense violence. Courageous CORE Freedom Riders not only compelled the Kennedy presidential administration to contest segregation but also activated scores of Civil Rights protesters.

In short, the Freedom Rides of 1961 propelled CORE into national prominence. CORE utilized the momentum of the Freedom Rides to assume a greater role in the nonviolent direct-action southern Civil Rights struggle of the 1960s. As Meier and Rudwick noted: "In the two years following the Freedom Rides CORE broadened the scope of its activities. Moving increasingly away from the public accommodations issue its program emphasized housing and job problems in the north and included an important voter registration program in the south."[20] The period from 1963 to 1964 would constitute the zenith of CORE's influence as an effective Civil Rights organization during its integrationist phase. CORE assumed an influential role in many of the major Civil Rights events occurring in the mid–1960s, such as the 1963 March on Washington, the Mississippi Freedom Summer in 1964, and the various northern freedom movements. Nevertheless, intraracial membership strife over the future of CORE signaled the end of the organization's integrationist phase.[21]

CORE and Black Nationalism: 1966–1979

Despite the passage of significant federal legislation (the Civil Rights Act of 1964 and the Voting Rights Act of 1965), the quality of life for the majority of African Americans remained unaltered. At this critical juncture the southern-based nonviolent integrationist Civil Rights Movement had stalled. A reassessment of the effectiveness of the integrationist strategy ultimately led to the advocacy of the Black power doctrine. This new political strategy profoundly impacted the mainstream Civil Rights coalition. In some instances support for the Black power concept exacerbated schisms within the civil rights alliance. The allegiance to the Black power perspective also adversely affected relationships within the biracial memberships of Civil Rights protest groups. Finally, in other cases, such as CORE and the Student Nonviolent Coordinating Committee (SNCC), Black power sentiments radically transformed the ideological orientation of the organization. From 1966 to 1979 CORE sharply departed from its historical roots and principles. During this period the organization supplanted the goal of integration with the objective of Black self-determination. It transformed itself from a biracial organization to one with an overwhelmingly Black membership. The once pacifist protest group committed to Gandhian principles of direct action now advocated the legitimacy of armed self-defense.

While CORE formally adopted the Black Power doctrine during its 1966 national convention, the organization's shift toward Black nationalism did not occur instantaneously. An early sign of membership disenchantment with the goal of interracialism appeared in a 1964 editorial published in *Rights and Views,* a publication of CORE's Harlem chapter. The editorial lamented that "they [civil rights leaders] are worried about the effect of rioting on the civil rights bill and on the movement generally. But it takes no great mind to realize that the civil rights bill means hardly a hill of beans to the junkie, the unemployed, the unemployable, and the school drop-out rioting in Harlem and other ghettoes."[22] Dissenters within CORE advocated grassroots community organizing by attacking the problems of inadequate housing, poor health care, and underemployment rather than the mere desegregation of the United States. Black nationalist proponents within the organization also stressed a Black leadership imperative. During the 1965 convention pro-nationalist CORE members proposed a resolution requiring that all local CORE affiliates have a majority Black leadership, yet they withdrew the proposal after the well-respected James Peck and James Farmer voiced their opposition. CORE Black Power advocates eventually solidified the organization's Black nationalist transformation with the passage of a 1968 resolution barring Whites from membership in the organization.[23]

James Farmer's resignation in 1965 to assume a position in President Lyndon B. Johnson administration's War on Poverty left a leadership void at a critical juncture in CORE's history. Floyd McKissick, a member of the original Freedom Ride, the Journey of Reconciliation, assumed the organization's leadership mantle in January 1966. McKissick, a Durham, North Carolina, lawyer with a long history of Civil Rights activism, was CORE's second ranking leader. His Black Power leanings made McKissick a favorite of CORE's nationalist faction. For example, McKissick invited members of the Black Muslims to address the delegates of the organization's 1965 national convention. McKissick's invitation to Black separatists indicated his attentiveness to the growing nationalist sentiment both within CORE and in the larger Black community. This newfound nationalism reflected CORE's attention to the requisites of internal legitimacy stemming from the Black community. McKissick defeated George Wiley, a university professor and influential CORE national staff member who favored interracialism, for CORE's top leadership position.[24]

As national director of the organization, McKissick firmly aligned CORE among Black Power ardents. During the first national convention of McKissick's administration in 1966, CORE delegates adopted a resolution declaring their allegiance to the Black Power doctrine. CORE activists also passed a resolution condemning United States involvement in the Vietnam War. The organization's antiwar position coincided with the views of an emerging cadre of Black Power proponents across the nation. Meier and Rudwick noted that "on the Vietnam War issue CORE's position had already been jelled by McKissick, who had become an outspoken critic of the war."[25] Finally, under McKissick's leadership CORE also strayed from its Gandhian principles and pacifist roots. CORE delegates followed McKissick's lead by passing a resolution differentiating between nonviolence and self-defense. Historian Akinyele Umoja suggests that the confluence of class, leadership, organizing styles, and the local cultural milieu led to CORE's newfound acceptance of armed resistance.[26] Thus, as Robert Allen has astutely noted, "CORE was reshaping itself. It was attempting to organize and respond to the new militancy, which had infected certain parts of the Black middle class as a result of the rebellions initiated by the Black masses."[27]

In doing so, CORE sought to respond to Black grassroots demands, thereby enhancing its internal legitimacy undergirded by the Black community. McKissick turned CORE inward toward the Black community for its policy directives and funding. Early in his tenure he moved CORE's headquarters to Harlem from downtown Manhattan in a symbolic gesture to the emerging call for Black Power. Programmatically, the McKissick administration sponsored activities designed to empower the Black poor. One program centerpiece under McKissick's leadership was the Baltimore "Target City" project, which launched a comprehensive attack on poverty in the city. CORE activists organized Black workers to form the Maryland Freedom Union, politicized welfare mothers, developed tenant associations, sponsored job training, and lobbied for quality education. Unfortunately, CORE's Target City efforts were short-lived. In the spring of 1967, within a year of its inception, the program was discontinued due to inadequate funding and acrimonious staff relations.[28]

CORE's second major project during the early days of its Black nationalist period was based in Cleveland, Ohio. In 1967 the Ford Foundation awarded the Cleveland chapter of CORE a generous grant ($175,000) for leadership development, job training, and voter registration. Subsequent funding from the Ford Foundation brought CORE an additional $340,000. While Cleveland enjoyed substantial funding, the source of the funding ran counter to the dictates of the Black Power doctrine. Black nationalist dissenters within CORE harshly criticized McKissick for his reliance on funding sources external to the Black community. McKissick resigned from the national director position after a mere two-year stint.[29]

During the 1968 national convention CORE delegates selected Roy Innis, a charismatic proponent of Black nationalism, to succeed McKissick. Thirty years after his initial ascension to the leadership position, Innis still holds the position of national director. Born in St. Croix, Innis migrated to the United States with his family at thirteen years of age. He entered the Civil Rights struggle in the 1960s and soon became an influential member of a Black nationalist faction within the Harlem chapter of CORE. In 1963 he spearheaded the ouster of the chapter's biracial socialist-leaning leadership. Two years later he assumed the chairmanship of CORE's Harlem chapter. In addition, Innis also served as the executive director of the Harlem Commonwealth Council, an economic development organization. The latter position would significantly shape Innis's conception of the Black power doctrine. Under Innis's leadership, CORE's Harlem chapter avidly supported Black nationalism. He championed the emerging sentiments of Black nationalism, which propelled his rapid ascension to the national leadership of CORE. During CORE's historic 1966 convention Innis was at the forefront of the organization's adoption of the Black Power doctrine. A year later, in 1967, he was elected second national vice chairman of CORE and appointed associate national director by Floyd McKissick.[30]

Under the leadership of Roy Innis, CORE subscribed to a reformist interpretation of the Black Power doctrine. In contrast to the proponents of the revolutionary version of Black Power who advocated an overthrow of capitalism, CORE proposed Black entrepreneurship. In a 1969 position paper Innis wrote:

> Blacks must innovate, must create ideology. It may include elements of capitalism, elements of socialism or elements of neither: that is immaterial. What matters is that it will be created to fit our needs. So then Black people are not talking about Black capitalism. Black people are talking about economic development. We are talking about the creation and the acquisition of capital instruments by means of which we can maximize our economic interests. We do not particularly try to define styles of ownership; we say that we are willing to operate pragmatically and let the style of ownership fit the style of the area or inhabitants.[31]

For Innis a pragmatic course of action was a key to Black liberation. "In my view," he explained, "Black people at this stage of development are not and should not be talking about some romantic thing called revolution, but rather a more pragmatic and necessary step called liberation."[32] Economically, Innis and CORE advocated the accumulation of Black capital by creating economic institutions to serve Black consumers. He proposed economic entities modeled on the Harlem Commonwealth Council, a nonprofit corporation funded by a state grant to invest in Harlem businesses.

Immediately upon assuming CORE's national director position, Innis initiated actions to centralize power within the organization. Specifically, he attempted to enforce a provision enacted during the 1965 convention which required all CORE affiliates to pay a one hundred–dollar assessment fee to the national office. Innis's efforts to consolidate power would become a trademark of this leadership style. He did not hold the organization's annual convention from 1971 to 1978. At one point during his leadership tenure, his wife, Doris, held the second highest position, national chairman, of the protest group. Moreover, CORE's decentralization also contributed to Innis's aggrandizement of personal power. Rudwick and Meier observed that "the very autonomy of the chapters contributed to the lack of constraints which they exercised upon the national organization."[33]

Not surprisingly, the unilateral decision-making authority of Roy Innis eroded the organization's legitimacy within the Black community. On several occasions Innis adopted policies that put him at odds with progressive forces within the Black community. Despite the rhetoric of "liberation" and "self-determination," CORE sided with Republicans and White segregationists on the desegregation of public education. As early as 1967, CORE advocated the creation of an independent school system in Harlem. In 1969 New York Black state legislators worked with CORE to accomplish the objective of establishing an independent Black school district. On the national level Innis proposed the creation of two school districts—one predominantly Black and one majority White—with independent autonomy for each district. He toured the South in 1979 promoting his proposal to education officials and southern politicians. He met, to no avail, with the governors of four southern states. CORE's brand of Black nationalism also led the organization to file a friend of the court legal brief in support of President Nixon's opposition to a Richmond, Virginia, busing plan.[34]

In late 1975 Innis announced CORE's plan to recruit Black Vietnam War veterans to fight in Angola's civil war on the side of the Union for the Total Independence of Angola (UNITA), a pro-Western faction eventually supported by the racist, White minority regime of South Africa. This ill-fated policy decision engendered criticism from all quarters of the Black community, integrationists and Black nationalists alike.[35] James Farmer, the paragon of CORE, formally resigned from the organization in protest of Innis's Angolan plan. Black leaders in the San Francisco Bay Area organized under the "Black Coalition against U.S. Involvement in Angola" to demonstrate during Roy Innis's scheduled address to the World Affairs Council. Innis's speaking engagement was canceled as a result of the controversy.[36] Congressman Charles Rangel, the chairman of the Congressional Black Caucus, called for a federal investigation of CORE's plan to recruit Black Vietnam War veterans to aid UNITA. Adel Krum, a leader of the demonstration against CORE in New York, angrily declared that "Innis and CORE are nothing but traitors to the Black race."[37]

Accusations of financial improprieties also plagued CORE during the mid–1970s. Innis was accused of questionable and excessive spending on travel and business entertainment. In 1976 a CORE delegation headed by Innis spent more than $180,000 during a two-month tour of Europe and Africa. Greg Harris, a journalist with the *Amsterdam News,* reported that the New York attorney general's office concluded that CORE misappropriated $301,282 in 1976. According to Harris, state auditors identified a host of questionable spending by Innis on such items as first-class airline tickets, extravagant dinners, and expenditures for landscaping of personal residences. Innis eventually agreed to an out-of-court settlement on the charges of financial irregularities, in which he consented to reimbursing $35,000 without any admission of guilt.[38]

In 1978 Alaska and New Jersey also initiated investigations into CORE's solicitation of charitable funds. The organization's legal woes stemming from its questionable fund-raising activities were further exacerbated by the assault of Ray Cunningham, a former CORE fund raiser, who was physically attacked by three members of Innis's so-called security team.[39] Dissident CORE members also filed a lawsuit against Innis accusing him of failing to account for charitable funds and not adhering to the constitutional bylaws of the organization. They requested that the New York State Supreme Court vacate Innis's national director position. Former leader Floyd McKissick, who joined the dissidents to remove Innis from the organization's leadership position, declared that "CORE has strayed from the principles it was founded on. I don't believe in intimidating, members or anyone else, I believe in the democratic process. We (the founders) did not authorize a dictator be created."[40] After a five-year legal battle the New York State Supreme Court eventually declared Roy Innis the legitimate national director of CORE. The court ruled that the dissidents lacked authority from the organization's charter to remove Innis from office.[41]

While Innis withstood this challenge to his leadership by disenchanted CORE activists and eventually prevailed against the series of court injunctions prohibiting CORE from soliciting funds, the organization floundered into the next decade. The cumulative impact of Innis's questionable policies, legal difficulties, and opposition significantly diminished CORE's internal legitimacy within the Black community. Indeed, by 1980 political scientists Lucius Barker and Jesse McCorry concluded that CORE had "all but faded from the scene."[42]

CORE and Black Conservative Politics: 1980 to the Present
Although CORE did not completely vanish from the political landscape, it remained embroiled in controversy throughout the early 1980s. In February 1980 the United States Postal Service launched an investigation of CORE's fund-raising activities. Federal officials alleged that CORE violated statutes regulating the solicitation of charitable contributions. Further compounding CORE's legal woes were several pending lawsuits. Citibank sued the organization for failure to repay two loans secured in 1977 and 1978 totaling $58,000. A New York landlord also sued Roy Innis and his former wife Mary for $35,000 in unpaid rent. Innis's legal problems continued when he was arrested in August 1981 on assault charges in connection with the beating of an individual who had stolen a radio from his car, which was parked outside of CORE headquarters. Eventually exonerated after a two-week jury trial in 1982, Innis remarked: "I have been persecuted by government officials for the past four years and it's like Russian roulette. If they keep trying sooner or later they get you on something. They are after me because I am the last of the Black dissenters."[43]

Innis's critics, however, extended beyond government officials and law enforcement officers. In November 1980 disenchanted CORE members impatient with the gradualism of a prior lawsuit sponsored a national convention held in Columbia, South Carolina, to remove Innis from the leadership of the organization. One dissident, Theo Mitchell, who headed the South Carolina chapter of CORE, complained that Innis used the directorship for "personal gain, egotism and grandiose plans."[44] CORE delegates ousted Innis and replaced him with Waverly Yates, who headed CORE's Washington, D.C., affiliate. Innis immediately filed a legal suit to contest his ouster. As noted previously, a 1983 ruling by the New York State Supreme Court found that the dissident faction did not have charter authority to convene the 1980 national convention. The New York State Supreme Court declared that "the fact remains that neither the CORE constitution then in existence nor that ratified in 1968 authorized a national convention to be called in such a fashion."[45]

In the midst of this organizational turmoil, CORE moved further to the right of the political spectrum, which signaled a new phase for the Civil Rights organization. CORE's conservative transformation in the early 1980s coincided with the emergence of a Black conservative leadership cadre spawned by Republican conservative ideologues. The election of Ronald Reagan as president in 1980 marked the resurgence of the Republican Party and the ascendancy of conservatism in American politics. Republicans won three consecutive presidential elections (1980–1992) and recaptured the United States Senate. In 1994 the GOP also gained control of the United States House of Representatives.

Conservative dominance in the national political arena enhanced the visibility of Black conservatives. Mack Jones, a distinguished scholar of African American politics, has argued persuasively that "the rise of the new Black conservative as a national movement was orchestrated by a constellation of conservative think-tanks, foundations and publishing outlets."[46] Shortly after the election of President Ronald Reagan, the Institute of Contemporary Studies, a conservative think-tank, organized the Fairmont Conference on Black Alternatives to mobilize Black conservatives from across the nation. On another occasion the Hoover Institute sponsored a national conference to establish the New Coalition for Economic and Social Change, a Black conservative organization created to challenge the leadership of the NAACP. The newly formed New Coalition for Economic and Social Change soon received funding and cosponsorship from the Heritage Foundation, a prominent conservative entity, to host the "Rethinking the Black Agenda" conference during the fall of 1982. Several other Black conservative organizations such as the Lincoln Institute for Research and Education, led by J. A. Parker, and the Council for Black Economic Agenda were also the beneficiaries of funding from White conservative patrons. In sum, White conservative elites sought to elevate Black conservatives as an alternative to the traditional Civil Rights establishment.[47] Innis adroitly exploited these partisan developments in order to reinvigorate CORE.

Roy Innis responded to these overtures from the political Right by maneuvering CORE among the ranks of contemporary Black conservatives. Consistent with the logic of the clientage theoretical construct, Innis selected political objectives that paralleled the interests of powerful White conservative ideologues in order to enhance the influence of CORE. His overtures to Republican ideologues included endorsing conservative political nominees, advocating conservative ideals, forming political alliances with conservative partisans, and publicly attacking the traditional Black leadership strata.

Innis derived conservative political capital from the contentious senatorial confirmation hearings of the Reagan presidential administrations. Although the Edward Meese appointment as attorney general of the United States was roundly opposed in 1985 by the liberal and Black political establishment, Innis endorsed the Meese nomination. Innis dissented again from African American political officialdom when he testified on behalf of Robert Bork during the 1987 confirmation hearings of the Supreme Court nominee. Innis told the Senate judiciary committee that he was "very impressed with [Judge Robert Bork's] faithfulness to civil rights."[48] Innis was only one of three African Americans to testify in support of the Bork nomination, which was eventually defeated by the Senate. Innis later opposed the Civil Rights establishment in 1991 when he endorsed Clarence Thomas's nomination to the Supreme Court. Speaking before members of the American Legislative Exchange Council, an organization composed of conservative state legislators, Innis characterized Thomas as "a great man and a great Supreme Court nominee." He further proclaimed that, "as a Black conservative, Clarence will do more in two months on the court than (retired justice) Thurgood Marshall did in the last 10 years."[49]

Innis also departed from Civil Rights orthodoxy on various partisan and policy issues, which further reflected the organization's strong conservative orientation. Beginning with the 1932 historical election of President Franklin D. Roosevelt, the Black vote has been decidedly Democratic. In a 1984 position paper, entitled "A Call for Black Americans to Develop Bold New Political Tactics and Strategies," Innis recommended that African Americans "abandon the sinking 'one party' ship of the democrats" and join the Republican Party. He further argued that "the successful desegregation of the Republican Party can be one of the most important and healthy political developments for the Black community and the country at large."[50] Under the proposed strategy Innis urged African Americans to vote for President Ronald Reagan in the 1984 elections. While Innis was not the first African American political observer to warn against the Democratic Party stranglehold on the Black electorate, his uncritical acceptance of conservative policy views raises the specter of political opportunism.

Similar to his White conservative compatriots, Innis adopted a hard-line position on crime. Whereas protesting police brutality was a focal point of CORE during its Black nationalist stage, assisting the police in the arrest of suspected criminals became the new priority of CORE in its conservative phase. CORE's former freedom patrols, which monitored the law enforcement officials to reduce police abuse, were supplanted with Innis's proposal to deputize armed citizens who would augment police officers. The right of citizens to bear arms constituted an integral component of the proposal. Innis explained: "Hoodlums are only brave when the odds are all in their favor, when they can predict what's going to happen. If he hears of this plan, that there are a growing number of Citizens legally armed and trained, when he plans to victimize his next prey he has to think, 'Is this prey really a prey?' Today, that same predator doesn't have to worry."[51]

Consistent with his White conservative counterparts, Innis also championed welfare reform. Innis charged the nation's welfare system with "perpetuating serial welfare recipients." He therefore avidly supported Congress's recent reform of the country's welfare policy. Innis explained that "there should be conditions and contractual obligations to receive welfare."[52] He attributed his welfare policy agreement with conservatives to his version of pragmatic Black nationalism. According to Innis, Black sufficiency, particularly at the individual level, was essential to the practice of pragmatic Black nationalism. Consequently, he shared the conservative disdain for affirmation action. Innis vehemently argued that affirmative action was "dehumanizing to Black people" and "an insult," since "Black people can successfully compete against white people."[53]

Innis's anti-busing stance also placed him at odds with the traditional Civil Rights establishment. He has been a staunch opponent of the traditional model of school desegregation. Instead of transporting Black schoolchildren across town to learn with White children, Innis recommended greater educational choice for Black parents. Consequently, he favored educational vouchers, another conservative policy mainstay. Vouchers, maintained Innis, would broaden the opportunity to receive a quality education so that "Black children can have the same leg up as the Kennedy's have."[54] Innis's conservative metamorphosis has spawned several alliances between CORE and prominent conservatives. In his quest to combat crime, Innis joined forces with Tony Imperiale of Newark, New Jersey. After meeting on a tri-state radio talk show in 1983, Innis and Imperiale agreed to form a grassroots anticrime movement. Imperiale, a former Newark city council member and Republican state senator, once directed George Wallace's presidential campaign in the state of New Jersey. Generally viewed as a White racist by many in Newark's African American community, the outspoken Italian American leader has been a longtime opponent of African American empowerment in the city. Nevertheless, Innis posed for a *New York Post* photo opportunity in which a smiling Imperiale referred to Innis as "the Black Imperiale."[55]

Prompted by a tough law-and-order stance on crime, Innis publicly supported Bernard Goetz, the so-called subway vigilante. Goetz, a White New Yorker, was charged with the premeditated shooting of four African American youths whom he accused of attempting to rob him. Innis volunteered to defend Goetz free of charge. Innis's emphasis on a citizen's right to bear arms also led to joint efforts between CORE and the National Rifle Association (NRA). In 1986 the NRA awarded CORE a five thousand dollar grant to develop an anticrime program in Brooklyn. Under this program CORE provided instruction for acquiring a gun permit. In 1990 CORE filed a friend of the court brief in support of the NRA lawsuit that challenged a Dayton, Ohio, city ordinance prohibiting the sale of semiautomatic weapons. CORE claimed that the city's gun ordinance discriminated against African Americans. The legal brief filed in support of the NRA stated, "CORE is convinced that those who conclude they should arm themselves against the crime running rampant in many poor minority neighborhoods, which are rarely if ever afforded adequate police protection, should have the right to do so."[56] Historically, the National Rifle Association has not enjoyed strong ties to the African American community, yet CORE's opposition to all forms of gun control offered entree to the powerful gun lobby.

Finally, Innis's unabashed criticism of the mainstream Black leadership has undoubtedly endeared him to powerful conservative political actors. The presence of an alternative Black conservative leadership voice provides White conservative ideologues with a sympathetic ally in the African American community. Roy Innis has adroitly assumed the "attack role" of the Black conservative leadership voice. The once outspoken critic of White racism now reserves his harshest criticism for Black political leaders. For example, he lamented that "we have a group of Black leaders who feel they have some special charge to apologize, to alibi, and just plain lie for criminals. No element in this society is so solicitous of criminals as [the] Black leadership."[57] He frequently refers to the traditional Black leadership as race hustlers, a view often promulgated by Republican conservative ideologues.

Innis's challenges to the Black leadership establishment were not confined to verbal jousting. On several occasions he threatened to campaign against several Democratic incumbents. At a 1985 fund-raising event honoring the new state chairman of the New York Republican Party, Innis announced his intention to oppose Congressional Black Caucus member Major Owens, who represented New York's Twenty-third District in the House of Representatives. Although Innis never campaigned against Owens, he entered the 1993 New York mayoral Democratic primary to unseat David Dinkins, the incumbent and first African American mayor of New York City. While his announced plans never materialized, Innis also threatened to challenge Governor Mario M. Cuomo in the Democratic Party's 1994 statewide primary elections.[58]

During CORE's conservative configuration, it has sponsored a limited number of programs. With the exception of "project independence," CORE has undertaken few ongoing activities. Its major recent activities have included a legal defense fund, which assisted individuals who defended themselves against criminals, an immigration assistance program, and an antidrug task force and job training placement. In fact, CORE has operated largely as a fund-raising apparatus. While its job training placement program has a one-person staff and meets three mornings each week to train on five outdated computers, the fund-raising arm of the organization has five full-time staff members and twenty to twenty-five telephone solicitors. According to George Holmes, the organization's executive director, patron members of CORE as well as corporations all across the nation are targeted.[59]

Telephone solicitations were further supplemented by two fund-raising award banquets. Since 1984 CORE has sponsored the Dr. Martin Luther King Jr. Ambassadorial Reception and Awards Dinner. Ironically, Innis, a staunch critic of the late Dr. King during CORE's prior Black nationalist stage, now exploits King's name to raise monies for CORE. During the 1998 King banquet Innis had the audacity to honor a Washington, D.C., talk show host who previously made several disparaging remarks about the late Dr. King. CORE initiated a second fund-raising event the "Harmony Awards and Celebration Roast and Dinner" in 1993. These two affairs were largely responsible for the organization's estimated $1.4 million annual budget. Despite CORE's concentration on fund-raising activities, the organization has been riddled with debt during much of its conservative configuration. In 1994 CORE owed nearly three million dollars in debt, court judgments, and federal tax penalties. The *New York Daily News* reported that the organization's "fiscal affairs [were] in such disarray that an independent auditor took the unusual step of refusing to certify its bookkeeping."[60]

Conclusion

At the onset of the twenty-first century CORE, the one time torchbearer of direct action protest for a just and humane society, has become a mere mockery of its proud legacy. Once a pacesetter in Black opposition to the Vietnam War, CORE recently honored Gen. William Westmoreland, the commanding officer of the United States Armed Forces in Southeast Asia, during the annual King fund-raising banquet. Under the leadership of Roy Innis CORE has evolved from an effective Civil Rights organization into an impotent Black conservative interest group.

Innis's explicit shift to the right of the political spectrum has elevated his stature among prominent conservative politicians such as former President Ronald Reagan and Rudolph W. Giuliani, the former two-term mayor of New York City. Indeed, Giuliani once complained that CORE's Martin Luther King Jr. annual fund-raising banquet "got no coverage the next day in the papers."[61] Innis's endorsement of conservative ideas has made him a mainstay on the conservative banquet circuit. He has addressed several national conservative organizations such as the American Legislative Exchange Council. Most important, CORE's adoption of a conservative policy orientation enhanced its funding attractiveness to conservative foundations and corporate America.

CORE's linkage to prominent conservative ideologues has undoubtedly increased its external legitimacy with powerful benefactors. This newfound external support has failed, however, to improve CORE's tenuous ties to the Black community. CORE's absence of internal legitimacy minimizes the organization's ability to represent Black people in the post–Civil Rights era.

Six

Claude A. Clegg III

"You're Not Ready for Farrakhan"

The Nation of Islam and the Struggle for Black Political Leadership, 1984–2000

October 16, 1995, was a clear, radiant day in Washington, D.C. As the morning sun arced against an azure sky, tens of thousands of people, predominantly African American and male, began assembling on the Mall in front of the Capitol Building. The occasion was the "Million Man March," a carefully planned mass demonstration intended to dramatize the capacity of Black men to organize and gather in large numbers as well as their potential as a progressive social force and political constituency. Additionally, the event was billed as a day of atonement and reconciliation, an opportunity for African American men to experience a collective brotherhood and camaraderie that would inspire them to excel in their multifarious roles as fathers, husbands, workers, and citizens. Into the afternoon speakers and entertainers poured oratory and song into vast, ever-shifting waves of onlookers, heightening the synergy that the multitude itself had created from its sheer density and immenseness. A bird's-eye view of the event revealed a moving, human collage of every hue—accented with flags, posters, dreadlocks, bowties, and Kente patterns—which was vivid and alive in an almost surreal way. As the event drew closer to the keynote address, the gathered masses focused increasingly, anxiously, on the platform before the steps of the Capitol, where the final, sorely anticipated speech would bring this most remarkable day to a crescendo. Gradually, they came together to stand and watch as one, wholly aware that they themselves, now numbering well into the hundreds of thousands, were the momentous occasion, notwithstanding the coming orator, who had initially summoned them to the capital.

After a rousing introduction by a uniformed associate, a nattily dressed group of Black men, appearing animated by some urgent, lofty purpose, descended the Capitol stairs. As they approached the rostrum, Louis Farrakhan, chief minister of the Nation of Islam, emerged from their midst. A light ruddy-brown-skinned sexagenarian, Farrakhan confidently took his place behind the podium, flanked by militarily attired followers. The occasion had not found the minister visually unprepared for his role. As characteristic of his public appearances, he was elegantly appareled in a black pin-striped suit, fashionably complemented by a gray bowtie and matching pocket square. Effective dietary and exercise regimens camouflaged his sixty-two years, as did other cosmetic touches, such as his large square-framed designer glasses. Greeted with reverberating applause and shouts of "Allah-u-Akbar" (God is great), Farrakhan seemed vital and self-possessed before his sprawling audience. To be sure, this kind of adulation was not new to him. For years he had packed arenas and auditoriums around the country with thousands who gladly paid the cost of admission for a chance to lose themselves in his fury. But on that autumn Monday he had the attention of the world like never before, with an audience of as many as one million literally at his feet. On that day, if not on many subsequent ones, he was the most politically influential African American on the planet.

Louis Farrakhan's central role in Black politics by late 1995 had evolved over a decade's time. He had first come to national attention during the 1984 presidential campaign, when he served as an informal aide of Democratic candidate Jesse Jackson. The story of his ascent in the nuanced, intrigue-laden world of Black political culture is one of propitious timing, personal talent and ambitions, hidden agendas, and fragile alliances, often torn asunder as quickly as they were forged. This chapter analyzes the political context and historical conditions that both made Farrakhan's advancement possible and, ironically, improbable. Also, the many, sometimes mutually exclusive, constituencies that he cultivated over the course of almost two decades, ranging from Black elected officials and Middle Eastern dictators to the federal government and Jews, are examined in detail. Additionally, given that Louis Farrakhan was as much a media creation as he was a private individual and the head of a very insular religious organization, his manipulation of the press—and its manipulation of his image—is central to understanding his dialogue with and meaning to others and thus is sensitively dealt with here.

In essence this chapter maintains that for many years Louis Farrakhan was a shrewd politician in his own right, able to follow the political winds as deftly as any player of modern politics. His most durable political skill was undoubtedly his ability to excite the masses of African Americans with his message of racial pride, economic self-help, moral reform, and quasi-Islamic millenarianism.

This talent was responsible for both his political leverage with officialdom and the populist wave that he navigated all the way to the Million Man March. Interestingly, much of Farrakhan's message in the 1980s and 1990s was a throwback to the 1960s, when the conservative Black nationalism of his mentor, Elijah Muhammad, held sway among Blacks disaffected by the slow pace of racial change. Thus, as a testament to both the seeming timelessness of these ideas and the desperate conditions among large numbers of African Americans during the late twentieth century, Farrakhan was able to package this message in a way that appealed to literally millions of Black people.

Despite his charismatic presentations, Farrakhan's personal idiosyncrasies, coupled with his ideological commitments and organizational agendas, have substantially limited both his effectiveness and longevity as a factor in mainstream partisan politics. His understanding and tolerance of politics as a pragmatic process for mediating conflict through compromises and coalitions grew over time. Yet, by the mid–1990s, he had crafted and broken alliances with political officials in almost every strata of government and subsequently learned much about the imperfections and impermanence of political realities. Significantly, during this period Farrakhan managed to create for himself a potentially powerful, though politically untried, base in African American communities. While his decline in American politics was much more rapid than his rise, he did challenge the premises upon which Black participation in American politics was predicated, and his leadership suggested, if temporarily, new possibilities.

Beginnings: The Nation of Islam, Jesse Jackson, and the 1984 Presidential Campaign

Like very few events in American history, the pursuit of the U.S. presidency by Jesse L. Jackson energized African Americans with currents of expectation and pride which were unusually palpable. Jackson, a Black Baptist minister and social activist, had been a close associate of Civil Rights leader Dr. Martin Luther King Jr. in the 1960s and had maintained, even during the conservative presidencies of Richard Nixon and Gerald Ford, a reserve of political capital, and ambition, which guaranteed him stature in some quarters of the African American community. His politics, like those of many Blacks, were Left-leaning. Thus, he championed strong government protections for Civil Rights, the social safety nets of the welfare state, workers' rights, redistributive tax and spending programs, and a liberative foreign policy designed to effect change in places such as White minority–ruled South Africa and Israeli-occupied Palestine. The election of Republican Ronald Reagan in 1980, the retreat from liberalism and some of the gains of the Civil Rights Movement, along with a ravaging recession, forced both African Americans and political progressives onto the defensive. Although he was a popular president, the reactionary Reagan was anathema to people of Jackson's political ilk and easily aroused a slate of challengers in the 1984 presidential election. Solidly backed by the Black electorate, Jackson made a historic bid for the Democratic nomination, causing seismic shifts in the landscape of American politics and Black electoral participation. While the larger White voting population would ultimately determine Jackson's political fate, his campaign was markedly affected by a singular alliance that he would forge with Louis Farrakhan, the little known leader of the religious group the Nation of Islam.[1]

Farrakhan had gained a hearing and an audience in the Black community via a route much different than that of Jesse Jackson's. Being the offspring of West Indian immigrants, the Muslim leader was attracted to the Nation of Islam, then led by Elijah Muhammad, by its message of Black self-help and initiative, racial pride (and chauvinism), moral asceticism, and its iconoclastic, though largely rhetorical, denunciations of Whites as "devils" doomed for destruction.[2] This group, which Farrakhan joined in 1955, was often the vocal, adversarial counterpart of Civil Rights organizations, which were leading the movement toward racial integration and Black enfranchisement. Whereas groups such as the National Association for the Advancement of Colored People (NAACP), the Congress of Racial Equality (CORE), and the Southern Christian Leadership Conference (SCLC) stressed nonviolence, Christian brotherhood, desegregation, and voting rights as the main themes of the Black struggle for equality, the Nation of Islam proclaimed economic nationalism, territorial separatism, and divine judgment by their god, Allah, as the remedies for White America's reluctance to address inequities between the races.[3]

Over the course of the 1960s and 1970s Farrakhan swiftly ascended the ranks of the Muslim movement, replacing ousted, and later slain, Malcolm X as both minister of the New York mosque and as the group's national representative. When Muhammad died in 1975, his son Wallace inherited the movement, drastically overhauling the Nation's philosophy and practices so as to reinvent it as a traditional Muslim sect, shorn of its racial teachings and open to White adherents. Farrakhan, still partial to the old teachings of Elijah Muhammad, stayed in the reformed Nation of Islam for about two years before departing to start his own movement. Appropriating the former title of the parent organization (which Wallace Muhammad had since changed to the World Community of Islam in the West), Farrakhan reverted back to the racialized Islam of his deceased teacher and quickly acquired a small following. In 1982 his Nation of Islam, based in Chicago, attracted forty-five hundred people to its Saviour's Day convention, an indication of its gradual, but steady, growth.[4]

Prior to the 1984 presidential campaign Louis Farrakhan and Jesse Jackson had been acquainted with each other for some time. The two men had met passingly during the tumultuous 1960s. In 1972 Jackson had lent moral support to Farrakhan when Mosque No. 7, his New York cell of Muslims, was assaulted by police. Additionally, at Saviour's Day 1975 Jackson generously eulogized the recently deceased Elijah Muhammad before thousands of gathered Muslims. It was not until 1979, however, when Jackson visited Syria and successfully convinced President Hafiz al-Assad to release captured American pilot Robert Goodman Jr., that the relationship between he and Farrakhan began to congeal. Farrakhan had journeyed to Syria with Jackson's delegation, and his knowledge of Arabic and Middle Eastern culture proved valuable. Following their return to the United States, lines of communication between Farrakhan's Nation of Islam and Jackson's People United to Save Humanity (Operation PUSH), a Civil Rights group, remained open. As the political conservatism and economic decline of the first Reagan Administration settled over the country, the two clergymen witnessed firsthand many of the social repercussions of these phenomena in Chicago, where they both resided. In subsequent meetings these images of privation and hopelessness substantially shaped their discussions.[5]

On Thanksgiving evening 1983 Farrakhan visited Jackson at his home, where they conversed about the upcoming presidential contest. The Baptist minister had by then decided to seek the Democratic nomination and sought the Muslim leader's assistance. Certainly known to Jackson, Farrakhan could be useful in several ways. His Muslim following in Chicago and elsewhere, already well organized and disciplined, could be employed to canvass Black communities and spearhead voter registration projects. Their sporadically published organ, the *Final Call,* could be instrumental in publicizing the campaign, given its estimated press run of twenty-five thousand copies by February 1984. Most important, Farrakhan himself was an eloquent speaker, with a keen talent for stirring, if sometimes impetuous, orations. He was an increasingly popular speaker in some quarters of the African American community and could reach audiences that Jackson and other politicians could not.

Although Farrakhan's assistance would fortify, at least initially, the credibility of the Jackson campaign among some African Americans, this alliance was, indeed, a symbiotic one in which Farrakhan, too, would benefit. Massive press coverage of Jackson in the following months would cast an intense spotlight on Farrakhan and his Nation of Islam. Especially since the Muslim leader agreed to provide Jackson with guards ("Fruit of Islam") until he was assigned Secret Service protection, Farrakhan was guaranteed at least a symbolic role on the campaign trail. On a number of occasions he served as the candidate's introductory speaker. Eventually, Farrakhan and his followers, with their curious mix of Islamic heterodoxy, Black chauvinism, and moral austerity, would claim a share of media attention in their own right. This would not occur, however, before Jackson's novel run for the presidency gave them entree into a larger world.[6]

As the 1984 campaign season began, Farrakhan was genuinely excited about Jackson's candidacy. Historically, the Nation of Islam had eschewed politics, claiming that the electoral system was irreparably racist and corrupt. Styling itself as principally a religious group, the Muslim movement embraced divine retribution and Black territorial separatism as its primary political doctrines. Yet by the 1960s Elijah Muhammad was willing to admit that "the judicious use of the ballot box" might gain Blacks a measure of "freedom, justice, and equality." Farrakhan, citing Muhammad's position and inspired by Harold Washington's successful 1983 bid to become the first Black mayor of Chicago, arrived at similar conclusions a generation later. "If a politician arose among us who was fearless . . . and would not sell us out," he contended, "that kind of politician deserved and should get the full backing and support of our entire people." To him Jesse Jackson appeared to be a politician entitled to such support.[7]

On February 9, in an unprecedented display of this new spirit of political engagement among the Muslims, Farrakhan led as many as twelve hundred people to the Chicago Board of Election to register to vote. During this occasion the Muslim minister praised Jesse Jackson, encouraging "those who feel alienated and locked out of the electoral process" to back his run for the presidency. Accompanied by his wife, Betsy, Farrakhan, "with a sober mind, a clear [conscience] and with deep humility," registered to vote for the first time in his life. It was clearly a turning point for him. Now his vision of the future, despite his persistent separatist rhetoric, pointed toward a secular, civil identity for the Nation of Islam, in which a burgeoning political realism and activism might conceivably have an ameliorating effect on the conditions of African American life. In this extraordinary moment his optimism about the Jackson campaign led him to declare voting by Blacks as obligatory and imminently pertinent to their survival. "We have no choice between violence and voting," he counseled. "I would rather see us vote."[8]

Farrakhan's ardor about the Jackson candidacy was common among African American voters, especially among those, like himself, who had registered solely for the purpose of electing a Black man to high office. The intensity of his zeal as a campaigner for Jackson was particularly striking, however, given the largely self-imposed fringe role that Muslims had traditionally played in Black political life. It was as though Farrakhan, and many other African Americans, had been waiting, longing, for a meaningful discourse with the national political culture, an exchange that would invert the static terms of their historical relationship with race by stressing their Americanism over their Blackness. The possibility, even the improbability, of a Jackson victory in November was electrifying for African Americans, especially in the context of a renaissance in conservatism which thrived on the racially coded rhetoric of the Reagan Administration regarding busing, welfare, affirmative action, and "constructive engagement" with apartheid South Africa.

Before an audience at Princeton University in mid-February, Farrakhan was irrepressibly charged with an almost ecstatic buoyancy over the Jackson campaign. He glorified the candidate in messianic terms, stating at one point, "If you listen to Jesse talk, he sounds like the Christ." According to Farrakhan, the sheer fact that he "would dare run, knowing the climate, is a sign that a higher power is urging him." As the case with many others, the Muslim minister reveled in the seeming audacity of a Black man to seek the U.S. presidency, debating "the best that the Democratic party has to offer." In a personal aside he told how Jackson's vision of a just and equitable society had enthralled young people, including his grandchildren, who donned campaign buttons and huddled around the television whenever the candidate received coverage. Farrakhan cajoled, sermonized, and demanded that the audience vote for Jackson as well as offer its assistance to his fledgling campaign. To applause he proudly asserted, "Now, I've got someone to vote for" and encouraged his listeners to "make your vote and your voice heard for Jesse."[9]

In retrospect the early, heady days of the Jackson candidacy had not prepared him or his advocates for the damage that both words and deeds would inflict upon his already slim chances of winning the Democratic nomination, let alone the presidency. To be sure, obsessive scrutiny of his campaign by the press and inelegant attacks by his political opponents occurred early on and could hardly have been surprising. After all, Black people were not the only Americans transfixed by what was perhaps the most fascinating political saga since the resignation of President Richard Nixon in 1974. Nonetheless, Jackson would become vulnerable to withering criticism in ways that he probably could not have imagined prior to announcing his candidacy in November 1983.

Most unfortunately, some of the harm was self-inflicted and nearly lethal to his bid for the White House. Illustratively, in casual conversation Jackson was overheard making disparaging references to Jews as "Hymies" and New York as "Hymietown," comments that ended up in newspapers across the country. At first he denied the reports but eventually apologized, labeling the remarks as "insensitive" and "wrong." By late February 1984 outraged members of the Jewish community had mobilized against Jackson's candidacy to the point that he felt it necessary to single out Jews as being responsible for most of the disruptions to his campaign and threats against his life. It is very probable that Jackson's "Jewish problem" was scarcely avoidable and would have starkly emerged at some point in his bid for the presidency. His relationship with the Jewish community had been strained for years, weakened by his embrace of Palestinian nationhood and a literal embrace of Yasir Arafat in 1979. His reported slurs were not only a blunder, however, but a distraction that would take on a life of its own throughout the primaries. Making a volatile situation explosive, Farrakhan, who had provided the manpower to defend Jackson from physical harm, vocally assailed his detractors in ways that the candidate would soon regret.[10]

At the Saviour's Day convention of the Nation of Islam on February 25, the Muslim minister announced to a crowd of ten thousand that Jackson had received over one hundred threats against his life—an assertion later confirmed by the Federal Bureau of Investigation. Farrakhan advised Jewish critics to settle their differences with the candidate through civil dialogue. Short of that, he said, whatever hostility they harbored toward Jackson should be expressed in the ballot booth. "We can stand to lose an election," he conceded, "but we cannot stand to lose our brother." The minister, who had firsthand knowledge of the physical dangers that accompanied Jackson's candidacy, took very seriously the attacks levied by Jews and others. The verbal assaults had become much shriller by this time, exemplified by a provocative "Jews against Jackson" demonstration in front of his campaign headquarters five days earlier. At one point in his oration Farrakhan asked rhetorically, "If you harm this brother, what do you think we shall do?" In reply he promised, in a tone infused with visceral anger, "If you harm Jesse Jackson, in the name of Allah, that will be the last one you harm."[11]

Farrakhan himself had had an ambivalent relationship with the Jewish community prior to Saviour's Day 1984. As a youth, he had grown up around Jews in the Lower Roxbury neighborhood of Boston. Many of his classmates and teachers had been Jews, and his fondness for the violin was directly related to his enchantment with the music of Jewish-born composer Felix Mendelssohn. But, along with seeing Jews as neighbors and even people to be admired, he also saw them as despised merchants, landowners, and powerbrokers in Black Roxbury. By the 1960s the community was bitterly divided along racial lines, and many African American residents resented continuing Jewish influence over the housing and retail market of the neighborhood, even as many of them relocated to exclusive White suburbs. As a member of the Nation of Islam, Farrakhan's early ambivalence was substantially supplanted by a doctrinal suspicion of Jews, as both White people and as Jews. Like many other African

American leaders, he was more sympathetic to the Arab side of the Middle Eastern conflict and had cultivated political links with anti-Zionist crusaders such as Libyan leader Muammar Qaddafi. Yet it was not until the 1984 presidential campaign, when some Jews attempted to derail the Jackson candidacy, that the Muslim minister publicly aired his views before the national media. Confronted by a motivated, politically influential opposition, his vitriolic broadsides against Jews would eventually become one of his most widely reported preoccupations.[12]

Jewish disdain for Jackson quickly rubbed off on Farrakhan, who had an unabashed penchant for arousing their ire. In response to being compared to Adolf Hitler, the Muslim minister replied during a March 11 radio address that "Hitler was a very great man," even though he had despised Blacks and wickedly murdered Jews. His remarks, of course, gained ample press attention. His later attempts at clarification, insisting that he had meant that the Nazi leader had been "wickedly great," hardly mollified Jewish displeasure and came too late to matter in the presidential race. In the same March 11 speech a threat to "one day soon . . . punish . . . with death" Milton Coleman, the Black *Washington Post* journalist who had reported Jackson's anti-Jewish slurs a month earlier, triggered a review by the U.S. Attorney's office into the possible criminal intent of the remarks. While Farrakhan back-pedaled from the ominous language of his talk and publicly reassured others "that the lives of Milton Coleman and his wife and family are sacred to me," it was Jackson, not his Muslim ally, who most acutely felt the political repercussions of such pronouncements. To his chagrin and detriment the patent reluctance of Farrakhan to apologize for or retract such intemperate statements, or to avoid making them, surfaced prominently during the spring campaign as both a notable character flaw of the Muslim minister and as a bane to Jackson's candidacy.[13]

Following this and other caustic exchanges between Farrakhan and campaign opponents, Jackson was sharply pressured to distance himself from both the Muslim minister and his tirades. At every opportunity the media pummeled Jackson with questions about Farrakhan. In an April 8 appearance on "Meet the Press" the candidate was visibly unsettled by queries about the March 11 address. Asked whether he would repudiate Farrakhan for remarks that Jackson admitted were "a bit inciting and distasteful," he declined and termed the line of questioning "a form of harassment." Three days later, on the "CBS Morning News," Jackson stressed his disapproval of "violence and threats of violence" but again refused to sever his ties with Farrakhan. Unsurprisingly, his chief rivals for the Democratic nomination recognized the political expediency of heightening the pressure on Jackson by denouncing his Muslim associate. "It was an outrage," Walter Mondale said of the March 11 talk. "It is and should be condemned." Emphatically, Gary Hart concurred. All candidates should "dis-associate in every way possible from anyone threatening physical violence or harm against anyone else."[14]

On a number of levels things were not quite that simple for Jackson. First, as he had stated during a number of interviews, his Christian code of ethics stressed forgiveness and redemption, ideals that had undergirded the ethos of the Civil Rights Movement. While the media and others seemed to be asking that he repudiate not only the views and utterances of Louis Farrakhan but also his person, even his right to exist, Jackson held that to do so would be unchristian, given that he did not have "the moral power to condemn" individuals, only their actions. In addition to this religiously inspired stance, the candidate believed that the whole controversy surrounding his relationship with Farrakhan had been unduly sensationalized by the press and his political enemies. Although he personally found some of the sentiments of the Muslim minister repugnant, the whole matter was a minor episode in a much larger story, and to concentrate on what Farrakhan said, primarily for the consumption of his followers, was an unwarranted distraction. In a spring meeting with his staff he excoriated others' fixation on his Nation of Islam ties and the media's eagerness in reporting Farrakhan's comments about Milton Coleman. He vowed to continue his affiliation with the Muslim leader, despite efforts "to write him out of our race—the human race." Whatever votes were lost due to the alliance "we never did have" in the first place, according to Jackson, and in any event they would not have compensated for the "loss of our self-respect" had he bowed to pressure. Into the summer Jackson saw the whole affair as an effort to divide his campaign and alienate Black voters over nothing more than "foolishness."[15]

A significant factor in Jackson's decision to resist calls to abandon Farrakhan was the expanding notoriety of the Muslim among African Americans. It had become quite clear to him and others that the campaign was not only creating Jesse Jackson as a political phenomenon; it was also recasting Louis Farrakhan in a mold much larger than the hermetic world and culture of the Nation of Islam. The ten thousand people who attended his Saviour's Day convention in February suggested his growing influence, but there were other discernible indicators. In February Mayor Marion Barry of Washington, D.C., honored him with an official "Louis Farrakhan Day" and referred to him as "one of the single most significant spokespersons for the dispossessed and the downtrodden." Black clergymen such as Rev. T. J. Jemison, president of the National Baptist Convention, and A.M.E. bishop John Hurst Adams, head of the Congress of National Black Churches, refused to disown their "Black brother," Adams arguing that Farrakhan "speaks for many more Blacks than just his followers." Negative coverage in White media venues did little apparent damage to the Muslim minister's image among African Americans. Actually, his willingness to exchange barbs with the press, presidential candidates, Jews, Whites, and even Blacks was refreshingly attractive to many African Americans, especially among youth who were not old enough to have seen Malcolm X and other Black spokesmen doing the same thing a generation earlier.

Unfortunately for Jackson, by June the political trajectory of his campaign was veering beyond his control. As the July Democratic convention approached, he was still in last place in a field of three candidates. His electoral strength was most evident in southern states with significant Black populations and in liberal urban areas. Yet this multiracial constituency, which he styled the Rainbow Coalition, was not enough to win with. Although he garnered almost 80 percent of the Black vote in his home state of Illinois, Mondale, the Democratic frontrunner, won the state's primary with 41 percent of the total votes cast. Savaged by bad press and an array of vociferous adversaries, Jackson was obliged to groom himself politically for a supporting role at the Democratic convention to be held in San Francisco. He had made a historic bid for chief executive of the United States, but now, if Reagan were to be overcome in November, he would have to get in line behind Mondale and pay homage to party unity.[16]

Predictably, but still not entirely expectedly, there was one more bombshell from Farrakhan. It came in the guise of an incendiary attack on Israel. In a June speech he lambasted the creation of the Jewish state as "an outlaw act" supported by the United States and other nations whose collusion was "criminal in the sight of the Almighty God." He charged Israel with "injustice, thievery, lying and deceit," as well as practicing a "dirty religion." The tone and substance of the harangue had become vintage Farrakhan and was thoroughly within the Nation of Islam's tradition of rhetorical opposition to Israel and Zionism. In the context of the endgame of the Jackson candidacy, however, it was one attack too many.[17]

Jackson's political destiny now rested almost solely in the hands of people representative of the lightest color of his Rainbow Coalition. Whatever advantages Farrakhan had delivered to his camp had long since evaporated, and now it was only the convention delegates the candidate had accrued that mattered. Thus, tolerance of the Muslim leader and his increasingly cumbersome baggage was no longer necessary. The formal repudiation was carefully worded but direct, leaving no room for doubt. Issued on June 28 while Jackson was abroad in Cuba, the statement characterized Farrakhan's anti-Israel remarks as "reprehensible and morally indefensible" and as "damaging for the prospects of peace" in the Middle East. Regarding their turbulent alliance, the missive declared that the Muslim minister "is not part of this campaign." On a note of finality and as a balm to party elements that had been most offended by Farrakhan, Jackson described himself as a "Judeo-Christian" and declared that "I will not permit Min. Farrakhan's words, wittingly or unwittingly, to divide the Democratic party, and neither anti-Semitism nor anti-Black statements have any place in our party." The long-avoided rupture was now a reality. Rather ironically, it occurred in the wake of Jackson's defeat, as opposed to being a tactic to forestall it.[18]

Although it may have been difficult to perceive at the time, Farrakhan, despite being subjected to a thorough character assassination by the media and others, weathered the trials and trauma of the 1984 presidential campaign much better than Jackson. Arguably, whereas the latter had failed to make his Rainbow Coalition a long-term, viable force in American politics, the Muslim leader entered the national stage, by way of the Jackson campaign, and enjoyed a previously unknown degree in popularity. Shrewdly and largely at Jackson's expense, he stayed in the public eye, regularly drawing press attention with statements and actions calculated to startle, fascinate, and outrage different segments of the population. While undoubtedly desirous of helping the Jackson campaign succeed, at least initially, Farrakhan eventually became invested in Black politics and the mass media in ways that allowed him to envision a future that was not necessarily congruous with the fortunes of Jesse Jackson. Thus, by late June 1984, when Jackson no longer needed the Nation of Islam leader, the converse was also true: Farrakhan no longer required Jackson's presence or influence to make himself palatable to African Americans. Where the Baptist preacher's campaign was ending, the Muslim minister's crusade was just beginning. It was a curious twist of fate, which left bitterness on both sides. Consequently, Farrakhan, while voting in the Illinois primary, would not cast another ballot for over a decade, having been disillusioned by the racial Machiavellianism of U.S. politics. As for his former ally, the pain ran even deeper. On future occasions when their public paths crossed, Jackson conspicuously avoided being photographed with the man who had so indelibly influenced his bold pursuit of the American presidency.[19]

Tempestuous Waters: Louis Farrakhan and the Black Political Establishment, 1985–1993

Saviour's Day 1985 attracted over fifteen thousand people. Not since the stewardship of the late Elijah Muhammad had the Nation of Islam drawn so many to its annual commemoration of the birthday (February 26) of W. Fard Muhammad, the fair-skinned mystic who founded the organization in 1930. The Chicago event was typically as much a self-aggrandizing tribute to the current leader of the Muslim movement as it was a salute of its founder, and, subsequently, Louis Farrakhan took center stage with his hours-long speeches. Yet this year the program was more controversial than usual.[20]

Libyan leader Muammar Qaddafi, known for his vituperative opposition to U.S. foreign policy in the Arab world, addressed the crowd by satellite. "This imperialist country must be destroyed," he declared. "We are ready to give you arms because your cause is just." Qaddafi denounced the oppression of Blacks and Indians in the United States and criticized the country for "committing this sin against you." Provocatively, he suggested that African Americans in the U.S. military should desert their posts and lay the foundations for "a separate and independent state . . . in America." After this address Farrakhan, who offered no response to the Libyan's commentary, dwelled on economic themes during his own talk. As he would do increasingly in coming years, he chided Black leaders for "looking to Washington" for guidance and went so far as to thank reelected president Ronald Reagan for cutting social programs. "Now you've got to look to yourself and organize," he counseled, "so together we will lift ourselves from this condition." For the thousands assembled, the convention turned out to be a grand spectacle, with its risqué political flavor and exotic pan-Islamic overtones. For Farrakhan it was one more audacious step toward realizing a more expansive vision of his leadership on the domestic and international scenes.[21]

The self-help motifs that Farrakhan stressed during his Saviour's Day sermon, and Qaddafi's appearance were part of a year-long concatenation of events which eventually would be advantageous to the economic program of the Nation of Islam. The Muslim minister's rancorous role in the 1984 presidential campaign, with its anti-Zionist invectives and nationalist fervor, gained the attention of principals in the Arab world who had similar views on Israel and U.S. foreign policy in general. His abrasive retorts to Jewish critics of Jesse Jackson reported by, in his words, the "Zionist-controlled media . . . increased my influence in the Arab world," though they did little to improve the candidate's odds of winning. Farrakhan's celebrity among selected Arab leaders was carefully nurtured over the coming years, but the first fruits of it emerged in the spring of 1985, when he announced that Qaddafi had agreed to loan him five million dollars, interest-free, for the purpose of inaugurating a "self-contained economic system" for African Americans. It was no mean achievement, since the mere symbolism of such a gesture illustrated the Nation of Islam's growing appeal and influence beyond U.S. borders. Also, five million dollars was a tremendous boost for an organization largely composed of Blacks from lower-class backgrounds. With the loan Farrakhan started People Organized and Working for Economic Rebirth (POWER), a marketing organization, which would distribute various toiletries and cosmetic goods to its members, who would in turn sell them retail.[22]

POWER never became the commercial avatar that Farrakhan had originally imagined. There were several obstacles, including insufficient capitalization, lack of professional personnel, and an outdated approach to retail enterprise, which barred the company from successfully competing in an already glutted market. Moreover, there were unexpected obstacles that hindered its progress. According to the minister, Jewish distributors, still incensed about his part in the 1984 campaign, successfully obstructed the marketing of his "Clean & Fresh" products. Even well-established Black-owned companies such as Johnson Products were pressured to back away from business agreements with the Nation of Islam, lest their own products be subject to boycott. Farrakhan, already convinced by the failed Jackson candidacy that Jews were against Black interests, was livid over this purposeful interference with his business plans. Years later he reported in an interview, "When I saw that . . . I recognized that the Black man will never be free until we address the relationship between Blacks and Jews."[23]

Farrakhan's chosen method of addressing what he saw as Jewish control of African American access to power and opportunity took the familiar form of a steady, brutal barrage of accusations and maledictions. On July 22 he spoke of the "wickedness" of Jews before a Washington, D.C., crowd of ten thousand and assured them that "Black people will not be controlled by Jews." He delivered a similar speech in Los Angeles before a comparable audience. But, unlike Jesse Jackson, who had tolerated his blistering orations, even as his services became more dubious and problematic for his campaign, Black leaders in both cities and elsewhere denounced the Muslim's message. Mayor Marion Barry, prodded by Jewish leaders, spoke out—although he did so seven weeks after the fact—against "the anti-Semitic impeachments" that Farrakhan issued that "didn't help our city at all." Barry was careful to add that he was not repudiating Farrakhan but was "very specifically" taking issue with his remarks. Tom Bradley, the mayor of Los Angeles, was less equivocal in his response to the minister's speech there, condemning Farrakhan, "bigotry, hatred, [and] violence" the day following his appearance.[24]

Perhaps caught off guard by censure from Black officials, the minister's first reaction was to berate his critics. He attacked Barry as a liar and hypocrite for having privately courted his influence, even as he publicly upbraided him "to placate the Jews." Additionally, he claimed that Jews had "dictated" that Bradley rebuke him as the price of their support for any gubernatorial bid that he might make. In defense of the mayors other Black officials entered the escalating war of words. Mickey Leland, Democratic representative from Texas and head of the Congressional Black Caucus (CBC), warned Farrakhan that his castigation of Black politicians was a "real mistake" and brought his credibility into question. On a similar note Washington, D.C., council member John Ray pointed out that "Barry and Bradley have been out there a long time fighting for . . . the rights of Black people." He added that no "reasonable-thinking person" sympathized with the minister's "anti-Semitic statements." In November officials in the Muslim's hometown took action. In the absence of Mayor Harold Washington the city council passed an anti-Farrakhan resolution by a margin of 31 to 14. According to sponsor Jerome H. Orbach, the action was a "moral imperative" meant to counter the mayor's public silence regarding the Muslim minister.[25]

In order to avoid being outmaneuvered in his rhetorical battles with Black politicians, Farrakhan's counterattacks became darker, with allusions to violent reprisal and death. On September 26, before a largely college-age audience at Morgan State University in Baltimore, he asserted that "Black leaders can not sell out another Black brother without consequences." Citing deadly Black infighting in South Africa, he intimated that "selling out your people" would result in the killing of culpable Black American leaders. On another occasion he stated his sentiments even more explicitly. For Black elected officials who betray their constituents and are unrepentant, "we will tar and feather them, we will hang them from the highest limb, we will chop off their heads and roll them down the streets." To him it was a fitting price for "working for the enemies, rather than working for ourselves." Rather disingenuously, Farrakhan often inverted the original terms of his dialogue with Black politicians, making himself appear as the injured, populist victim and his Black adversaries as treacherous aggressors. This is aside from the fact that the Muslim minister was often, purposefully or inadvertently, the instigator of these confrontations and the first to employ abusive language.[26]

This tactic of resorting to macabre terminology to denounce an adversary was not new to Farrakhan. He had used it publicly as early as 1964, when he warned that Malcolm X was "worthy of death" for having criticized Elijah Muhammad. Of course, almost identical language was used in reference to Milton Coleman, the *Washington Post* reporter, as recently as February 1984. This practice bespoke a homogeneous, corporatist view of African Americans which was authoritarian in nature and allowed very little individual dissent or variance from the imagined best interest of the Black commonweal, as (conveniently) defined by the Nation of Islam. It could take on a beguiling religious gloss, which portrayed Blacks as the chosen people of God (Allah) sharing a unique, collective origin, history, and destiny. Still, it easily morphed into a theological fascism when Muslim spokesmen were confronted with often legitimate criticism of their views and program. Even if it was no more than metaphorical bravado and rhetorical bluff in most instances, the morbid language stifled constructive discourse and exacerbated tensions between Farrakhan and Black elected officials.[27]

Throughout the late 1980s Farrakhan's most enduring criticism of Black politicians, especially mayors, was that they lacked real influence due to their profound dependence on White (and Jewish) patronage and support. He was fond of referring to them as Black managers of White enterprises. He believed that African American elected officials as a class sought favor with the White "establishment," which allowed them a small measure of power "as long as they play by the rules of the Devil." Based substantially on his 1984 experiences, the minister had a fundamental distrust of politicians and a deep skepticism regarding the efficacy of political participation as a means to Black empowerment. If politics gained Blacks access to the capital, skills, and opportunities required to develop their communities economically, then it was a worthwhile medium for them to utilize in their struggles. What Farrakhan saw in Black politicians, however, was "symbol without substance;" to him they were obsequious puppets who had no ideas or agendas outside of what their White bosses allowed. Further, the imperatives of politics, such as the need for pragmatic alliances and compromises, seemed to offend him morally in very basic ways. When Jesse Jackson announced that he did not want Farrakhan's assistance for his 1988 presidential campaign, the Muslim leader took umbrage. "If you won't walk with me Reverend," he contended in a 1987 speech, "you're a liar when you say you'll walk with Jesus." By the spring of the following year Farrakhan had softened his position, downplaying the significance of Jackson's rejection of him. He even lauded his former ally as a man of vision who would make a formidable chief executive. Nonetheless, his cynicism about politics dominated his thinking about Jackson and other Black politicians, regardless of how prophetic or inspired they seemed. "No politician can save nobody," he characteristically fumed in 1989. "No whore can save you!"[28]

Despite his public bickering with Black officials and his reflexive distaste for their profession, Farrakhan actually desired a relationship with recognized leaders of the African American community, even if only on occasion and largely on his terms. Many of them, in turn, earnestly hoped for a more productive dialogue with him as well. His ability to draw audiences of several thousand people in nearly every major city in the country was unique among Black leaders, a fact that was not lost on his admirers or enemies. African American politicians, particularly those beholden to predominately Black electorates, were usually careful not to provoke his wrath unnecessarily or to alienate constituents who paid hard-earned money to hear him speak. During the presidency of George Bush, Farrakhan sporadically made overtures to other Black leaders, which were often well received. He seemed to dislike being completely isolated from other African American representatives and organizations and could be graciously cooperative under the right circumstances.

Significantly, in April 1989 Farrakhan was invited to participate in the African American Summit held in New Orleans, where he called for greater Black unity and a healing of the rift between him and Jesse Jackson, who evidently tried to avoid the minister on this occasion. He also demanded federally funded reparations for Blacks and boldly charged the government with being responsible for the spread of AIDS and the crack cocaine epidemic in Black communities. In October the city council of Washington, D.C., passed a resolution recognizing Muslim efforts "to rid the Black community of the scourge of drugs," particularly in the Mayfair Mansions apartments in the northeastern part of the city. Encouraged by both the thawing of his relationship with some Black politicians and the public relations dividends that might accrue, the minister again shifted his stance on politics, conceding in an interview, "I'm beginning to feel more and more that we should use our strength politically." Consequently, after Mayor Barry of Washington was arrested during a federal sting operation, which found him smoking crack cocaine, Farrakhan announced that Muslims would be running for local offices in the Maryland-D.C. area during the 1990 elections. Underfinanced and facing seasoned incumbents, none of the Muslims won their contests, but their efforts were certainly a break with the apolitical tradition of the Nation of Islam. This conspicuous attempt to work for change within the political system and Farrakhan's alliance building with other Black leaders appeared to be conditioning the Muslim movement for a much greater role in American life.[29]

Higher Ground: Toward the Million Man March, 1993–1995

Ideologically, Louis Farrakhan remained notably constant in his views well into the first Clinton Administration. While the 1992 election of the Democratic president set a more liberal tone for American political culture, the basic conservatism of the Muslim minister still informed his vision of politics, economics, and morality. At least rhetorically, he still believed in the advisability of a separate Black state in the event that African Americans could not be equitably treated in the United States. On this score he announced at a 1993 Pan-Africanist summit in Gabon that he intended to request that African leaders "carve out a territory for all people in the diaspora" on the African continent. Regarding domestic politics, he remained skeptical of the electoral system and governing bodies. Uncharacteristically, he did extend his sympathy to President Clinton, who had "inherited a mess" from his predecessor. He even offered Muslim assistance in crafting a national health care system. Yet, when asked in a June 1993 interview whether he would ever become a candidate for public office, he demurred, since such a step, he claimed, "would severely limit my ability to tell the truth." Interestingly, his religiously inspired opposition to abortion, homosexuality, drug use, and a number of other practices and lifestyles noticeably intersected with the social conservatism of Christian fundamentalists and the right wing of the Republican Party.

In terms of his economic views the minister never seemed to evolve beyond a "bootstraps capitalism," which encouraged self-help and entrepreneurship in Black communities. A prominent strand of populism coursed through his message, most evident when he decried tax policies that favored the wealthy and corporate downsizing that had devastated the working class. Yet he offered few sophisticated, coherent solutions for the problems of poverty, unemployment, homelessness, and crime other than demands for collective uplift, personal responsibility, and reparations. Occasionally, his proposals did break with the traditional racial myopia of the Nation of Islam; for example, in his book *A Torchlight for America* (1993) he called for a "new relationship" with U.S. leaders which could benefit "the good of the whole." Yet, even his most innovative thinking tended to be variations of long-standing Muslim doctrines, which were often as unworkable as the original formulation. As a solution to crime and recidivism, for instance, he advocated sending Black inmates to Africa, "under Nation of Islam supervision."[30]

Aside from his staple doctrines, one of Farrakhan's most persistent themes during the 1990s was the need for Black leaders and organizations to unite in common cause. It was not a new imperative for the minister, for he and the Nation of Islam had been insisting on African American coalitions for years. Now, however, his appeals were more specifically focused on the realm of politics and intimated a greater willingness of the Muslim movement to become involved in public policy matters. The organization that Farrakhan was most interested in allying with was the Congressional Black Caucus, an influential group of African Americans in the U.S. House of Representatives. The minister's overtures began as early as the publication of *Torchlight,* in which he lionized the caucus for representing the poor and for submitting annual budgets to Congress which "would keep America strong." The group, or at least its chairman, Kweisi Mfume, a Democratic representative from Maryland, was receptive of Farrakhan's political advances, which in turn led to him being invited to a CBC town hall meeting in September 1993.

The theme of the CBC gathering was "Race in America," and a number of topics relevant to African American life, from societal racism and poverty to crime and the disintegration of families, were discussed. Significantly, several well-known Black leaders attended, including NAACP executive director Benjamin Chavis and Rev. Jesse Jackson. The convening of such a meeting was significant in itself, given the political and personal divisions that still existed among participants. The most remarkable feat, however, was the agreement reached between the CBC and Farrakhan "to work for real and meaningful change." The pact, or "sacred covenant" in Mfume's words, was to be identical to an arrangement that the caucus already had with the NAACP, in which the Nation of Islam would consult with the Black legislators regarding policy issues. The alliance was also meant to be a symbolic declaration of Black solidarity and independence, indicating that, according to Mfume, "No longer will we allow people to divide us."[31]

At least initially, the agreement seemed to be fortuitous for everyone involved. For the CBC an alliance with Farrakhan's Nation of Islam was a risky proposition, especially for those members who represented predominantly White constituencies. Nonetheless, the growing influence of the Muslims could hardly be ignored by the legislative group, particularly for those from districts with Black electoral majorities. Again, Farrakhan was exceptional among African American leaders in his ability to draw crowds. In October 1992 a speech in Atlanta attracted more people than the World Series game occurring the same evening. A month after the CBC town hall meeting he drew a capacity crowd of 16,500 in an appearance in the Los Angeles Sports Arena, and in December 25,000 New Yorkers and others flooded the Jacob K. Javits Convention Center to hear his message. With these regular attendance figures (and speaking fees up to twenty thousand dollars) Farrakhan's potential as an invaluable political ally was nearly impossible for many African American politicians to deny. Predictably, there were those who came forward to question the wisdom of the CBC–Nation of Islam agreement. The Anti-Defamation League, the American Jewish Congress, and several others asked that Mfume elaborate on the meaning of his organization's treaty with the Muslims. The caucus chairman obliged the request in two meetings with Jewish leaders and, in an October statement, affirmed the accord with the Nation of Islam. He was careful, however, to add that, while the CBC and Jewish organizations "may differ on some issues, we must nevertheless continue to work together."[32]

If the sacred covenant was ostensibly beneficial to the work of the CBC, it was also timely for Farrakhan. As with the legislators, there were intricate motives behind the minister's overtures to the caucus which must be taken into account in order to understand the value of the accord to him and his organization. Clearly, Farrakhan had a desire to be well regarded in influential circles in the Black community, for its own sake and as a reflection of where he was psychologically at that time in his life. He had turned sixty in May and had

been painfully reminded of his own mortality when he was diagnosed with pros-
tate cancer in 1991. As he faced the twilight years of his life, he had established
no readily apparent legacy to leave to the world outside of the Nation of Islam,
except for the alluring, and repulsive, images that he and the media had created from his fiery, controversial speeches. If he had perished in 1993, it would
have been difficult for non-Muslim observers to pinpoint his significance, beyond his conservative, but still potent, Black nationalism and the reams of news-
print which only partially captured his complex life. Unlike Elijah Muhammad,
who first made the Nation of Islam an enduring phenomenon, or Malcolm X,
whose extraordinary transformations and perennially available autobiography
created a posthumous following, Farrakhan's overall meaning was still hazy
and unsettled, for it was subject to change abruptly from week to week. A longing for life beyond his earthly years almost certainly influenced his reaching
out to the CBC and others. But there were additional factors that likely shaped
his decision as well.[33]

By the early 1990s the Nation of Islam had become a major recipient of government contracts, most notably relating to the provision of security for drug-
infested, violence-plagued public housing. This business with the state was a
huge coup for the Muslims, for between 1991 and 1995 their security enterprises secured over fifteen million dollars in contracts in nine cities, including
Washington, D.C., Los Angeles, and Chicago. One of the most obvious ramifications of these transactions was that they linked the fiscal health of the Nation of Islam to federal and local government agencies. Consequently, the
financial and contractual ties mandated that Muslim businesses receiving state
monies abide by established rules of conduct and accountability. This new dependency was certainly not lost on government officials, who supervised Muslim services and sometimes refused to renew contracts for entirely subjective
reasons. Neither were the implications lost on Louis Farrakhan, who softened
his antigovernment rhetoric at a time when the most lucrative contracts were
being acquired. The minister's desire for a relationship with the CBC and his
sometimes conciliatory tone toward the U.S. government were not wholly predicated on protecting economic interests that were becoming increasingly associated with state largess. Yet his appeal to the country's "political and economic
leadership," as stated in *Torchlight,* "with the hope of formulating a cooperative effort for the benefit of us all" certainly makes comprehensible the dialectic relationship between his efforts at rapprochement with government officials
and the Muslims' growing reliance upon state contracts.[34]

Despite the optimistic inauguration of the CBC–Nation of Islam alliance,
subsequent events exposed it to insurmountable difficulties. On November 29,
1993, Khallid Abdul Muhammad, the national spokesman of the Muslim move-

ment, gave a most controversial speech at Kean College in Union, New Jersey. Even considering the liberal rhetorical standards of the Nation of Islam, the talk was an indecorous indictment of Whites, and especially Jews. Sometimes feigning a Jewish accent, Muhammad's talk, entitled "The Secret Relationship between Blacks and Jews," was punctuated with mocking phrases, such as "Columbia Jew-niversity" and "Jew York City." At one point he intimated that Jews had provoked the Holocaust by overrunning Germany to the point that "a German in his own country would almost have to go to a Jew to get money." To Muhammad the same themes of Jewish greed and manipulation echoed across the Atlantic, where Jews had become the "blood suckers of the Black nation" in the United States. His extraordinary rant went on for three hours, sparing few of the groups believed to be enemies of Black people. In response to a question about South Africa, Muhammad proposed that, once Blacks had secured political power there, Whites should be given a single day to depart the country. For those who remained, his solution was brutally methodical. "We kill the women. We kill the babies, we kill the blind. We kill the cripples. We kill them all. We kill the faggot. We kill the lesbian," he coldly declared. "When you get through killing them all, go to the goddamn graveyard and dig up the grave and kill them a-goddamn-gain because they didn't die hard enough."[35]

Widespread reactions to the venom that Muhammad spewed at Kean College began to surface in January. Black leaders, including several members of the CBC, publicly responded to the diatribe, categorically condemning it for both its substance and tone. Benjamin Chavis of the NAACP termed it a "virulent strand of racism that must not go unchallenged." Similarly, William Gray, president of the United Negro College Fund, denounced the speech for its "racism and anti-Semitism," as did Jesse Jackson, who also asserted that Muhammad's superior, Louis Farrakhan, "must make a definitive judgment of the speaker, in that he spoke in his name." Caucus member Charles Rangel of New York, after reading transcripts of the talk, concluded that "clearly, we're dealing with a person who is very dangerous, bitter and, in my opinion, very sick." Quite significantly, Representative John Lewis of Georgia, who had been critical of the Nation of Islam in previous years, attempted to invalidate the CBC's pact with the Muslims by arguing, "I don't think a good majority of the caucus ever saw ourselves engaged in any type of partnership or covenant with the Nation of Islam." Of particular note, the CBC chairman Kweisi Mfume appeared visibly conflicted by the unfolding dilemma. In September he had warmly embraced an alliance with Farrakhan, perhaps without first deliberating its desirability with other caucus members, and was now under intense pressure to step away from it due to a single, though appalling, speech by a heretofore little known subordinate. For the time being Mfume vacillated and simply penned a letter to Farrakhan asking for clarification of his spokesman's words, which he later said had been "extremely agonizing for me to even read."[36]

Farrakhan vacillated too. Muhammad's speech had, ironically, put him in a position similar to the one in which his verbal attacks against Jews had placed Jesse Jackson during the 1984 presidential campaign. Accordingly, he could either jettison an ally, indeed, a follower, in order to remain on course toward the Black political mainstream, or he could refuse to censure him, a costly option in terms of his newly acquired political capital and credibility. Thus, the inopportune Kean College tirade threatened to unravel possibilities that the four-month-old pact had promised. To a striking degree Farrakhan was silent for several days after the first outcries about the speech reached the press, even neglecting to reply to Mfume's correspondence. But, to the amazement and shock of many, he refused to reprimand Muhammad even mildly during a speaking engagement in Harlem on January 24. Instead, he played to the crowd in a classically Farrakhanesque way. Jews were "trying to use my brother [Khallid's] words against me to divide the house," he charged, according to press accounts. "They don't want Farrakhan to do what he's doing. They're plotting as we speak." Undoubtedly, doctrinal hard-liners in the Nation of Islam delighted in their leader's flagrant resistance to the mounting pressures to rebuke his chief spokesman. In light of the indomitable image that Farrakhan had cultivated among his followers, his perceived need to make this pro forma gesture of defiance for his organizational base, while hardly excusable, is understandable. Others outside of the Muslim movement, people whom Farrakhan had courted politically, were dismayed, however, by his blatant and public refusal to penalize Muhammad. They felt betrayed that he had seemingly abused their confidence in such a callous fashion.[37]

Two weeks after his Harlem address the Muslim minister finally conceded that the Kean College invective had been "vile in manner, repugnant, malicious, mean-spirited and . . . against the spirit of Islam." Yet, even in condemning the speech and demoting his national spokesman, Farrakhan equivocated, insisting that he supported the unspecified "truths that he [Muhammad] spoke." To those who mattered most, it was far too little too late. At a February 2 news conference Mfume unilaterally repealed the CBC–Nation of Islam covenant a full day before Farrakhan's late criticism of his lieutenant. Perhaps expressing the majority view of the caucus, Representative Major Owens of New York maintained that the legislators would allow "no future consideration of any kind of covenant" with the Muslims. There was apparently minor dissent within the group, expressed best by Congresswoman Barbara-Rose Collins of Michigan, who believed it unfair that Black public officials were pressured to "condemn the individual and the remarks . . . [and] everybody who's associated with them." Nonetheless, her voice was a minority opinion that day on Capitol Hill. In the same afternoon the U.S. Senate passed a scathing resolution condemning the Kean College speech by a margin of 97–0. Three weeks later the House of Representatives, characterizing the November talk "as outrageous hatemongering of the most vicious and vile kind," did the same with a 361–34 vote. Both congressional measures were unprecedented in their castigation of a citizen's speech, which was, even in this case, federally protected by the constitution. To Louis Farrakhan, however, it was the damage to his accord with the CBC, along with the apparent litmus test ritual, which was most disturbing. "Correcting one another in public for the purpose of currying favor with the enemies," he averred after the collapse of the alliance, "is repugnant."[38]

One consideration that the congressional resolutions against Khallid Muhammad did not address or counter was that Farrakhan's infamy among Whites seemed to be inversely correlated to his popularity among African Americans. The minister himself was cognizant of this phenomenon, as evidenced by his baited offer to appear before the U.S. House of Representatives to answer questions about "anything that I have ever said in the past." (The members of congress declined, perhaps sensing that a damning live sermon from Farrakhan would produce a politically uncomfortable spectacle.) Moreover, several opinion polls taken among African Americans during the public ruckus over Khallid Muhammad seemed to confirm this trend. For instance, a study by the University of Chicago found that 67 percent of Blacks queried agreed that Louis Farrakhan was "a positive force" in their community. A *Time/CNN* poll revealed that 70 percent of African American respondents believed that the minister "says things the country should hear," 67 percent viewed him as an "effective leader," and 63 percent agreed that he "speaks the truth." It is very likely—though not shown in these studies—that Farrakhan's support among Blacks was uneven and subject to fluctuations based on differences in the age, gender, socioeconomic class, religious affiliation, and other defining characteristics of respondents. Still, if the poll figures were even approximately accurate, his notoriety among African Americans, even in the wake of congressional censure, was undeniably impressive in magnitude, suggesting the existence of literally millions of admirers.[39]

Many Blacks found Farrakhan, and the Nation of Islam, alluring for a variety of reasons. The minister's celebrity, his charismatic orations, and the austere pageantry of his public appearances—replete with contingents of well-dressed, clean-shaven Fruit of Islam and dignified, wholesomely attired women—reflected a long-established trend among prominent African American leaders.

Historically, Black American leadership has incorporated a substantial measure of showmanship, even an entertaining quality. Spokesmen, especially in the twentieth century, did not only have to provide guidance for the masses; they needed to perform leadership as well. Whether one considers the flamboyant Black nationalist Marcus Garvey, Elijah Muhammad's Nation of Islam, or the Civil Rights Movement, with its soulful anthems, engaging speeches, and dramatic street protests, Black leadership has been as much choreographed as improvised, if not more so. By the 1990s Farrakhan had fully mastered this style of presentation and understood its power to an uncanny degree.

Indeed, the minister, almost at a whim, could elicit passions from audiences based on very real grievances and sometimes outrageous fantasies. During his speeches he imparted to his Black listeners the vicarious pleasure of defying, even harming, the oppressor in a forum saturated with displays of Black power and control, masculine assertion and dominance, and the mass illusion of Black nationality in the microcosm of an auditorium. For theatrical effect the minister sometimes referred to himself in the third person, as if he, too, were admiring Louis Farrakhan and absorbing his message. For many attendees Nation of Islam meetings were a form of forbidden fruit, which instantly sated one's appetite for plain talk on taboo subjects. The minister's vilification of Whites, Jews, and others and his often simplistic characterization of problems, even his troubling conspiratorial propositions, reverberated with audiences, who, based on their experiences as African Americans, could make a dark, digestible sense out of even his most fantastical assertions. At bottom Farrakhan candidly and often purposefully offended the racial sensibilities of White people. Ultimately, this was enough to ensure him a hearing in some quarters of the Black community, a fact less reflective of the minister's irresistibility than the difficult realities of African American life.

Farrakhan's showmanship was not restricted to forums that Muslims created and controlled. By the mid–1990s he was a frequent guest on televised news programs and talk shows. Intellectually, his interviews tended to be shallow, in large part due to the line of questioning. His views on substantive issues, such as public education, the economy, or health care, were almost never solicited. Instead, interviewers dwelled on controversial topics, such as his opinion of selected Black leaders, his role in the assassination of Malcolm X, his connections with Libya, and his conflict with Jews. Many of his admirers and foes in the media imagined him only in racial terms—as Black nationalist, Black Muslim, Black supremacist, and Black anti-Semite. For the most part he satisfied, intentionally and inadvertently, these constructions of him, although he increasingly tried to transcend their limitations.

Being an articulate, telegenic man, Farrakhan was always well prepared for the camera. In interviews his attitude was typically cheerful, highlighted by immaculate, bold-colored suits and trademark bowties. He spoke in patient, instructive tones, rarely interrupting questioners, except to chuckle about an unexpected compliment or poorly concealed slight. During a 1994 interview with Barbara Walters, his voice struck soft, even caressing, chords as the "20/20" reporter relentlessly grilled him on Khallid Muhammad's notorious speech. Yet, in a 1996 appearance on "60 Minutes," he nearly incinerated journalist Mike Wallace during a flaming condemnation of American history and foreign policy. Notwithstanding this episode, his televised conversations were mature, pleasant affairs, which made him seem much less the irrational demagogue than his newspaper coverage did. He could appear meek, and surprisingly endearing, even as anxious interviewers pressed him to explain video clips of the other Farrakhan, in all of his high-decibel ferocity.[40]

Although he had lost political capital during the public uproar over Khallid Muhammad, Farrakhan's stock was still valuable in high places. By 1994 his popularity had reached a critical mass politically. No public gathering of national Black leaders for any important purpose could avoid including him, lest its credibility come into question. This political axiom was perhaps clearest to NAACP executive director Benjamin Chavis, who had been endeavoring to make the Civil Rights organization more appealing to a broader, younger audience of African Americans. At a summit of Black leaders in June 1994, the NAACP head again affirmed the "unity pledge" that had been made at the September town hall meeting. "Never again," Chavis declared, with Farrakhan at his side, "will we allow an external force to attempt to dictate who we can meet with." Considering that CBC members, including Kweisi Mfume and Donald Payne, of New Jersey, were present, there appeared to be at least a preliminary attempt to mend wounds resulting from Khallid Muhammad's speech and its acrimonious aftermath. But, perhaps predictably, the response to Farrakhan's inclusion in the meeting was mixed.[41]

Upon hearing about the Baltimore gathering, some Jewish groups threatened to demonstrate outside of the NAACP's headquarters to protest the organization's embrace of the Muslim minister. Although Chavis deemed it expedient to release a statement condemning racial intolerance, he also insisted that the proposed protest by Jews would only serve to worsen their relationship with African Americans. It was an uncharacteristic public assertion of independence by an NAACP official, especially regarding the organization's intention, despite charges of anti-Semitism, "to get the leadership to the table," including Farrakhan. Unfortunately for Chavis, his overtures to the Nation of Islam would be greatly overshadowed by a devastating sexual harassment suit filed against him on June 30, along with the August disclosure that NAACP debts totaled three million dollars. Despite these storm clouds, there was still enough good news resulting from the meeting to make it a qualified success. Significantly, on the second day of the conference Jesse Jackson, who beforehand had attempted to dissuade people from attending, was seen "chatting amiably" with Louis Farrakhan. The two men reportedly even talked a while privately, away from inquisitive reporters and camera lights. After the event the Muslim minister spoke warmly of the former presidential candidate. Although he suggested that Jackson had strayed away from "his base" in the Black community, he obviously yearned for a renewed alliance with him. "He and I must never be seen as enemies of each other," Farrakhan contended, "but must be seen as brothers who may have some legitimate differences but we will come together to work for the common good of all of our people."[42]

By the time crippling arrears and an unseemly sex scandal racked the NAACP, Farrakhan had started thinking in grander terms about the possibilities of his own leadership. Claiming inspiration from God, he began publicizing a plan to assemble one million Black men in Washington, D.C., as a show of African American strength, solidarity, and potential. His intention was to center Black males as the fulcrum of the African American community upon which everything else pivoted, including political empowerment, economic advancement, family stability, and moral responsibility. Patterned after the 1963 March on Washington, the Million Man March, as it became known, would dramatize the ability of Blacks to organize a logistically challenging event, but, at the same time, it would highlight, and in a sense crown, a single Black leader and affirm the magnitude of his support. The months-long preparation for the march, slated for October 16, 1995, aroused tangible excitement throughout the country's Black communities. Some African American men intended to make the trek to the capital expressly to see Farrakhan, but many more wanted simply to be part of something epic and transcendentally fraternal. As mentioned earlier, the march was primarily to be a day of atonement and reconciliation for Black men, who had supposedly shirked or in other ways left unfulfilled their obligations as fathers, husbands, brothers, and citizens. Yet the march also had an elaborate written agenda, which included calls for a more just U.S. foreign policy, corporate investment in African American communities, and universal health care insurance. Regarding politics, the mission statement of the Million Man March encouraged "Black united fronts" and future leadership summits to strengthen collective decision making. Most notably, it offered a post-march blueprint of action, which emphasized the need for "a massive and ongoing voter registration of Black people as independents" and the imperative of "creating and sustaining a progressive independent political movement."[43]

On the day of the march the capstone message was delivered by Farrakhan, following several long hours of speeches, songs, and waiting. The minister's preachy, rambling oration, entitled "Toward a More Perfect Union," ricocheted from topic to topic, with many distracting asides and little overall coherence. He offered an array of exotica to the Black legions gathered in front of the Capitol, ranging from numerology and Masonic mysticism to biblical allegories about American slavery and extended commentary on the Egyptian architectural influences on nearby buildings. The themes of atonement, unity, and reconciliation did wind through the talk, as did the usual Muslim prophecies regarding Blacks as chosen people and the coming divine chastisement of the United States for its wickedness. At one point the minister stated, as if addressing President Clinton and the Congress, that the "real evil in America is the idea . . . of white supremacy." As he had increasingly done over the past few years, he extricated physical Whiteness from racist mentalities and behaviors, thus departing from the racial essentialism and determinism inherent in traditional Nation of Islam teachings. "White supremacy is the enemy of both white people and Black people," he proclaimed. "White supremacy has to die in order for humanity to live."

In relation to Black political organization, he stressed that African Americans should both join groups, including the NAACP, CORE, and the Urban League, aiming to uplift their communities, and endeavor to register eight million eligible voters. Alluding to his belief that many Black groups and leaders were controlled by Whites, he advocated the creation of an Economic Development Fund, which would make Black organizations financially independent and self-sustaining. Perhaps the most memorable part of Farrakhan's speech was a series of pledges that he led his audience in reciting, essentially committing themselves to be better, more responsible members of their communities. As twilight unfurled, his two-and-a-half-hour presentation, which seemed much longer, ended with desultory applause. After greeting several people clustered around him, the minister departed from his thinning audience almost as quickly as he had appeared.[44]

By many standards the Million Man March, as a singular event, was a resounding success. The imagery of so many Black men gathered for noble reasons was overwhelming in itself, but the exuberant feeling of immeasurable connectedness with humanity which pervaded the event easily eludes description. Notwithstanding the spiritual ambiance of the march, for many listeners Farrakhan's speech, given the occasion, was quite disappointing. His mystical treatise, intertwined with historical anecdotes and prophetic revelations, perhaps fulfilled the expectations of his followers but provided little nourishment for those who had come to hear a practical plan of action for ailing Black communities. In essence the speech was problematic because it was classical Farrakhan—the same kind of esoteric lecture that one might hear in a typical Nation of Islam meeting. Fortunately, the momentousness of the march was much larger than the messenger and his message. Although no other contemporary Black personality could likely have succeeded in bringing so many Black people together at once, the communal energies and cooperation generated by both preparations for the march and the event itself created dynamics that were beyond the control of any one individual or organization. Thus, after October 16 the question became what would this multitude of men do once they returned to their communities, not what would Louis Farrakhan do once he arrived back at his Chicago mansion.[45]

To be sure, the massive display of Black unity evinced at the Million Man March only temporarily masked tensions and divisions among African American leaders and organizations. Not everyone had heeded Farrakhan's call to Washington, nor were they pleased with the idea or his central role in the proceedings. For instance, Henry J. Lyons, president of the National Baptist Convention, flatly refused to endorse the march, declaring, "We ain't marching behind no Farrakhan." Likewise, the NAACP, now under new leadership, did not officially support the event but did not ban individual members from participating. The CBC, which had gone through so much with the Muslim minister over the past year, was late in announcing its approval of the march. Not wholly unexpected, some of the most cogent criticism came from women's groups, which were dismayed by both their exclusion from the event and its patriarchal overtones. The organizers of the march had been careful to include preeminent African American women, such as writer Maya Angelou and Civil Rights pioneer Rosa Parks, but these gestures were hardly enough to preempt feminist opposition. "Yes, we share the rage and pain and anguish that fuel this march," one recently organized group conceded. "But our needs are not served by men declaring themselves the only 'rightful' leaders of our families, or our communities and of our ongoing struggle for justice." Professor Mary Francis Berry, chairwoman of the U.S. Commission on Civil Rights, was more blunt in her disavowal of the demonstration. In a letter to the *Washington Post* she maintained that she did not "trust Louis Farrakhan or Benjamin Chavis to lead us to the Promised Land."[46]

Similar to some women's groups, Jesse Jackson saw much more symbolism than substance in the Million Man March. While compelled to endorse the gathering by the weight of its inevitability, he later pointed out that the march had been "disconnected from public policy... and from our political leadership" and thus could not be readily used as leverage in the halls of power in Washington, D.C. His criticism rang truer as days passed, even though his own speech at the event had been finely attuned to public policy issues, such as education, racially discriminatory prison sentencing, and the welfare bill in Congress. Ironically for Jackson, things had come full circle by October 1995. Whereas Farrakhan had been pulled onto the national stage by his 1984 presidential campaign, now, at the Million Man March, the Baptist minister was obliged to bask in the glare of the Muslim's ascending star. Certainly the irony was not lost on Jackson, who had never spoken before a crowd the size of the one Farrakhan had assembled. Nonetheless, the experience did not seem to draw him appreciably closer to the Muslim minister.[47]

At least briefly, the march did gain the attention of high officials in the federal government but not to any meaningful degree. President Clinton, who was in Texas on the day of the gathering, praised the participants for "standing up for personal responsibility" but cautioned that "one million men do not make right one man's message of malice and division." Newt Gingrich, the Republican speaker of the House of Representatives, was neither a fan of the Muslim ministers nor well liked among Blacks generally, but he did recognize that, "if the pain level is great enough for him [Farrakhan] to be a leader, then we all have a lot bigger challenge to lead." Senate Majority Leader Robert Dole was far less charitable to Farrakhan, whom he labeled "a racist and anti-Semite, unhinged by hate." As the presumptive frontrunner for the 1996 Republican presidential nomination, Dole found it politically opportune to criticize Clinton for not having "the moral courage to denounce Louis Farrakhan by name." The fact that top elected officials, Republicans and Democrats alike, were so dismissive of the march certainly suggests how "disconnected from public policy" it appeared, in Jesse Jackson's words, from the vantage point of Capitol Hill and the White House. There were a few other political rumblings, such as a proposal to the president by six congressmen to establish a bipartisan commission to study race relations. Yet the Million Man March and its aftermath were strikingly notable for their dismal failure to affect government leaders or their agendas in any substantive way.[48]

Crossroads: The Nation of Islam and Black Politics into the New Millennium, 1996–2000

Following the Million Man March, it was clear that the demonstration had meant different things to different people. There were those who hoped that the event would invigorate African Americans to tackle the serious problems of poverty, crime, teenage pregnancy, drug abuse, and hopelessness in their communities. Others had hoped that the event would send an explicitly political message that would awaken federal and local governments to the power of Black votes. Still others were satisfied with the symbolism of approximately one million Black men coming together for fellowship and moral renewal. It is difficult to determine what Louis Farrakhan had wished for in the aftermath of the march. He certainly had talked much about atonement and reconciliation among African Americans. In a *Newsweek* interview published on October 30, he spoke of abandoning party loyalties and forging "a Third Force or a Third Power out of Republicans, Democrats and Independents." But beyond these vague statements he offered no concrete plan of action regarding political empowerment or much else. Strangely, he seemed willing to allow his greatly enhanced political credibility to wither as the glow of the Million Man March faded. A few weeks after the October demonstration Farrakhan actually departed the country for a twenty-three-nation tour of Africa and the Middle East. Outside of his inner circle the move came as a surprise to most and appeared peculiarly timed. The Muslim minister offered no public explanation for his trip until he arrived back in the United States in early 1996. In the meantime he made whirlwind visits to a number of countries, including Iraq, Iran, Libya, Saudi Arabia, Sudan, Nigeria, Ghana, and South Africa, where he was generally received as a foreign dignitary.[49]

At Saviour's Day 1996 Farrakhan, faced with growing criticism of his lack of "follow-up" work after the Million Man March, invoked divine revelation and religious rhetoric to justify his sudden trip to the East. "My job was to get up quickly and get out of America," he announced, "and connect the Nation of Islam and Black America to Africa, to the Middle East, and to the Muslim world." His answer may have satisfied many in his audience of twelve thousand, but it did not impress critics, who believed that the minister had selfishly used the success of the march to peddle his celebrity to Third World countries. To those disaffected by Farrakhan's tour he had not only squandered the opportunity actually to lead African Americans during a historical moment pregnant with possibilities. He had also poorly chosen his friends from among dictatorships, such as Iraq, Iran, Sudan, and Libya, which he knew to be on bad terms with the United States.

In retrospect Louis Farrakhan appears to have missed a quite unique opportunity to seize the reigns of leadership in the wake of the Million Man March. At that historical juncture he was undeniably the most watched and influential Black person in the United States and had the rapt attention of millions. There are so many hypothetical paths that he could have taken, such as making the march explicitly political and forcing the federal government and other state agencies to dialogue with him and his million men about substantive issues. Alternatively, he could have simply passed up his Eastern tour and visited various U.S. cities to keep the constructive energies generated by the march alive. At the very least he could have avoided further alienating himself from African American leaders, the U.S. government, and others by avoiding such a controversial tour of countries avowedly anti-American in their politics and foreign policies. The failure of Farrakhan to take any of these paths suggests that he did not primarily view the Million Man March as the springboard that would propel him into national prominence as an important player in mainstream politics. He certainly paid a lot of lip service to the idea of Black political mobilization in the aftermath of the march. He even registered to vote again in 1996, after a twelve-year hiatus from the ballot box. Still, whatever vision he had of his future leadership had little to do with effectively influencing public policy, the electoral process, or American political culture in general. The Million Man March did not even seem to be conspicuously transformative for him, beyond perhaps his personal faith and commitments. By Saviour's Day 1996 he was exhibiting old patterns of unpredictable, unaccountable, and controversial leadership, which had marginalized him in the past and broken many hopeful alliances with others. He brought no new ideas to the table and was characteristically hostile toward those who illuminated his shortcomings.[50]

During the five years that followed the Million Man March, the only novel theme that is easily discernible in Farrakhan's words and activities is that of reconciliation. As mentioned earlier, this was a guiding motif of the October 1995 demonstration, and the Muslim minister, now in his mid-sixties, appeared to be reaching out to a broader, but not necessarily politically minded, audience. For example, during Saviour's Day 2000 he embraced Warith D. Mohammed (formerly Wallace D. Muhammad), the son and organizational heir of Elijah Muhammad, in a gesture of detente, which suggested that his Nation of Islam was moving closer to a more traditional, nonracial version of the Muslim faith. Two days later Nation of Islam officials announced an accord with a number of Orthodox Jewish groups, an achievement that had seemed near impossible a few years earlier. In May Farrakhan publicly commiserated with Attallah Shabazz, a daughter of the late Malcolm X, and expressed regret for having outspokenly contributed to the hostile atmosphere that led to her father's assassination. Quite significantly, during the October 16 Million Family March, a more inclusive iteration of the 1995 event, Farrakhan told an interracial audience of thousands that "the mutual respect between people and the mutual love between people . . . will save humanity." Days before the event he had credited his recently resumed struggle with cancer with helping him to "feel the pain of anyone who suffers on this planet." A universalist strand of thinking had been in his ideology since the early 1990s, however, although it was frequently obscured by his conflicts with Jews and others. Following this event, which once again gave his leadership a political makeover, Louis Farrakhan has been much less visible and vocal and thus not at the center of public controversies. Now, close to age seventy, he will likely continue to attract the spotlight, only this time his cognizance of his own mortality, coupled with a desire for a less ambiguous legacy, will likely be more evident.[51]

In studying the two most dynamic decades of the life of Louis Farrakhan, one is struck by his intellect, charisma, and media savvy as well as the wealth of experiences, both American and international, which created and molded his public persona. He was, and is, a master propagandist of the Black experience in United States, weaving together truth and fantasy, religion and nationalism, into a message that resonated with perhaps millions of people over a generation. In addition to these observations, one is struck, too, by the realization that Farrakhan's life as a public figure reveals no overarching, realistic strategy for tackling the problems of African Americans. Certainly there were fascinating, romantic prescriptions offered by the Muslim minister, such as the resettlement of Black convicts in Africa, African American secession from the United States, and the euphoric Million Man March. Moreover, the Nation of Islam offered a puritanical moral code designed to combat drug abuse, recidivism, and welfare dependency as well as abortion and homosexuality. But in the early years of the twenty-first century Farrakhan has constructed no grand philosophy or practical program beyond small-scale entrepreneurial capitalism, passionate invectives against perceived enemies, and heavy doses of messianism and apocalyptic imagery.

On the surface Louis Farrakhan reinvented himself on a number of occasions. He fluidly passed between confrontational and conciliatory moods, from political engagement to apolitical aloofness, and through alliances of all sorts, even with the U.S. government. Moreover, it was quite apparent as early as 1984 that media attention, along with the celebrity and public theater that accompanied it, was an end in and of itself. Yet his ideology and vision were less elastic than his publicity tactics and short-term agendas. He rarely offered anything wholly new and consistently mimicked the conservative morality, economic nationalism, and racial chauvinism of his predecessor, Elijah Muhammad, only slightly adjusting these ideas to fit a late-twentieth-century context. Ironically, his Black separatism, defiant unpredictability, and iconoclasm, and even his old-fashioned moral code, were his main draw, especially when coated with the shiny gloss of eloquence and street vernacular which he artfully employed during his orations. For many African Americans he was cathartic, routinely saying things that they wanted to hear but would not dare say publicly. When he told an audience in 1984, "You're not ready for Farrakhan," they, in fact, were, just as they were ready for Jesse Jackson's unprecedented run for the presidency. To his followers and admirers the Muslim minister was the premier showman who actually performed leadership. Aside from whether they really believed all of what he had to say, the show, the spectacle, was often good enough to beckon them back for more.[52]

Seven

F. Carl Walton

The Southern Christian Leadership Conference

Beyond the Civil Rights Movement

What I would like to develop is an SCLC that is known programmatically more than one that is driven by personality. Historically, it was driven personality-wise.
—Martin Luther King III

The Southern Christian Leadership Conference (SCLC) was founded in 1957 in Atlanta, Georgia. Like other civil rights groups, the SCLC was established to improve the political and social conditions of Black Americans. The SCLC is characterized by its use of nonviolent direct action. This method was manifested predominately through marches that were organized to protest segregated facilities throughout the southern United States. It was supplemented in the early 1960s by the sit-in movement, which was orchestrated mostly by college students who ultimately organized to become the Student Nonviolent Coordinating Committee (SNCC).

In the post–Civil Rights era the SCLC has been primarily led by an old guard knowledgeable of the traditional means of forging change but perhaps less adept at utilizing new methods that are more relevant to today's society. It faces the challenges of appealing to a generation of people who have more diverse experiences than its original constituency. It also operates in an environment in which racial discrimination remains a defining feature of American society, even though it does not appear in the same overt manner that it did during the peak of the Civil Rights Movement. It is against this backdrop that the SCLC operates.

The SCLC is particularly challenged in accomplishing its objectives in the post–Civil Rights era for several reasons. First, its leadership is not as dynamic as it used to be. Indeed, during the Civil Rights Movement the SCLC was headed by one of the most charismatic leaders of the twentieth century, Dr. Martin Luther King Jr. Much of the group's success was attributable to King's ability to mobilize the masses of Black Americans and to express his message articulately. Additionally, the issues affecting Black people during the Civil Rights Movement could be applied broadly, regardless of an individual's socioeconomic standing in the society. Today many of the important problems affecting Blacks are not as easily definable and are often class based and thus mainly affect individuals based upon their socioeconomic class.

Furthermore, some of the success of the movement came about because of the negative responses of White Americans to the overt racism of many White southern leaders. Examples are Bull Connor's blatant violence against marchers in Birmingham, Alabama, in 1963 and the harsh treatment of the voting rights protesters in Selma, Alabama, on Bloody Sunday in March 1965. The racism practiced in the post–Civil Rights era is often subtle. As a result, public support is more difficult to acquire because many potential supporters and even benefactors do not realize that a problem exists or are not able to agree on the proper solution.

The SCLC also now exists in a period when affiliation with a strong Black organization is no longer necessary for leaders to achieve power. The work of the SCLC and other groups to achieve voting rights for Blacks in the United States (especially the South) resulted in increased voting, which brought about the election to public office of many powerful and charismatic Black leaders. As a result, some of the energy and talent that could be a part of the inner circle of the SCLC are now mainstream government officials. These individuals do not rely exclusively on Civil Rights organizations as a base of support. Moreover, these Civil Rights organizations do not possess the necessary financial resources to support a political campaign fully or other aspirations of politicians.

Finally, during its early years the SCLC functioned mostly in response to crisis situations in various cities and regions. The SCLC was usually called to address the most overt instances of discrimination. In most cases the SCLC would implement a successful protest action, which would result in some improvement of the conditions in a particular area. While there was a group effort, King was generally the focal point of the SCLC's actions.

Since much of the success of the SCLC during the Civil Rights Movement is attributable to King's charismatic leadership, a central question of the post–Civil Rights era is: Can a single leader be expected to generate a response to societal ills or to be the focal point of the response? Singular charismatic leadership is a problematic concept in an era when the Black community generally is more diverse, educated, and opinionated and more of its people are qualified to lead than before. A second question is: How does a group like the SCLC respond to the changes in a society that no longer provides conditions under which its efforts were most effective? Does it change its approach, or does it seek leaders from another generation? During the Civil Rights Movement the SCLC's winning strategy was the protest march. As opportunities for Blacks increased and overt barriers to integration diminished, organizational strategies that center on this tactic are considered less successful than others and therefore lack mass support.

In the face of all the transitions that have occurred in the United States since 1968, the underlying factor affecting the success of any organization is its ability to provide programs and activities that are relevant to the needs of its various constituencies. Generally, organizations achieve the goal of relevance by providing incentives to potential members and participants. James Q. Wilson finds that: "the behavior of persons occupying organizational roles (leader, spokesperson, executive, representative) is principally though not uniquely determined by the requirements of organizational maintenance and enhancement and that this maintenance in turn, chiefly involves supplying tangible and intangible incentives to individuals in order that they will become, or remain members and will perform certain tasks."[1]

The SCLC faces the task of establishing a new agenda and new methods of action that will be adequate incentives to encourage the desired involvement of Black Americans, particularly its young adults. The SCLC's attempt to revitalize itself has thus included capitalizing on its past by electing Martin Luther King III as its fourth president.

In general, the literature on the SCLC has focused on the life and work of Dr. Martin Luther King Jr., rather than the activity of the organization. In many cases there is the impression that the activity of the SCLC between 1957 and 1968 directly parallels King's life and work. This chapter will provide an analysis of the work of the organization.

The Founding and Structure of the SCLC

The first organizational meeting of what later became the SCLC was held in Atlanta, Georgia, on January 10–11, 1957. It was initially called the Southern Negro Leaders Conference on Transportation and Non-Violent Integration. The document of the first organizational meeting of the SCLC stated that:

1. The church had functioned effectively as the institutional base of protest movements.
2. Aggressive nonviolent action of Blacks was necessary if the system of segregation was to be overthrown.

3. An organizational mass force was needed to supplement the activities of the NAACP, which was under fierce attack throughout the South.
4. Movements could be generated, coordinated, and sustained by activist clergy and organized Black masses working in concert.

At that meeting the participants also decided that there would be new protest movements focused on voting but modeled after the bus boycott and that there was a pressing need to create an organization to unify the southern movements.[2]

The initial membership of the organization consisted of ministers who were leaders of their respective local movements. Nine of these men emerged as leaders of the newly formed SCLC. They were Rev. Dr. Martin Luther King Jr., leader of the Montgomery Bus Boycott, president; the Rev. C. K. Steele, leader of the Tallahassee bus boycott, first vice president; the Rev. A. L. Davis, leader in the bus protest of New Orleans, second vice president; the Rev. T. J. Jemison, leader of the first mass bus boycott in Baton Rouge in 1953, secretary; the Rev. Fred Shuttlesworth, leader of the mass direct action movement in Birmingham, corresponding secretary; the Rev. Ralph Abernathy, a leader in the Montgomery bus boycott and King's confidant, treasurer; the Rev. Kelly Miller Smith, local NAACP president and activist in Nashville, chaplain; and Lawrence Reddick, a scholar at Alabama State College and activist of the Montgomery bus boycott, SCLC historian.

The SCLC was organized to be a southern-wide organization of organizations. As such, the membership was made up of other organizations rather than individuals. The cooperative organizational structure that characterized the Montgomery Bus Boycott provided the model for which the SCLC ultimately emerged as a southern-wide organization of organizations. As a result of this structure, when there was a need within local communities for protest activity, the SCLC was the umbrella organization that was available to provide resources to enhance and strengthen the local effort.[3]

Because of the ministerial presence, Aldon Morris, author of *The Origins of the Civil Rights Movement,* refers to the SCLC as a church-related protest organization. The original SCLC had thirty-six formal leadership positions, including the executive staff, administrative committee, and executive board. Nonclergymen filled four of the thirty-six positions. Most of the important decisions were made by the administrative committee, which consisted of thirteen individuals, eleven of whom were ministers. Morris concluded that a movement organization with a charismatic leader rooted in a mass-based institution was more likely to mobilize masses of people than a movement organization without such a leader. Hence, charismatic leaders such as Martin

Luther King Jr. played a crucial role in the mobilization process and the building of an internal organization. In addition to providing the general support of
the southern-wide organization and the presence of a charismatic leader, the
SCLC brought direct action workshops, voting clinics, and mass rallies to many
local communities across the South.[4]

Morris also argues that the SCLC during the late 1950s and early 1960s crystallized and strengthened the internal organization of the Civil Rights Movement because it functioned as the decentralized political arm of the Black
church. The church provided the SCLC with leadership, institutionalized charisma, a mass base, and other social resources. It, in effect, linked the various
local movements that emerged across the South during the late 1950s into a
region-wide organization of organizations. The first executive director was Rev.
John Tilley of Baltimore, Maryland. Ella Baker was the first associate director. The SCLC kicked off its first major organizational campaign, the Crusade
for Citizenship, in 1958. The goal of the crusade was to enfranchise southern
Blacks by organizing a mass-based political movement for the explicit purpose
of acquiring the vote. It began officially on February 12, 1958, when the SCLC
held simultaneous meetings in twenty-two southern cities. In spite of the
group's effectiveness during this period, there was still a lack of formal organization. This early informality grew out of the charismatic and fluid personal
relationships characteristic of the Black church. Ministers often carried the
same style into their direct-action organizing, showing little regard for formal
bureaucratic behavior.[5]

From Civil Rights to Post–Civil Rights

During the final years of King's life, particularly after the passage of
the Civil Rights Act of 1964 and Voting Rights Act in 1965, the Civil Rights
Movement was perceived as successful. The success of the Civil Rights Movement impacted the SCLC greatly. First, the group was perceived as largely responsible for the success of the movement, considering that it achieved a
number of victories in various localities. Second, because of his success in the
South, King began to consider issues relevant to Blacks in northern cities. The
movement out of the South to Chicago, a nonsouthern city, represented the
first significant departure from the initial focus and goals of the organization.
In doing so, the SCLC began to lose its historic connection to local leadership.
Ultimately, its attempt to work through a network of national leaders took it
away from its true source of power.[6]

Third, actualizing this newly granted legally sanctioned equality was more
difficult to accept by Whites than was the act of working for the achievement
of equality. Whites who were in full support of the movement realized that their

lives were going to change with regard to the availability of resources if the Black community was truly to gain equality. Fourth, the support of Whites and the nonviolent posture of Civil Rights activists began to dissipate. The Black community was becoming impatient with the traditional Civil Rights Movement. The Black Power Movement had emerged, and the Black Panther Party had been established in Oakland, California, in 1966. These two events were outward manifestations of the move away from the SCLC's approach to acquiring Civil Rights gains through nonviolent direct action. The Black Power Movement had left the South and did not rely on the leadership of Black ministers and participation of the Black church for its support base.

Before his death King's final project was the Poor People's Campaign, which was an effort to highlight poverty in the United States. One manifestation of the SCLC's support for poor people was the willingness of its members to travel to Memphis on behalf of striking sanitation workers. During the first march in Memphis violence broke out. Nonetheless, the SCLC planned a second Memphis march. In order to reduce the chances for more violence, King met with the Invaders, an organization that had sparked violence in the first march. During this meeting King explained:

> The SCLC did not have funds to finance their community organizing plans but he would make some phone calls to organizations that might. He also promised to have Andrew Young sit down with Cabbage (the leader of the Invaders) and prepare a proposal describing their ideas. He emphasized the importance of their peaceful cooperation in Monday's (April 8, 1968) march would be. He spoke of how he appreciated their past difficulties with adult leadership, and asked that they trust his commitment that the treatment would not reoccur and that SCLC would work with them on their plans. The youths understood the terms and accepted the exchange.[7]

The difficulty experienced by King in implementing the Poor People's Campaign as well as the problems experienced in Memphis, Tennessee, with maintaining nonviolence as the posture of the movement, foreshadowed the challenges that Civil Rights activists were faced with after King's death.

The Abernathy Years: 1968–1977

Martin Luther King was so adamant that Ralph Abernathy succeed him as president of the Southern Christian Leadership Conference that he revised the bylaws of the organization's constitution. King proposed that Abernathy become the vice president at large of the organization, that he would still be the financial secretary-treasurer, and that in the case something happened to him Abernathy would automatically become president.[8] The board approved this proposal by King. On April 4, 1968, the day of King's assassination, Ralph David Abernathy became the second president of the SCLC.

As King's successor, Ralph Abernathy walked into a precarious situation. He was the full-time pastor of the West Hunter Street Baptist Church in Atlanta, Georgia. He had always pastored while serving as King's chief lieutenant in the Civil Rights Movement. Beyond becoming SCLC's president, Abernathy took office at a time when the Black community was realizing many of the advances that the SCLC had fought for over the first eleven years of its existence. In order to keep the organization afloat, he would have to prove the organization could resolve a problem or crisis and, more important, find a significant funding source. Until the time of King's death most of the SCLC's money had been raised by his speaking engagements.

As Abernathy took office, he did so realizing that there were some particular challenges facing the organization. He cited reasons for these challenges:

1. The first reason for the decline in influence was the remarkable success in eliminating virtually all statutory barriers to Black advancement and equality. Legal segregation in most areas had been eliminated either by action of the U.S. Supreme Court or by passage of legislation in the U.S. Congress.
2. The shift of the battleground from the South to the North also cost the SCLC some support.
3. The doctrine of nonviolent protest had increasingly come under attack by newer and younger Black leaders who neither understood what was being done by the existing organization nor cared about the progress that had been made.
4. The focus of the later years was no longer on race alone but on the disparity between the rich and the poor, and there were people who opposed racism as a matter of principle but who did not want to see the economic apple cart upset.
5. Finally, after a decade of fighting for racial justice, many people, Black and White, were weary of the struggling and were ready to give up. Financial supporters were also becoming weary.[9]

Aside from the challenges and the internal struggles, there were doubts about Abernathy's ability to lead the organization by part of the SCLC's inner circle. As Adam Fairclough noted:

Stanley Levinson and others wanted to see some form of collective leadership emerge within SCLC, as well as a greater degree of democracy and shared decision-making. King had the unique ability to appeal to a variety of groups and audiences: he could communicate with students, clergymen, intellectuals, white liberals, and Blacks of all classes. In order to sustain this broad appeal, SCLC now needed to project a number of personalities. Abernathy was strikingly popular with southern Blacks, especially the rural poor; Young appealed to northern white liberals; Jackson had created an impressive following among Blacks in Chicago. Jackson in particular had the kind of mass appeal that SCLC sorely needed.[10]

Yet, because of King's wishes, Abernathy remained the leader of the SCLC. Eventually, top lieutenants James Bevel, Andrew Young, Stanley Levinson, Jesse Jackson, and finally Coretta Scott King broke formal ties with the SCLC and pursued their own goals.

The initial activities of Abernathy's presidency can be characterized as a continuation of those that were carried out during King's presidency. The first major action was the implementation of the Poor People's Campaign, which had been initiated by King. The campaign was officially opened on May 12, 1968. A main feature of the Poor People's Campaign was the establishment of Resurrection City in Washington, D.C. On May 13, 1968, the Resurrection City on the Capitol Mall was dedicated. An additional highlight of the Poor People's Campaign in Washington, D.C., was the Solidarity March held on June 19, 1968. Abernathy was the keynote speaker, and people came from throughout the United States to support the SCLC effort to bring the plight of poor Americans to the forefront of the nation's attention. Abernathy in response said: "Unlike previous marches, which had been held in Washington, this march will not last a day, or two days, or even a week. We will be here until the Congress of the United States decides that it is going to do something about the plight of the poor people by doing away with poverty, unemployment, and underemployment in this country."[11]

In carrying out King's goal to find ways to support poor people, the SCLC had taken on a battle that it could not win by waiting on the government to provide a program. It was an issue that was not winnable by an isolated activity. In his speech Abernathy retorted: "We will stay in Washington and fight nonviolently until the nation rises up and demands real assurance that our needs will be met. . . . I don't care if the Department of Interior gives us another permit to stay in Resurrection City . . . I intend to stay there until justice rolls out of the halls of Congress and righteousness falls from the administration, and the rough places of government agencies are made plain and the crooked deals of the military-industrial complex become straightforward."[12] Establishing Resurrection City was among the first of the activities of the organization which indicated its move toward predominately symbolic activities.

In this attempt to bring together poor people of all nationalities in the United States to show that poverty was not only a racial issue, the SCLC was once again moving away from the base that had made it a successful movement. In doing so, it had to respond to the issues that existed between the different minority groups. The problems were insurmountable. For example, in Resurrection City all of the Indians wanted to live together, as did all of the Blacks, all of the Mexican Americans, Puerto Ricans, and Whites. Every single group found its own little neighborhood within Resurrection City.[13] The leadership brought these people to Washington, D.C., with the notion that there would be some unity of purpose yet realized that the participants were not able to step outside of their own issues and biases against one another. Soon after the march the movement in Washington began to break down. The number of people participating waned, and the SCLC's ability to control those who were there weakened. After the permit for location of the Mall expired, and was not renewed, Abernathy and his counterparts were arrested as they sought to demonstrate on the grounds of the Capitol. Resurrection City was dismantled, and the SCLC's first major activity since the death of Martin Luther King ended. In Abernathy's words, their first and only confrontation with the federal government was over, and the victory they had won was too ambiguous for people at that time to appreciate it fully.[14]

There were less positive characterizations of this campaign. Adam Fairclough found that the

> SCLC had violated the basic canons of non-violent protest. Instead of leading the press it found itself responding to criticism; it lost the initiative. Instead of gradually escalating the protests to create a sense of drama and momentum, it let the campaign drift aimlessly. The demonstrations and sit-ins did not get underway until late May and they were badly planned and poorly led. They allowed the camp dwellers to let off steam but did not form part of any coherent strategy. In Birmingham and Selma, King went to jail during the early days of the campaign in order to set an example and to inspire supporters. When Abernathy went to jail in Washington, the campaign was over. [15]

The problems experienced by Abernathy in attempting to pursue the goals of the Poor People's Campaign was an early sign of the difficulty that he was to have in Charleston, South Carolina.

The Charleston campaign commenced when Dave Livingston, a White activist, invited the SCLC to help organize Black hospital workers. By going there, Abernathy saw an opportunity for an unambiguous victory. This potential victory was important in order to reestablish the credibility of nonviolence as a means of social change. The unionization of Charleston could be victorious, not just for Blacks but for labor throughout the country.[16]

The Charleston government responded to the SCLC's pressure by refusing to recognize any union, stating that they were protected by a South Carolina law prohibiting any government agency from negotiating with a union. SCLC lawyers pointed out a key factor while they were in Charleston: "This is not a law passed to discriminate against Blacks. It falls under an entirely separate category of law, and we would not be in a strong position if we attempted to challenge it."[17] This marked an early realization by the SCLC of its transition toward fighting laws that were not set up specifically to discriminate against Blacks, even if Blacks were disproportionately affected. As they went about their Charleston efforts, Abernathy knew that in order to draw real attention he would need to be arrested. He and many others were eventually arrested for illegal picketing and were sent to jail. Once there, he sent word to the press that he would not allow himself to be bailed out of jail but would remain inside in order to dramatize the plight of hospital workers.[18]

Charleston was instructive for the SCLC and its leader. They realized that new strategies were required to deal with the economic situation and with the change in responses of young marchers to violence from law enforcement. Abernathy reflected on these events:

> I must say here that the sporadic violence that was beginning to break out during our marches was a sign of the times more than a deliberate change in style on the part of SCLC. We had continued to workshop our people in Charleston, just as we had always done. But the country as a whole had gone mad . . . and there were Black militants who were determined to provoke more of the kind of rioting that occurred during the nights immediately after Martin's death . . . Unfortunately, when the police and guardsmen confronted us, sometimes with bayonets, our people retaliated by hurling stones and bottles over the heads of the marchers and into the ranks of the police.[19]

This kind of activity also became a critical factor, as nonviolent direct action had been a major theme of the movement. If the organization was not able to preserve this form of protest, it would be on the brink of a major identity crisis.

As the strike continued and Abernathy remained in jail, the Charleston movement gained momentum when the AFL-CIO announced that, if the strike continued, it would get involved.[20] During the negotiations in Charleston and Abernathy left jail after a two-week stay, he issued the following statement: "Although no agreement has been reached at County Hospital, I have decided in good faith to place my trust in the people of Charleston and to call upon them to reach a satisfactory settlement at the County Hospital. . . . Accordingly, I have accepted my release from jail, and ordered my staff to continue the suspension of non-violent activities through the weekend. I have been assured that the people of Charleston County want a settlement and they can use this time to reach a just conclusion of this strike."[21]

Abernathy counted the victory in Charleston as not only an accomplishment for the SCLC but also a personal one. He saw this as the first indication that people were beginning to believe that the SCLC would have a life and a purpose beyond completing the projects already begun by King.[22] Other significant activities during his tenure as president included:

—In 1970 the SCLC led a march against repression following killings at Jackson State and Kent State Universities.

—In 1970 the SCLC backed Black and White steelworkers who won a strike in Georgetown, South Carolina.

—In 1971 there was a Wall Street demonstration against racism, poverty, and the military-industrial complex.

—In 1972 the SCLC started voter registration drives for Blacks, students, and poor people at campuses and communities across the United States.

—In 1973 the SCLC assisted and coordinated the mobilization of the massive lobby-ins of sixty-five thousand people in Washington, D.C., against Office of Economic Opportunity (OEO) cutbacks by the Nixon Administration.

—In 1974 a National Amnesty Program was presented to the Congressional Black Caucus.

—In 1975 the SCLC led two thousand people in support of Joan Little and organized a mass protest to expose the murders of five Pensacola, Florida, Black men.

—In 1976 the SCLC pushed the Humphrey-Hawkins Full Employment Bill, continued opposition to the death penalty, and joined the Continental Walk for Disarmament and Social Justice.[23]

Despite its small victories, the SCLC faced a number of challenges during Abernathy's presidency. The organization experienced a financial collapse after the Poor People's Campaign, and the staff had dwindled from 125 to 61. In 1972 the decline in contributions became so severe that another 21 staff members had to be dropped. By 1973 only 17 remained on the payroll.[24]

In 1977 Abernathy resigned as president of the SCLC. In his autobiography he alludes to the scenario surrounding his resignation. Amid the financial difficulties that the SCLC was facing, he had received a call from Chauncey Eskridge, the chief fund raiser for the group, who told Abernathy that they could not "continue to operate unless we do something to generate funds, and said that he wanted to come to Atlanta to meet with him to discuss the future of the organization."[25] Abernathy perceived this meeting with Eskridge, Joseph Lowery, and other members of the board as an opportunity to come up with a campaign to revitalize the organization. After Eskridge gave an overview of the SCLC's financial woes, he turned to Abernathy and made the following statement: "Mr. President, We appreciate everything you've done for the organization and the movement, but, well, we feel you've outlived your usefulness. We feel we have to have a change. . . . We need new blood. . . . We need new life."[26] After resigning as president of the SCLC, Abernathy announced that he would run for the United States Congress. Even though he lost the election, it gave him the opportunity to withdraw gracefully from the SCLC.[27]

A look at the activity of Abernathy's era shows that the SCLC had moved from an organization of local organizations based in the South to one that sought a more national presence. This, of course, was a departure from its original thrust in spite of the fact that it was continuing to use methods employed in the early years of its organizational history. Arguably, this shift brought about the question of whether the SCLC could remain viable as the premier Civil Rights organization.

Unfortunately, after Abernathy's resignation his political activities created more distance between the Black community and him. He unsuccessfully ran for a seat in Congress and tried to develop programs to decrease African American dependence on welfare. In both of these efforts he considered conservative president Ronald Reagan's ideas as being consistent with his views. He also looked beyond his traditional constituency to support his agenda. Abernathy cited two reasons for supporting Reagan's presidency: "First, he had advocated and initiated job training programs to remove people from welfare. Second, . . . it was time for Blacks to show some openness toward the Republican Party, provided the party showed an openness toward us."[28]

While Abernathy enlarged his sphere of influence, his support for Ronald Reagan had a negative affect on his relationships with other African American leaders. Most noted was his sometimes difficult relationship with Joseph Lowery, who had become his successor as SCLC president.

The Joseph Lowery Years: 1977–1997

Upon Abernathy's resignation Joseph Echols Lowery was first appointed acting president. He was elected president at the next National Convention, and in 1977 he became the organization's third president. Lowery was a founding member, the first vice president and later chairman of the board of the SCLC, a position he held until becoming president. During his administration Lowery undertook a number of activities that came to characterize his administration:

—He raised the annual two million–dollar budget and kept the SCLC visible.

—He participated in efforts to extend and strengthen the Voting Rights Act for twenty-five years by undertaking a twenty-seven hundred–mile pilgrimage through five states and seventy-three cities in 1982.

—He was in the forefront of attacking U.S. businesses that had contracts with South Africa's apartheid regime and was among the first five people arrested in November 1984 at a protest at the South African Embassy in Washington, D.C.

—He kicked off one of the earliest programs to address the AIDS crisis in the Black community.

—He led efforts to reduce crime and teenage pregnancy.

—He led efforts to expand economic opportunities for Black entrepreneurs, which include a 1989 agreement that SCLC signed with Shoney's, Inc., which provided ninety million dollars in business opportunities for minority entrepreneurs and the nationwide restaurant chain.[29]

In addition, under Lowery's leadership the SCLC inked a pact with Publix food store chain to bring 750 Blacks into management over a five-year period, spend a minimum of forty million dollars with Black vendors, and make ten million dollars in philanthropic contributions to civic and community groups. Lowery says he was able to win these concessions from Publix because he threatened to boycott and picket the store. Despite what naysayers argued, Lowery maintained that direct action campaigns still worked.[30]

One of the significant occurrences toward the end of Lowery's administration was the reenactment of the Bloody Sunday March across the Edmund Pettus Bridge. There were a number of speakers present, including Congressman John Lewis, Coretta Scott King, and Rev. Jesse Jackson. Each of these individuals, who had previously been key players in the work of the SCLC, expressed what they perceived to be present ills of society. Ironically, of its early leadership only Lowery remained a high-ranking member of the SCLC. Lewis is in elective office as a member of the U.S. Congress—as a beneficiary of the work and sacrifices he had made in the 1960s. Reverend Jackson has founded two organizations: People United to Serve Humanity (PUSH) and the Rainbow Coalition. He later merged these organizations. Coretta Scott King decided to preserve her husband's legacy through the Martin Luther King Center for Non-Violent Social Change.

Throughout the 1980s voting rights for African Americans and threats against affirmation action were important issues for the SCLC. The organization highlighted affirmative action at its Thirty-eighth Annual Convention in New Orleans, Louisiana, because it believed that African Americans were losing support for the policy. For instance, during a panel discussion on this topic the theme emerged that "the civil rights movement once so adept at capturing the public with stirring imagery and oratory has been outfoxed by Republicans using the same tactics."[31] SCLC members argued that conservatives were gaining support for their opposition to affirmative action by appealing to the masses of the White race—those who are perhaps the have-nots who need someone to blame for their misfortune. Blacks end up being the scapegoats. On the other hand, the SCLC and other groups who boast of the benefits of affirmative action generally refer to the advances of a middle-class segment of the Black community who are mostly college educated. Blacks at all socioeconomic levels have to be brought to the point where they feel affirmative action programs apply to them. These are the kinds of issues that confronted the Lowery administration; they bring about the question of whether this kind of movement is effective at mobilizing Blacks around such broad policy issues like affirmative action.

Another initiative of the Lowery administration was the gun buy-back program. The program, established in 1995, has been continued by Martin Luther King III as a response to the shooting of Black youths during early 1999. In these buy-backs guns are put into a coffin and buried.

After stepping down from the presidency of the SCLC, Lowery reflected on the organization's viability: "While we need the middle class for leadership and support, we also need to remember that there's a whole lot of folks down there who have experienced very little of the benefits of the movement, still poor, badly housed, and in low wage jobs. This needs to be addressed."[32] Upon his election Martin Luther King III characterized Lowery's administration by describing Lowery as "under the gun everyday": "In the 21st century, we cannot address every issue. We can't be all things to all people. We'll have to carefully pick our battles."[33]

Lowery's administration continued with nationally focused efforts. Under his leadership the SCLC had either consciously or subconsciously grown away from its initial reliance on church-based leadership and on the church as a major base for support. Furthermore, few of its activities were specifically targeted toward localities in the southern United States. This was the case in spite of the fact that Lowery was a minister and also one of the founders of the organization.

Perhaps one of the most controversial decisions made during his administration was Lowery's eventual decision to support the 1991 nomination of Clarence Thomas to the Supreme Court. Thomas, a staunch conservative, had received a wave of support from the African American community after his nomination. Lowery was sensitive to the Black community's seeming support for Thomas and advised his followers to refrain from publicly criticizing the nominee. Ultimately, Lowery's actions turned into at least tacit support for Thomas's nomination.[34]

The Thomas affair was an indication of the lack of effective leadership by the SCLC. Believing that it was important to support a judicial appointment because of skin color and not ideology represented a failure to analyze the possible detrimental impact that Thomas's confirmation could have on African American lives. The SCLC's reaction to the nomination represented the need for its leaders to look beyond race and take a serious look at values and ideas.

Martin Luther King III as President:1998–Present

Martin Luther King III was elected president of the SCLC in 1997 and officially took office on January 15, 1998, the birthday of his late father. His election as the organization's fourth president signaled the transition from the old guard to the next generation. Recently, however, questions have risen about the effectiveness of his leadership. In particular, people have asked whether or not he is providing adequate incentives for SCLC members, as well as potential members, to get involved. In an interview soon after his election, he indicated his sensitivity to this issue. "The most important thing we've got to do is realize that we are a grassroots organization and mobilize at the grassroots level. . . . For whatever reason, we as an organization have to be more reactive than proactive. What we've got to do is develop a plan that calls for activism, that causes us to be proactive."[35] He goes on to address his philosophy further by saying:

We have to define very specific issues and hone down on the ones that we can best address. That way, we become known for a particular area of expertise. We want to get more involved with young people who don't know very much about the organization. Part of my job is to go out and reach these young people with program activity. One of the things I want to do is develop a youth training institute. I don't want to be part of the developing of a messiah complex. I'm more concerned about developing the kind of institute that can develop many leaders, so that if something happens, there ought to be a number of people who can take over the organization.[36]

As a result of these goals early in his tenure, King subsequently hosted a retreat to generate an action plan for the SCLC as it moved into the new millennium. The programmatic thrust of the transition plan presented by King was developed around four tenets: love of self, love of family, love of community, and love of God. These programs include "SCLC Nonviolence Training," the "Call to Manhood," and the SCLC's "Leadership Academy and Health Initiatives." In addition, the SCLC agenda includes grouping senior citizens with children who would normally be home alone in afternoons, finding fathers safe and affordable housing, reordering educational priorities, and establishing juvenile justice and alternative sentencing programs.[37] These plans are intended to provide an incentive for youth and other segments of the Black community to become involved in SCLC programs. The programs represent the use of a new set of strategies for addressing the problems that affect the Black community.

Prior to the 2001 Annual Convention, King faced one of his greatest challenges when Claud Young, chairman of the SCLC board of directors, questioned his effectiveness. Young charged that King had failed to communicate effectively with the SCLC, had failed to raise enough money, and had taken frequent stints away from the organization's headquarters. These criticisms led to King's seven-day suspension and a threat of termination.[38]

In the midst of this controversy there was a major call for unity among SCLC members and supporters. Rev. Jesse Jackson, president of the Rainbow/PUSH Coalition, commented favorably on his working relationship with King on national Civil Rights issues: "I have seen him inspire youth and argue the case for civil rights and social justice at church and on television with confidence . . . he deserves the support of the civil rights community and as a son of the SCLC, I feel compelled to speak out."[39] After four years in office King had had to justify his legitimacy as president. In spite of the attacks, at the 2001 annual convention he restated his vision and goals: "We had a great convention. We have discussed issues ranging from racial profiling to health issues like HIV and AIDS. . . . But we still have much business to do. We are embarking on major challenges, and we are pledged to be a bigger, better, more responsive organization."[40]

Additionally, at the end of the convention both King and Young iterated that they both were continuing in their offices and pledged that the organization would be a more responsive one. According to King: "It is important to leave here with unity. We want the world to know that we are a strong unified organization. We are not divided. We have a board, a chair and most of all a president who will continue to chart the course of the organization."[41] While not speaking against King, Young seemed to stand by his prior assessment: "No one told him he was wrong in his assessment of the organization and its direction . . . the stuff that I have gotten across to the nation was that it was time to light a fire . . . the Board had to come out of the convention with an agenda to address the issues confronting the nation. We have to have a better presence."[42]

Conclusion

From its inception the SCLC was different from other Civil Rights organizations in various ways. It became the most dependent on its charismatic leader and was dependent on a crisis or overt discrimination in order to implement its strategy of direct action or to pursue its organizational objectives. While other Civil Rights organizations based their activities on such things as legal maneuvering and economic empowerment, as in the case of the NAACP and the National Urban League, the SCLC drew its power by directly attacking overt injustice. The SCLC did not emphasize or promote long-term projects. As a result, its membership concentrated on short-term direct-action projects in contrast to a more systematic and structured process. Without that long-term approach, the SCLC has had to change its philosophy, not just in words but also in its personality as an organization.

To be certain, the economic issues that King started to grapple with at the end of his life, the issues that both Abernathy and Lowery sought to deal with, are not adaptable to quick solutions. The earlier Civil Rights Movement activities attacked specific laws or policies that were changeable by government action. Many of the issues that confront the Black community today are the very same ones that government policy makers have had difficulty resolving for decades. In that regard there are no immediate answers. By hiring Martin Luther King III, the son of the organization's most charismatic leader, the SCLC sought to generate interest in its organizational agenda and the concerns of its constituency.

During the Civil Rights Movement, and even into the Abernathy and Lowery administrations, the leadership relied on being arrested in order to draw attention and support to a particular cause. Ralph Abernathy recounted his time in Charleston, South Carolina, in 1969: "We expected to be arrested. We would accept the sentence, stay in jail long enough to rally additional support, and then bail ourselves out."[43] Although this tactic continues to be used by Civil Rights leaders, including the Rev. Jesse Jackson, it is much more a symbolic act than anything else. One also must examine whether or not it is still the most effective way to rally support and also whether masses of people are as willing to spend time in jail as they were when they were necessarily being directly affected, as during the Civil Rights Movement.

Additionally, in terms of its constituents, the SCLC has lost one of its most important bases, the ministers and their willingness to bring along their congregations to support the activities of the organization. Ministers in the 1990s tend to focus on their own plans for economic development and do not necessarily require the support of an outside Civil Rights organization. In addition, they have their own resources and often focus their efforts on projects that specifically benefit their congregation or the area in which their church resides.

In its early years the SCLC was successful in part because of the church base. Lowery's selection as president even makes a statement to that effect. In 1997 the SCLC elected its first nonministerial president as a sign that it was no longer a minister-led organization. Was it also a signal from the board of directors that that kind of leadership was no longer applicable and that the organization needed a new kind of leader? Martin Luther King III has the challenge of redefining the organization not just in its mission and its approach but also in its ability to communicate this new mission and way of conducting business to prospective participants and supporters of the group's activities. Unfortunately, the recent public criticisms of King may have reduced the hopes that the SCLC can return to its former glory.

Eight

Karin L. Stanford

Reverend Jesse Jackson and the Rainbow/PUSH Coalition

Institutionalizing Economic Opportunity

The Rainbow/PUSH Coalition Wall Street Project, launched on January 15, 1997, represents Rev. Jesse Jackson's effort to promote economic inclusion.[1] Its purpose is to create new opportunities for African Americans and other minorities in corporate America and on Wall Street. The project's objectives include expanding minority access to capital; urging corporate America to become trading partners with African Americans, Hispanics, and other disadvantaged groups; building investment vehicles to close the vast wealth disparities in the United States; and fighting for greater diversity in senior-level management in American corporations.

The Wall Street Project is not the first economic initiative led by Rev. Jesse Jackson. During the height of the Modern Civil Rights Movement, Jackson was the national director of the Southern Christian Leadership Conference's (SCLC) Operation Breadbasket. Later he founded Operation PUSH, Inc. (People United to Save Humanity), with the mission to promote political and economic inclusion for African Americans. Perhaps the best known of Jackson's organizations is the National Rainbow Coalition, the organization that provided structure to Jackson's historic 1984 and 1988 campaigns for the presidency. Although the National Rainbow Coalition was founded to organize America's poor, working-class, and minority groups under one umbrella for political empowerment, it too pursued economic empowerment initiatives.[2] Jackson is currently the president of the Rainbow/PUSH Coalition, the result of the merging of National Rainbow Coalition and Operation PUSH, Inc.

Jackson's economic initiatives boast of several successes. Under Operation

Breadbasket and Operation PUSH the African American community benefited from opportunities that had not been available in the past. Particularly in Chicago, major corporations that had previously refused to employ African Americans began to do so. In addition, more African American businesses received contracts, and African American financial institutions received more recognition and income.[3]

Even in its infancy the Wall Street Project can claim several victories. In its effort to increase economic opportunities for African American and other disadvantaged businesses, the Wall Street Project has brokered deals with corporations to increase their use of minority vendors and suppliers. Successful negotiations were concluded with such companies as Digital Equipment Corporation, a subsidiary of Compaq Computer Corporation, the second largest computer company in the world.[4] In regard to internal corporate matters, the Wall Street Project was intricately involved in the negotiations to persuade Texaco Inc. to settle a $176 million dollar racial discrimination case and forced the company to set hiring and procurement goals that would ensure equal opportunity within its corporate ranks. Similar negotiations were held on behalf of Mitsubishi Corporation employees who had filed a sexual harassment suit and disgruntled African American employees of the Boeing Company.[5] The Wall Street Project has also negotiated with corporate owners and chief executive officers to allow African Americans to bid on and purchase companies in areas where they have previously been excluded. For instance, telephone giant Ameritech Corporation sold part of its wireless telephone business to the GTE Corporation and Georgetown Partners, an African American finance and investment service firm based in Maryland.[6] In another Rainbow/PUSH Coalition negotiated deal, Spectronics, an Atlanta-based minority-owned telecommunications construction company recently partnered with CenturyTel, the seventh largest telephone provider in the country, to purchase over 100,000 telephone lines from GTE. Spectera, the newly formed company, now owns a large telephone company in Missouri.[7] Initiatives such as these which promote ownership of businesses and corporations are essential if African Americans are to participate fully in the U.S. economy.

Unfortunately, these kinds of initiatives and achievements of Rev. Jesse Jackson and the Rainbow/PUSH Coalition have largely gone unnoticed by scholars. Part of the reason for this dearth of analysis of Jackson's economic initiatives results from his large political persona. Another reason may be the tendency of scholars to accept the unabashed criticism of Jackson and the Rainbow/PUSH Coalition by the mainstream press. Yet Jackson's historic economic empowerment activities force a thoughtful examination of his economic perspective and programs.

This chapter explores the economic initiatives of Rev. Jesse Jackson and the Rainbow/PUSH Coalition in the post–Civil Rights era. First, I will consider the history of Jackson's involvement and leadership in economic initiatives during the Civil Rights Movement, illuminating how Jackson has drawn upon the experiences and philosophical approach of Dr. Martin Luther King Jr. and the Civil Rights Movement to formulate his perspective and structure his initiatives. Second, I will examine the economic initiatives of Operation PUSH, the organization founded by Jackson to promote economic and political development for African Americans. Exploring the work of Operation PUSH will help unearth the myriad of strategies utilized by African Americans at the end of the Civil Rights Movement to address their economic concerns. Then, in discussing the economic strategies behind the Rainbow/PUSH Coalition Wall Street Project, I will highlight the organizational structure and methods of the project as well as examine the factors responsible for its accomplishments and failures. Finally, I will address criticisms of Jackson's programs to promote economic opportunity. Indeed, Jackson's economic initiatives have not gone uncriticized by socialists, liberals, and conservatives. If one follows the trajectory of Jackson's economic initiatives, however, it is evident that his approach is pragmatic, not offending the primary structure of capitalism yet also incorporating leftist ideals that promote using the state's apparatus to support his call for inclusion to promote prosperity for all Americans.

The Civil Rights Movement and Economic Opportunity
One popular criticism of the Civil Rights Movement is that it lacked a clear and concise economic agenda. According to such analysts as Manning Marable, even after legal segregation was abolished and the Voting Rights Act passed, the United States's "political economy was still profoundly racist."[8] A second criticism of the movement is that its goals—giving Blacks the right to share the same lunch counter, stay in the same hotels, and go to the same schools as Whites—largely appeared to be those of the African American middle class. To the African American lower classes in inner-city neighborhoods in the North, these goals were considered symbolic.[9] To this class the Civil Rights Movement would not deliver jobs and a decent place to live. Evidence of this perspective and of dissatisfaction with the lack of economic opportunity were the riots that occurred in a number of cities throughout the summers of 1964, 1965, and 1967 and the eventual call for "Black Power" by young Civil Rights activists.[10]

Although the critics are correct that the Civil Rights Movement did not explicitly challenge the United States's economic hierarchy, they fail to acknowledge that it influenced the nation's economy. The first successful boycott by the movement profoundly affected the economy of Montgomery, Alabama. By using a strategy that required withholding African American economic resources, the boycott had such an impact on the economy that the city of Montgomery was forced to negotiate a settlement with the Civil Rights activists.[11] Ultimately, the refusal of African Americans to patronize Montgomery's buses allowed them the opportunity to demonstrate their ability to influence political outcomes through monetary means. The effectiveness of the Montgomery Bus Boycott spawned similar boycotts throughout the South.

A second way in which the Civil Rights Movement affected the economy of the South was related to its integrationist goals. Certainly, it was necessary to break down the barriers of segregation in order for African Americans to participate fully in the U.S. market-driven economy. With its physical mobility restricted, the African American community could not expand its businesses, obtain necessary products, and even gain training in new areas of commerce. Desegregation was necessary if African Americans were going to attempt to benefit from the United States's economic largesse.

Another economic consequence of the Civil Rights Movement was the vast expansion of federal welfare efforts aimed at the urban poor from 1964 to 1970. The most significant aspect of this expansion was the "War on Poverty" declared by President Lyndon Johnson and the creation of the Office of Economic Opportunity. Although the War on Poverty was not a direct response to specific goals of the movement, the general objective of equality was its impetus. The War on Poverty encompassed programs that emphasized employment, work training and study, small business development and loans, Head Start, and others.[12] These programs provided the financial, social and educational resources and training needed to boost African American economic mobility.

Indeed, Dr. Martin Luther King Jr. recognized the limitations of addressing legal segregation primarily through legislation and obtaining voting rights. Hence, right after the signing of the Voting Rights Act in 1965, King began to explicitly focus on economic rights and the problem of poverty. Led by King, the Southern Christian Leadership Conference (SCLC) began conducting demonstrations in Chicago for open housing while planning a "national poor people's campaign" that was to be a massive civil disobedience crusade calling attention to the plight of the nation's poor.[13] The campaign would end with a "March on Washington" for economic justice and call for an Economic Bill of Rights. King felt so strongly about the fight for economic justice that his opposition to the Vietnam War was not only on behalf of peace but also to call attention to the enormous amount of resources that were being diverted from the War on Poverty. Understanding the importance of economic justice, the SCLC agreed to support a strike of garbage workers in Memphis, Tennessee, where an assassin eventually killed King.[14]

Finally, SCLC attempted to institutionalize its economic focus by establishing Operation Breadbasket. In his final book, *Where Do We Go from Here?* King outlined the agenda of Operation Breadbasket as securing more and better jobs for African Americans by using the economic power of its community.[15] The program was named Operation Breadbasket because its goal was to bring bread, money, and income into the baskets of Black and poor people.[16] Operating under the framework of Black capitalism, Operation Breadbasket urged Blacks to fight for their share of U.S. economic wealth.

As the economic arm of the SCLC, the strategy of Operation Breadbasket was based on the "selective patronage" campaign instituted by Rev. Leon Sullivan in Philadelphia in 1958. Sullivan's campaign was designed to reduce African American unemployment by boycotting companies that refused to comply with his request for fair job opportunities.[17] Joined by a group of four hundred ministers, Sullivan formed "small visitation committees," which provided information to companies on the needs of African Americans. Their task was to ask top company executives to employ African Americans in specific numbers and categories. If the company refused, it would be boycotted.

Sullivan's program was successful. In just "four years the Black community of Philadelphia successfully boycotted twenty nine companies," with other firms meeting their demands to prevent them from calling for a boycott.[18] The success of the selective patronage campaign led to its expansion to other cities. When King became aware of the success of the program, he asked Reverend Sullivan to help him develop a similar program for the entire country.[19]

King named his version of the selective patronage campaign Operation Breadbasket. On February 1, 1966, he outlined the concept and program to more than three hundred ministers at Jubilee Temple in Chicago.[20] In the South, Operation Breadbasket focused on Atlanta and was led by Fred Bennette. Only two years after joining the SCLC, King selected the twenty-four-year-old Rev. Jesse Jackson as the northern director of Operation Breadbasket.

SCLC's Operation Breadbasket

Based in Chicago, Operation Breadbasket thrived under Jackson's leadership. Starting with the same objectives of Sullivan's program, Jackson "enlisted the support of enough Black clergymen to make a city-wide economic boycott of carefully selected businesses feasible and effective."[21] This steering committee of about one hundred clergy eventually grew to include small and large African American businessmen and professionals, who expanded the scope of the program. Eventually, consumer clubs were formed, and negotiations included contracts. [22]

Jackson's leadership of Operation Breadbasket was considered a success for African Americans in Chicago. *Ebony* magazine reported that in just fifteen months of Jackson's leadership, Operation Breadbasket had negotiated agreements with Chicago food chains, soft drink firms, and dairies. These negotiations opened approximately two thousand jobs worth fifteen million dollars in annual income to the African American community of Chicago.[23] *Time* magazine reported that in those two years under Reverend Jackson's leadership, Operation Breadbasket had produced three thousand jobs for African Americans and "boosted South Side Negro's income by $22 million."[24] In August 1967 Jackson was eventually appointed the first national director of Operation Breadbasket.[25]

As its national director, Jackson established programs that would involve larger numbers of African Americans in promoting economic growth and wealth in their communities. In 1968 Jackson initiated a Black Christmas and a Black Easter; both programs aimed at persuading African Americans to shop at African American–owned stores. During holiday celebrations Jackson also encouraged African Americans to open their savings accounts in African American–owned banks. "Children were also treated to a visit from a new Santa image, called Black Soul Saint."[26] During that same year Jackson organized a promotional festival for African American businesses called "Black Expo." Black Expo was highly successful and was by far the largest event of its type. Hundreds of thousands of people attended the event, including high-visibility politicians, entertainers, and Black and White entrepreneurs. Out of Operation Breadbasket came the Breadbasket Commercial Association (BCA), started in 1970 to help Black entrepreneurs build on their expertise in marketing, production, finance, and other areas essential to growth.[27]

These programs, however, did not interfere with the boycott strategy. Operation Breadbasket's first national boycott was against A&P Grocery Stores, at that time one of the largest supermarket chains in the United States. A&P owned forty stores in Chicago's African American neighborhoods, but all of its employees were White. Jackson called for a boycott after A&P management refused to negotiate with the Civil Rights leadership. With enormous support from the African American community, that boycott was successful. Within four weeks A&P management agreed to hire 268 African Americans at various levels in the company. The chain also agreed to stock such African American products as Grove Orange Juice, Mumbo Barbecue Sauce, and Joe Louis Milk.[28] That successful national boycott was followed by other national boycotts, such as those against the Black Tea Company and Seven Up Bottling.

The success of Operation Breadbasket can be attributed to several factors. First, after gaining the passage of Civil Rights and voting rights laws, Whites were more willing to negotiate with African American leaders in an effort to avoid the kind of public confrontations they had witnessed during the height of the Civil Rights Movement. Whites had also become aware of the economic potential of African Americans and wanted to retain or expand their customer base. In addition, the removal of legal barriers to African American physical mobility made it easier for them to seek business and employment opportunities in other venues. And, finally, the work of Rev. Jesse Jackson provided the kind of charisma and oratorical and negotiating skills needed to galvanize and mobilize leaders and followers. His charisma and negotiating ability accounts for his ability to get corporate leaders to support his programs. Indeed, the mentoring Jackson received from King contributed to his growth and development. Jackson's experience as one of King's lieutenants exposed him to King's philosophy as well as his method. And, finally, Jackson had the consent of the African American community to negotiate on their behalf. That consent came from his status as a minister and from his status as a disciple of King.

Nonetheless, Operation Breadbasket had its problems. Structurally, with a small budget and eight staff members, there were not enough resources to organize a national effort. Even Jackson argued that SCLC's national commitment was evident primarily in its rhetoric.[29] For Operation Breadbasket to have become a national effort, African American consumers needed to be organized locally and nationally, which would have required an enormous amount of resources for information, training, and organizing.[30] Another problem with Operation Breadbasket was its inability to monitor all of the companies it had targeted effectively. Certainly, many of the companies failed to live up to the entire agreement made with Operation Breadbasket. With the lack of resources, it was difficult to follow up with those companies and to provide the national African American community information about their shortcomings. Moreover, because of rampant discrimination, there was an abundance of complaints and calls by the African American community to target specific companies. The lack of an adequate internal infrastructure and resources, however, prevented the staff from pursuing many of those complaints.

Notwithstanding these criticisms, Operation Breadbasket's efforts led to the hiring of more African Americans and more opportunities and contracts for African American entrepreneurs. Largely due to Jackson's leadership, SCLC's economic programs gained national prominence. After King's death and Jackson's departure from the SCLC, Jackson continued to promote economic opportunity for African Americans. Using the ideas of the Selective Patronage

Program and Operation Breadbasket as his foundation, Jackson devised and instituted programs that would further the case of economic opportunity under the banner of Operation PUSH.

Operation PUSH, Inc.

As SCLC made Civil Rights the cutting edge issue of the 1950s and 1960s, Operation PUSH made economic opportunity the issue of the 1970s and 1980s. Operation People United to Save Humanity (Operation PUSH) was founded by Rev. Jesse Jackson in 1971 on Christmas Day. Its basic thrust was economic opportunity and political empowerment. Hence, through its voter education and registration drives, Operation PUSH was instrumental in registering millions of voters and consequently influencing the outcome of local and state elections.[31] Its economic initiatives also made an impact. Similar to Operation Breadbasket, Operation PUSH promoted economic opportunity for African Americans and persuaded Fortune 500 companies to utilize the talent of African American workers and businesses.

At its beginning the economic initiatives of Operation PUSH were based on the ideology and strategy of the selective patronage programs of Reverend Sullivan and Martin Luther King Jr. Eventually, however, Jackson devised his own theoretical explanation and strategies for Operation PUSH's economic initiatives. The main tenets of Jackson's economic philosophy included concepts such as control, reciprocity, and parity. In what he called a "Kingdom Theory of Economic Control" Jackson argued that African Americans must control their own economic destiny. To gain that control, however, African Americans must know how to use and benefit from their own resources.[32] Reciprocity meant a mutually beneficial relationship with American corporations and financial institutions. Jackson argued that the African American community needed economic reciprocity, not "just social generosity, meaning an equitable return on the African American consumer dollar."[33] The third tenet of Jackson's theoretical framework is parity, which required that African Americans receive a fair return on their investment with corporations. Control required that African Americans have ownership in the means of production. Ultimately, Jackson emphasized the idea that African Americans must shift their focus "from charity to parity, from aid to trade, from social generosity to economic reciprocity, from welfare to our share."[34]

As Jackson's programmatic thrust and strategy evolved, one could distinguish it from that of Operation Breadbasket. Jackson began to focus on developing and expanding basic African American economic institutions such as banks and radio stations. Yet building and expanding institutions required that new opportunities be made available for ownership, wealth, and control. Therefore, Jackson advocated the implementation of a "Marshall Plan for African Americans" financed by U.S. corporations and financial institutions.[35]

The Marshall Plan was dependent upon Jackson's ability to persuade major corporations to provide a share of their business to African American entrepreneurs and institutions. Operation PUSH selected companies that sold products that African Americans were known to consume. The tactic was to request contracts, deposits, and employment opportunities for African Americans. If a company refused, then Operation PUSH would initiate a boycott. Internally, the PUSH International Trade Bureau conducted the boycotts. The Trade Bureau, which was membership based, allowed its members to benefit directly from the resulting covenants with national and local corporations.

Also distinguished from Operation Breadbasket were the Jackson-led negotiations of Operation PUSH. Jackson pursued goals that were more ambitious than those under Operation Breadbasket. He not only demanded senior-level management positions for African Americans but, consistent with the Marshall Plan idea, sought shelf space for African American–made consumer products, retainers for African American lawyers, deposits for African American banks, advertising for African American publications, and contracts for African American janitors, garbage collectors, and manufacturers. In addition, Jackson expanded the strategy of boycotts to target not only individual corporations but also national product chains and entire industries. Hence, companies in the food and beverage industry such as Coca-Cola, Kentucky Fried Chicken, and Burger King became targets for African American inclusion. Key to these discussions were franchising opportunities. By focusing on such well-known products and franchises, Operation PUSH had the advantage of boycotting nationally known brands with which African Americans were very familiar, and therefore the boycotts potentially would have a greater impact.

In the three years after its founding Operation PUSH successfully negotiated multimillion dollar covenants with several nationally known chains such as General Foods, Avon Products, the Joseph Schlitz Company, Quaker Oats, Miller Brewing Company, and others.[36] Jackson also negotiated an African American–Hispanic agreement with the Southland Corporation. The same principles of reciprocity, control, and parity were embodied in each covenant.

The covenants represented economic growth for African Americans and the corporations. One example was with the Burger King Corporation, which was negotiated on behalf of the Minority Franchise Association. In that covenant Burger King was asked to increase its loans to minority-owned banks, increase the amount of dollars spent with minority advertising agencies, use minority accountants and insurance services, enhance minority franchise opportunities, and expand employment and management opportunities.[37]

Another example of how Operation PUSH engaged corporations to promote economic opportunity occurred in 1981 with a campaign against Coca-Cola. In 1980 and 1981 Operation PUSH examined Coca-Cola's company practices. While African Americans constituted about 14 percent of Coca-Cola's total domestic business and while their consumption of soft drinks was three times that of Whites, Coca-Cola did not have an African American on its board of directors. It had five hundred bottling franchises and nearly four thousand wholesale distributorships, yet none were African American. In addition, Coca-Cola spent $343 million in 1979 on advertising, yet less than half of 1 percent was with African American firms.[38] In 1981 Operation PUSH launched a campaign against Coca-Cola with the slogan "Don't Choke on Coke."[39] The negotiations to secure better economic relationships between Coca-Cola resulted in an agreement with Coca-Cola which pledged to name African Americans to its board of directors and to make wholesale distributorships and bottling franchises available.[40] Specifically, in the covenant Coke agreed to appoint thirty-two African American wholesalers within the year to lend $1.5 million to African American entrepreneurs entering the beverage industry and to name an African American to its board of directors. The first African American board member was Donald F. McHenry, who was named in 1981.[41]

Operation PUSH's economic programs under Jackson's leadership were successful. Jackson had created more employment opportunities, had successfully negotiated covenants for the first time with national Fortune 500 companies, and had put together successful "Buy Black" campaigns. By 1974 Chicago had gained a reputation for having the largest and strongest financial base of any African American community in the nation. Ultimately, Chicago became known as the Black business mecca.[42]

In November 1983 Rev. Jesse Jackson announced that he would run for the presidency of the United States. His campaign was organized under the banner of the Rainbow Coalition, a "progressive, Black-led, multiracial, anti-corporate, and anti-imperialist movement that took an electoral form."[43] Jackson's economic ideology was consistent with the ideas he had espoused during the 1970s as head of Operation PUSH. During the campaigns, however, Jackson's policies emphasized the need for economic inclusion and economic justice.

Jackson's economic policies emerged from his decision to make his candidacy the voice of the disadvantaged. With the help of progressive scholars and policy experts, Jackson put forth an economic agenda that was vastly different from the other legitimate contenders for the presidency of the United States.

One can derive some sense of Jackson's economic perspective by reviewing his 1984 and 1988 campaign platforms and speeches. The 1984 Jackson Campaign Platform was called the "New Directions Platform." It was a "people centered platform" and promoted a plan to rebuild the nation's cities. It included a full employment policy, increases in funding for the Jobs Training Partnership Act and the Youth Incentive Employment Act, and funding and protection of workers from plant closings.[44] Jackson's plan would reduce the budget deficit and stop the deterioration of U.S. cities.[45]

The details of Jackson's 1988 economic policies can be found in *Keep Hope Alive,* Jackson's published 1988 campaign documents. The 1988 campaign slogan was "Reinvest in America," which advocated ideas similar to the 1984 effort. In campaign documents entitled "Paying for Our Dreams" and "Investing in America," Jackson outlined his economic prescription for the United States. The plan included such items as a Worker's Bill of Rights and a Fair Minimum Wage and Pay Equity plan. Central to Jackson's economic plan was the establishment of a National Planning Board and a National Investment Program. The National Planning Board would target distressed communities and would also assist in resolving problems between management and employees by mobilizing workers to work in the nation's interest and to offset the deterioration of the U.S. economy.

Jackson's National Investment Program would create jobs and build infrastructure. Its foundation would rest upon the use of federal guarantees to shift 10 percent of $600 billion in assets of U.S. public pension funds to secure investments for small business loans, the development of low-income housing, and neighborhood revitalization projects.[46] In addition to these efforts Jackson would establish an American Investment Bank that would finance large infrastructure projects and rural and urban development projects.[47] Modeled after the World Bank, this plan would leverage pension fund capital to allow the American Investment Bank to loan funds at a low interest rate for such development projects.[48]

Specifically regarding the economic status of African Americans, Jackson had always considered them an underdeveloped nation within a developed nation.[49] He argued that, in order to develop itself, the African American community had to create a formula for development that is centered on its relationship with corporate America. From Jackson's standpoint corporate America continued to relate to African Americans as consumers and workers but not as copartners in development, production, ownership, and shared wealth. Jackson argued that the relationship had to change to one that was based on reciprocity and parity.[50] Throughout his campaign Jackson also supported affirmative action to promote minority business ownership, education, and employment opportunities.[51]

Jackson's economic critique also attacked the trickle-down policies of the Reagan Administration, argued for a reduction of the budget deficit by slashing the defense budget, and advocated for the nation's allies to pay more for U.S. troops stationed in those countries.

An analysis of Jackson's economic agenda would suggest that he incorporated elements of progressive and conservative policy orientations. On the conservative side he argued to strengthen U.S. corporations, which would support American national interest domestically and internationally. On the progressive side, however, he called for the involvement of the federal government in private sector economic decisions. He also promoted affirmative action and government / private sector partnerships to improve the U.S. economy. In Jackson's economic platform there was also a critique of capitalism. This critique is evident in his economic development program, which would involve national economic planning.

As expected, criticisms of Jackson's plan came from conservatives and liberals. Conservatives argued that Jackson's planning board would socialize the United States. Moreover, his plan to slash the defense budget would severely jeopardize the nation's defense. Socialists argued that Jackson's plan merely set forth proposals to make capitalism more efficient through national planning. Furthermore, as critics Rodney D. Greene and Finley C. Campbell argued in their article "The Jesse Jackson Economic Platform of 1984: A Critique and an Alternative," the platform guided capitalism and would tie workers even more tightly to the capitalist classes instead of promoting a militant antiracist working-class movement to fight for its interest against capitalism.[52]

To the detriment of the much-needed analysis of Jackson's economic agenda, it did not receive the kind of attention it warranted. Unfortunately, Jackson's economic agenda was foreshadowed by the media's focus on issues of race. Thus, issues related to racism in party politics, anti-Semitism, and a potential White backlash received more attention than Jackson's economic plan.

Operation PUSH suffered financially from Jackson's run for the presidency, but the organization did not fold. Operating with a scaled-down staff and fewer resources, the organization continued to fight for economic justice. Throughout the 1980s Operation PUSH negotiated several covenants with major corporations. Before the 1984 campaign Operation PUSH signed an economic covenant with the Heublein Corporation in March 1982. The Seven Up Company and Operation PUSH signed an agreement in 1982, and a covenant was signed with Miller Brewing Company in June 1984. Operation PUSH and Ford

Motor Company signed an agreement to continue its relationship in December 1988, and a restated covenant was signed among Burger King, the Minority Franchise Association, and Operation PUSH in 1986. An agreement between Adolph Coors Company and a Coalition of Hispanic Organizations was signed in October 1984, and a National Economic Pact was established between Adolph Coors Corporation and a national coalition that included Operation PUSH, the National Association for the Advancement of Colored People (NAACP), and others. A covenant was signed with WBBM-TV, a division of CBS, in December 1985 and a subsequent review was conducted in May 1986. Operation PUSH also continued to evaluate companies, for instance, conducting a review of the Seven Up Company in 1984. In addition, Revlon signed an Economic Pledge with Operation PUSH in 1987.[53]

After the 1988 campaign, Operation PUSH gave some attention to the negative consequences of globalization. It targeted U.S. shoe companies, such as Nike and Adidas, and their perceived support for illegal child labor. An unsuccessful boycott of Nike followed. The Nike boycott was thwarted mainly because it lacked the support of African American celebrities and sports heroes such as Spike Lee, Michael Jordan, Bo Jackson, and John Thompson, all of whom had formal financial ties to Nike. John Thompson and Michael Jordan issued statements in support of Nike, and "Bo Jackson submitted a statement that attacked PUSH so specifically that it was judged too incendiary to release ('What the hell did PUSH ever do for my family?') was one of its lines."[54] Nonetheless, Operation PUSH also continued to push the Jackson campaign's economic agenda through its own programs. A "Rebuild America Campaign" was the focus of the organization's work in the early 1990s. It promoted the tenets of Jackson's economic agenda through public awareness campaigns, conferences, and marches.[55] Those same ideas led to the founding of the Rainbow/PUSH Coalition's Wall Street Project.

Deracializing Wall Street: Continuing the Fight for Economic Justice

Operation PUSH and the Rainbow Coalition merged in September 1995.[56] The goal of the merger was to pool the resources of both organizations so that they would operate more efficiently and effectively. The new organization, the Rainbow/PUSH Coalition, continues to fight for social, political, and economic justice. Its general programs focus on education, voter registration, and public policy issues to uplift the disadvantaged. Its economic programs are organized under the International Trade Bureau and the Wall Street Project.

Similar to the Trade Bureaus of Operation Breadbasket and Operation

PUSH, the Rainbow/PUSH Coalition's International Trade Bureau focuses its efforts on providing opportunities for minority businesses. The International Trade Bureau covers twelve different business sectors and works closely with the local offices, such as the LaSalle Project, a Rainbow PUSH economic initiative located on LaSalle Street in Chicago.[57] The LaSalle Street office is charged with facilitating partnerships between leading corporations and minority businesses that have achieved the kind of stability that will enable them to be considered strategic partners for Fortune 1000 companies.

It is the Wall Street Project, however, which challenges the United States's greatest financial institutions to integrate African Americans and other disadvantaged Americans fully into its ranks. In this regard African Americans should become high-ranking employees in U.S. corporations, share in the ownership of those same corporations, as well as be good consumers of loyal companies. In addition to its work with corporations, the Wall Street Project also challenges the nation's financial institutions to create opportunities to assist inner-city and rural communities in generating jobs and income for their residents.

The Wall Street Project builds upon the successes of the Civil Rights Movement, the Black Power Movement, and the economic programs of SCLC, Operation PUSH, and others. Indeed, it was the work of Civil Rights Movement activists and organizations which forced the federal government to enact laws that made it difficult for American institutions and companies to discriminate against African Americans. Because of that kind of activism the average household income of African Americans has improved, the number and diversity of minority-owned businesses has increased, and African American spending power has risen substantially. Yet these accomplishments do not negate the continued economic malaise of the African American community. For instance, even though average household income among African Americans has improved, in 2000, 22.1 percent of African American families were considered poor compared to 7.5 percent of White families. Also in that same year only 47.2 percent of African Americans owned their own houses compared to 71.1 percent of Whites.[58] And, while growth of African American firms has been impressive, the numbers are much better for other minority groups. In 1992 minorities owned about 12.4 percent of the country's 17.2 million firms, up from 9.8 percent in 1987. The number of Hispanic firms grew by 76 percent and Asian firms by 56 percent, while African American firms grew by only 46 percent.[59]

The answers to solving the problem of economic opportunity and mobility for African Americans in the post–Civil Rights era are different from those of the past. No longer can analysts charge blatant legal barriers as the primary reasons for racial disparities in wealth and income. For example, Thomas

Boston's research suggests that the most difficult barrier to achieving upward mobility for African American entrepreneurs is securing financing and credit.[60] Studies have found that African Americans have a lower success rate than nonminorities in obtaining loans, even when factors such as business experience, knowledge, size of firm, and industry are taken into consideration. African American executives in corporations also complain of barriers to advancement. Most argue that there is an invisible, impenetrable barrier that prevents African Americans from reaching the highest levels in corporations, regardless of their accomplishments.[61] In addition, programs and laws, such as affirmative action and set-aside programs designed to increase opportunities for African Americans and others who have faced discrimination, are under assault. The inability to secure adequate financing for African American businesses, the assault on programs such as affirmative action, and the problems experienced by African American executives in attempts to become senior-level managers prompted the founding of the Wall Street Project.

Through the Wall Street Project the Rainbow/PUSH Coalition has made African American business development and economic mobility the centerpiece of its agenda. Described by Rev. Jesse Jackson as the "capitol of capital," the Rainbow/PUSH Coalition targets Wall Street because it is the most important economic arena in the United States. Wall Street houses the New York Stock Exchange and most of the nation's prestigious investment firms. It is also one of the arenas that remains the domain of White males, despite integration of other sectors in U.S. business.

The Wall Street Project, located in New York City, is staffed with nine professionals whose work is focused on finance, investments, banking, and other wealth creation and sustaining arenas.[62] Wall Street Project staff are also housed in other Rainbow/PUSH offices: the automotive division is located in Detroit, Michigan, and the Media and Telecommunications project is located in Washington, D.C., also home to the Federal Communications Commission, the federal regulatory body of media and telecommunications industries. The entertainment work comes primarily out of the Los Angeles Bureau; work related to increasing opportunities for minorities in the technology arena is housed in East Palo Alto, California; and the LaSalle Street office is located in Chicago.

The Wall Street Project hosts a Trade Bureau of over five hundred members. Similar to SCLC's and Operation PUSH's Commercial Division of the past, the Wall Street Project Trade Bureau is an organization of minority business owners and corporate executives interested in gaining more access to capital, business opportunities, corporate board appointments, and senior-level positions in corporations. The Trade Bureau is guided by a twenty-five-member steering committee that helps determine the direction and strategy of the project, provide financing through fund raising and donations for the project and its staff, and determine target companies.[63]

Unlike the work of the past to create economic opportunities for African Americans by focusing on employment and contracts, the Wall Street Project is unapologetically committed to African Americans gaining a share of influence and control over America's financial institutions. *Partnership* is the operative term of the Wall Street Project. Hence, in addition to placing African Americans on corporate boards and in senior-level management positions in Fortune 500 companies, the Wall Street Project also emphasizes ownership opportunities.

The strategy of the Wall Street Project differs from the selective patronage emphasis of the past. Purchasing stock in corporations, attending and discussing diversity at stockholders meetings, and holding conferences with CEOs and senior management executives in corporations is the primary strategy. In those rare instances when a company refuses to work with the Wall Street Project, the organization institutes a public awareness campaign about the corporation, by broadcasting in various forums its concerns about the company's record. When that fails, then a boycott is considered. In the two years since its founding, the Wall Street Project has engaged at least thirty Fortune 500 Companies, including Texaco Inc., Mitsubishi Corporation, General Motors, R. R. Donnelley's and Sons Company, MCI/WorldCom, Citigroup, Travelers Property Casual Corporation, Southwestern Bell, Goldman Sachs Group, Pepsi Cola Company, and AT&T Corporation. As a result of the work of the Rainbow/PUSH Coalition's Wall Street Project, within a two-year period African Americans have been placed on boards of several corporations, including MCI/WorldCom, Mitsubishi Motors, Texaco Inc., Seagram Company, LTD/Polygram Records Inc., Sprint Corporation, Raytheon Company, and the Goldman Sachs Group.[64]

Perhaps the most important component of the Wall Street Project's work is also its most visible. The Wall Street Project staff devotes most of its time to increasing and expanding opportunities for the African American business sector. The rationale for this focus is related to the important implications that business ownership has for supporting community. African American–owned businesses have the capacity to generate jobs, contribute to the revitalization of communities, as well as provide wealth.[65] Recent studies have shown that successful African American–owned businesses principally employ African American workers, locate mainly in African American neighborhoods, and recruit heavily from low-income communities.[66] According to Thomas Boston, "Everytime we create 100 jobs in African American firms, 80 jobs go to African

Americans."[67] A survey of 224 African American business owners in Atlanta conducted in 1995 indicated that four-fifths of their employees were African American, one-fourth operate businesses in neighborhoods in which the annual income is less than $25,000, 62 percent of their customers/clients are non–African American, and 21 percent of their employees are from low-income inner-city neighborhoods. African American–owned businesses are about eight times more likely to employ African American workers than are all firms.[68] Therefore, they serve as a major focus for generating jobs for unemployed workers. For these reasons the Wall Street Project puts heavy emphasis on increasing the numbers and capacity of African American businesses. An example of one effort is in the automotive industry. Since 1990 more than 20 percent of all minority automotive dealers have failed. To improve that situation the National Association of Minority Automotive Dealers (NAMAD) asked Rainbow/PUSH Coalition to partner with them in their quest for more low-interest loans, training programs, and greater access to foreign car sales from automotive companies. The Wall Street Project Automotive Division responded by pursuing negotiations with such automotive companies as General Motors Corporation and Ford Motor Company. The negotiations resulted in a moratorium on shutdowns, pending an independent review of each company's relationship with minority automotive dealers. Both companies agreed to find better ways to support fledgling African American–owned dealerships, with loans and extended credit programs.[69]

In the arena of media and telecommunications the Rainbow/PUSH Coalition worked with Viacom International, a large media conglomerate, to sell radio stations to minority buyers. In that case Viacom International had not sought minority buyers after the Federal Communications Commission had ordered it to sell several radio stations in 1977. After Rainbow/PUSH's intervention, Viacom International sold two stations to African Americans and agreed to provide resources to African American organizations to fund research projects to explore minority media ownership, start a Minority Broadcast Education and Advocacy fund, and fund broadcast training scholarships.[70] With regard to financial services, the Wall Street Project has persuaded Fortune 500 companies such as Ford Motor Company, Southwestern Bell, AT&T Corporation, Bell Atlantic Corporation, and GTE Corporation to use the services of African American money managers. The organization has also worked with financial firms such as Citigroup Inc., Travelers Property Casual Corporation, Goldman Sachs Group Inc., and Merrill Lynch and Company to promote African Americans to senior-level positions, appoint African Americans to corporate boards, and finance more business deals by African American entrepreneurs.[71] In its effort to expand opportunities for African Americans in food distribution, the Wall Street Project was partly responsible for helping African American grocers, for the first time in history, to gain the opportunity to display their products at the Food Marketing Institute Trade Show in Chicago in 1998. The Food Marketing Institute Convention is the largest food tradeshow in the United States. The Rainbow/PUSH Coalition helped secure reduced booth rates for disadvantaged vendors and sponsored a workshop on "Supplier Diversity."

In addition to helping African American–owned businesses gain contracts and increase ownership opportunities in corporate America, similar to the work of Operation PUSH, the Wall Street Project continues to promote the products of African Americans within the African American community. In his article "Economic Self-Destruction: African American Consumerism in the 1990s" Robert E. Weems argues that in recent decades there has been a decline of support for African American businesses by the African American community.[72] This has occurred despite the rise in African American spending power. Weems points out that during the World War I era African American consumers spent approximately one-third of their collective disposable income with African American firms. Around 1944 African American consumers made nearly 28 percent of their major purchases at stores owned by African Americans. Today it is estimated that African Americans spend only 7 percent of their disposable income with African American–owned firms. Certainly, one of the reasons is White competition. White-owned companies, for example, now dominate the billion-dollar African American personal care products industry. In response to this reality, as well as to increased visibility of African American products, the Wall Street Project provides opportunities for African American entrepreneurs to network and showcase their products through conferences and exhibits.

And, finally, the Wall Street Project worked closely with the federal government to increase opportunities for minorities. Rev. Jesse Jackson encouraged President Bill Clinton, the Small Business Administration, and officials at the Office of Economic Priorities to consider his long-standing idea of a domestic Marshall Plan for urban and rural America. These discussions led to a White House program known as the "New Markets Initiative." The goals of the initiative were very similar to Jackson's Rebuild America initiative of the 1990s. It sought federal guarantees to provide support to inner-city and rural residents to obtain employment and to promote business development opportunities. Some of the most significant components of the initiative included: (1) tax credits worth up to 25 percent for investments in capital-generating vehicles, such as community development banks and venture funds; (2) American Private Investment Companies (APICs), which would provide up to $1.5 billion annually in private and government-backed funding to finance capital investments; (3) venture capital companies that would combine equity venture capital financing and technical assistance to small companies in lower-income areas; and (4) programs that would encourage large firms to work with small ones as technical advisors in the inner cities and in rural areas. President Clinton traveled throughout the country promoting the idea and also appeared on Reverend Jackson's talk show "Both Sides" to discuss its merits.[73] The president's office introduced legislation in the 2000 budget to establish the program. The New Markets Initiative was established and provides tax incentives and other programs to increase economic development opportunities in underserved communities.

The Rainbow/PUSH Coalition believes that advocating for ideas and programs such as the New Markets Initiative is extremely important in the quest for economic parity. Yet, as has been stated elsewhere, there are many critics of the Wall Street Project and its goals. One popular concern is that only a few African Americans will benefit from the work of the Wall Street Project, while the needs of the poor are disregarded. Noted scholar Manning Marable argues that the basic problem with minority-corporate partnerships is that they only benefit a small number of African American entrepreneurs and executives, which thereby fosters the illusion that U.S. corporations can be persuaded to support African Americans and other minorities. This illusion is problematic considering that the actions of corporations are rooted in public relation strategies and in response to threats of boycotts, which do not affect structural racism and prejudice.[74]

A second concern is whether or not these initiatives will only create greater wealth for a small elite and therefore perpetuate the exploitation of African American workers and the poor, given the capitalistic nature of business. These arguments support professor William Julius Wilson's fear that, when upwardly mobile African American families leave the ghettos, they take with them the kinds of social resources which are essential for sustaining critical institutions and services, such as churches, stores, and schools. According to Wilson, the consequences of "Black flight" create more class divisions in the African American community.[75]

Perhaps the most serious question is whether or not these kinds of economic programs, which primarily argue for inclusion and/or control of U.S. capitalism, can cure the economic ills of the African American community. Can programs such as Selective Patronage, Operation Breadbasket, and the Wall Street Project, with its primary focus on employment and support for African American businesses, somehow counteract capitalism's inherent unfairness and greed?

Earl Ofari Hutchinson would answer the question with a resounding no. He argues in "Black Capitalism and Consumers" that only the "federal government can provide the mass resources needed to revitalize African American communities." Hutchinson points to the growth of Black businesses from 1977 to 1980, when sales for the *Black Enterprise 100* nearly doubled from $886 million to $1.53 billion. According to Hutchinson, the increase was due to President Jimmy Carter's effort to strengthen federal programs that provided grants, loans, and technical training to minority businesses. He maintains that Black leaders are not realistic about the ability of Black businesses to create greater wealth for African Americans.[76] Likewise, Manning Marable maintains that greater emphasis should be placed on income distribution strategies and a campaign for living wages for families. Family-oriented, rather than individual-based, strategies have the potential to benefit entire communities rather than a few entrepreneurs.[77]

Notwithstanding these thoughtful critiques, programs such as the Wall Street Project will continue into the new millennium. Recognizing the need to close the wealth and income gap between African Americans and Whites, other Civil Rights organizations including the Urban League and the NAACP have also adopted economic development and opportunity programs.

Conclusion

This chapter explored the economic initiatives of Rev. Jesse Jackson and the Rainbow/PUSH Coalition in the post–Civil Rights era. It illustrated how Jackson relied on the philosophy and strategies of SCLC and Dr. Martin Luther King Jr. in his early approach to promoting economic opportunities and development for African Americans. This chapter also elucidated how the Jackson approach to economic development evolved into the Rainbow/PUSH Coalition Wall Street Project. Overall, the Wall Street Project has been successful in creating more economic opportunities for African American entrepreneurs, establishing programs that will increase the number of African American senior-level executives in Fortune 500 companies, increasing corporate board membership, and creating wealth for the African American community. Certainly, the approach of the Wall Street Program is pragmatic, not offending capitalism's profit motive but advocating government involvement in creating opportunities for African Americans. Until programs such as Affirmative Action are truly accepted and implemented; until federal and state governments accept that underserved communities require a massive infusion of resources for rehabilitation, until reparations are a reality, or until capitalism is defeated, such piecemeal approaches will have to suffice.

Nine

Todd C. Shaw

"We Refused to Lay Down Our Spears"

The Persistence of Welfare Rights Activism, 1966–1996

*Maybe the [newspapers] do not write about us anymore
and the country is not concerned about what is happening
to poor people, especially poor women and their children,
but we are still organized and fighting for our rights.*
—Johnnie Tillmon

Welfare Rights in a Post-Welfare Era?

By the time President Bill Clinton left office in January 2001, he had
made good on his campaign pledge to "end welfare as we know it," even though
few critics and supporters actually thought he would dismantle the Aid to Families with Dependent Children (AFDC) program. What had been a New Deal
entitlement for poor women and children became a Republican-inspired "block
grant" that devolved much of the old program's federal discretion to the states.
Underlying this overhaul of the American welfare system and this drastic shift
away from a federal guarantee to the poor was a view long in development:
welfare and thus the welfare state violated the American work ethic. It sapped
low-income citizens, especially African American women, of their capacity to
be independent and productive.[1]

"Workfare"—the assertion that recipients had an obligation to work in order to retain their benefits—assumed a new respectability among moderates.
In collusion with right-wing Democrats and conservatives, Clinton agreed to
sweep away a standard plank of the Democratic platform. Reflecting the new
consensus that welfare was no longer an entitlement, the new program was

called "Temporary Assistance to Needy Families," or TANF. Among its other restrictions TANF imposed on every recipient a five-year, lifetime cap of benefits if they were paid for by federal funds. In some states this meant only provisions for two years if a recipient failed to meet work requirements. Signed into law on August 22, 1996, the Personal Responsibility and Work Opportunity Reconciliation Act (PRA) brought into fruition one of the ten "Contract with America" pledges made by the Republican majority in Congress.[2]

From the perspective of antipoverty advocates, the law was draconian. The groundwork for the previous AFDC program, which became the most contested plank of the American welfare state, was established under the 1935 Social Security Act. AFDC provided cash grants to children whose parents were unemployed, were unable to provide them with support, or who had other unmet needs. Among other changes the TANF program eliminated even these moderate entitlements by giving states the additional authority to deny benefits to children born to welfare recipients or unwed parents under age eighteen. A lion's share of the projected savings of these reforms (75 percent of fifty-five billion dollars between 1996 and 2002) was derived from greatly tightened restrictions on food stamp allotments and benefits to legal immigrants.[3]

Civil Rights advocates voiced their vehement opposition to what they saw as shortsighted and punitive measures. Rep. John Lewis of Georgia, a Democrat, pleaded upon the House floor, "Where is the compassion? . . . Where is the sense of decency? Where is the heart of this Congress? This bill is mean. It is base. It is downright low." Marian Wright Edelman, president of the Children's Defense Fund, not only labeled the bill as a "moment of shame" but also hinted at disavowing her organization's relationship with the Clinton White House. Likewise, the National Association for the Advancement of Colored People (NAACP), the National Urban League (NUL), and their local affiliates railed against the passage of the bill in Washington.[4]

They joined a chorus of longtime, antipoverty and welfare rights activists who wanted to convince state capitols neither to lead a "race to the bottom" in engineering their own welfare restrictions nor to comply with the most austere features of the 1996 act. Marian Kramer, president of the National Welfare Rights Union, warned Republican Gov. John Engler and the Michigan legislature not to approve legislation in compliance with the federal restrictions, "We're here to defend the victims of poverty. . . . We want the [Michigan] House to have some backbone today and defend poor people."[5]

With current reforms as a backdrop, this chapter outlines the history of the welfare rights movement from 1966 to 1996. My methodology is a narrative analysis of primary and secondary sources. Unfortunately, the Welfare

Rights Movement is a neglected strain in the literature on Black economic justice activism during the post–Civil Rights era. Although men have too often occupied the recognized positions of Black political leadership, this research emphasizes that the indispensable leaders of the antipoverty movement have been African American and other women of color. Their leadership should come as no surprise given the disproportionate poverty and Aid to Families with Dependent Children (AFDC) enrollment rates of Black and Latino female–headed households.[6]

The Welfare Rights Movement expands our definition of what it means to be a "Black political organization" for, like the Civil Rights Movement, it was Black led but still fairly multiracial. This chapter contributes a unique analysis of this movement's history. It addresses a key question: How can any movement that asserts a right to welfare persist when the dominant thinking is that welfare is passé and that certainly no one has a right to welfare? During the nadir periods of the Welfare Rights Movement the few devoted activists who remained believed that the maintenance of an infrastructure for opposition, however fragmented, was necessary to reignite a mass countermovement on behalf of welfare recipients. Thus, these veterans effectively served as links between one movement high point for activism and the next, or what Tarrow calls "cycles of protest." Their ability to create a successful linkage between these cycles is what Taylor and others label the "abeyance process." In this process veterans lay the groundwork for future generations of activists by ensuring there are activist networks, protest repertoires, and collective identities to pass on. To make my case about the movement's persistence and its regenerative power, I employ these three concepts. But it is the resonant qualities of any movement's "master frame," or its public ideology and interpretive lenses, which determine its appeal to succeeding activists.[7]

Theorizing the Persistence of Poor Peoples' Movements

During the Civil Rights Movement activists expanded the scope of conflict, induced a public crisis, recruited allies, and provided various elites with motives for negotiating a new political equilibrium— for example, the 1964 Civil Rights Act. The greatest sanctioning power that marginalized citizens (racial minorities, the working class, the poor) have is the power to disrupt a delicate political stability that hinges upon public quiescence.[8]

Late in 1965 the scholar-activists Frances Fox Piven and Richard Cloward penned a paper entitled "A Strategy to End Poverty." They argued that an ad hoc Welfare Rights Movement should enroll all poor families who are eligible for welfare benefits. This would trigger a system-wide crisis to which public officials would have to contemplate a guaranteed income reform such as

Nixon's Family Assistance Plan.[9] After the movement they concluded that anti-poverty activists placed an inordinate emphasis upon the maintenance of movement organizations. "Organizations endure, in short, by abandoning their oppositional politics . . . by endeavoring to do what they cannot do [effectively sustain permanent organizations], organizers fail to do what they can do [compel further system concessions]." Furthermore, they noted that the National Welfare Rights Organization (NWRO) did not exploit "the momentary unrest among the poor to obtain the maximum concessions possible in return for the restoration of quiescence. It is by that criterion that it failed."[10] Maintaining an organization of the politically marginalized when its purpose is to confront those in power costs money. Even if initial pressure politics are successful, it is precisely those in power who may subsidize a group's continuance, thus the chances for co-optation increase.

Albeit, I extend upon the cycles of protest and abeyance process literature so as to present caveats to Piven and Cloward's otherwise convincing conclusion. These caveats are the internal factors of the abeyance process. Lingering organizations are useful to the degree that they are able to perpetuate and transmit activist networks, protest repertoires, and collective identities. I add to this framework that a general outcome of the abeyance process is a diversionary or incremental politics that may precipitate social change or at least a new protest cycle. Whereas disruptive politics are conceivably the power to invoke substantive reforms and social change by fundamentally challenging a political system, diversionary politics are a place-holder politics in that they: (1) lay the groundwork for more effective insurgency (even though a battle has been lost); (2) cushion the marginalized against taking the full brunt of an attack; or (3) create a diversion that buys activists more time. Organized rallies, protests, and press conferences by welfare organizers which simply call attention to a grievance may at the moment seem ineffectual. But this form of opposition consistently attempts to push the trajectory of the policy debate at least a little off center at each round and thus incrementally shift its final destination. It is the exertion of this type of insistent pressure—akin to a drop of water chipping away at a rock—for which long-term organizations are intrinsically suited.

As diagrammed in figure 9.1, the dynamics of any protest cycle and its subsequent abeyance process are calibrated by this cycle's respective master frame. Whereas an initial protest cycle likely produces disruptive politics, I hypothesize that succeeding protest cycles—or Protest Cycle A^{+1}—can produce either disruptive or diversionary politics based upon the movement's momentum. Of course, the Welfare Rights Movement is my case study to explicate my theory.

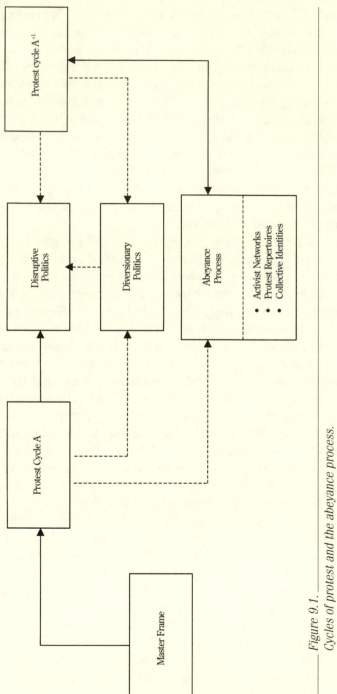

Figure 9.1.
Cycles of protest and the abeyance process.

Master Frames, the Cycles of Protest, and
the Abeyance Process

Despite Piven and Cloward's functionalist assertions about the primacy of tangible movement incentives, ideology still matters. David Snow and Robert Benford posited that the ability of activists to frame the ideals of and rationales for a movement selectively determines the success of that movement and its offspring. They explain that, like a linguistic code, "Master frames . . . provide the interpretative medium through which collective actors associated with different movements within a cycle assign blame for the problem they are attempting to ameliorate." In turn, cycles of protest are "sequences of escalating collective action that are of greater frequency and intensity than normal, that spread throughout various sections and regions of society, and that involve both new techniques of protest and new forms of organization."[11] Master frames are important to cycles of protest because, among other functions, they shape the duration, dispersion, frequency, innovation, and complexity of the latter. In effect, movement veterans innovatively preserve elements of initial ideals and tactics until the political environment is ripe for a new protest cycle. As indicated by the dotted line in figure 9.1 between "Protest Cycle A" and the "Abeyance Process" box, the abeyance process is a protest cycle in hiatus. Verta Taylor states that abeyance "depicts a holding process by which movements sustain themselves in nonreceptive political environments and provide continuity from one stage of mobilization to another." Although Taylor challenges Ephraim Mizruchi's assumption that abeyance structures rarely facilitate social change, she concedes, "As a movement loses support, activists who had been most intensely committed to its aims become increasingly marginal and socially isolated. . . . In short a movement in abeyance becomes a cadre of activists who create or find a niche for themselves."[12] Abeyance works because veterans and their residual groups provide refuge for an activist network, a protest repertoire, as well as a collective identity "that offer . . . participants a sense of mission and moral purpose."[13]

Networks, Protest Repertoires, and Collective Identities

It follows that Piven and Cloward are very concerned about long-term outcomes. For them the ability to staff a protest group that does little protesting is a hollow victory, and in that respect they are quite right. But they fail to see how standing organizations can be conduits through which the activist ties of one generation of a movement are reshaped and transmitted to the next. A movement that is embedded in or which serves as an anchor for an activist network of other movements may guarantee its posterity because it has allies or beneficiaries that indirectly further elements of its cause.[14] Additionally,

Piven and Cloward fail to recognize that disruptive politics is only one pole of a broader dimension we can call oppositional politics. Between the poles of mass collective disruption (e.g., riots, strikes, and revolutions) and covert, individual acts of resistance (e.g., graffiti, sabotage, and beating the system) is a range of collective insurgency whose immediate effects may not supplant the dominant order, but they do more than extend an index finger. Again, I call these politics diversionary politics.[15] Lastly, Piven and Cloward do not consider that organizations, with all of their failings, are useful because they hold out the prospect for providing the psychic and social incentives needed to maintain an oppositional presence, though they compete for resources at various times.[16]

In summary, I suggest that the Welfare Rights Movement persisted because it cultivated an activist network, protest repertoire, and collective identity that were useful in a post-welfare era. They passed along these protest resources and innovated upon them as necessary.

Before Abeyance: The First Welfare Rights Protest Cycle, 1966–1975

An overview of NWRO's organizational history will allow me to delineate the range of ideals, alliances, and tactics that were available to fan the embers of post–1975 activism. This examination will discuss the master frames that set the tempo for the movement's protest cycles and its abeyance processes. As mentioned, there were a number of constituencies and contemporaries that contributed to NWRO's origins. Of course, the organization's core constituents were Black, White, Latino, and Asian women who were AFDC recipients. Black women in all periods constituted the majority of activists; among the most prominent were Johnnie Tillmon from California, Beulah Sanders from New York, and Annie Smart from Louisiana.

The NWRO was formed in 1967 as a federation of preexisting local and state Welfare Rights organizations (WROs). The founders did not come to this experience as empty slates but, rather, as activists with prior organizing expertise and/or vital life experiences.[17] The core ideals were that poor women of color refused to accept poverty, racism, or sexism. Thus, they believed they had just as much of a right as more affluent citizens to demand that the government ensure them a minimum standard of living. Many of them came to this perspective through affiliations with several other activist groups, including neighborhood organizations, the Black Panther Party, the Civil Rights Movement, and Community Action Programs.

The Black and White Left also allied itself with welfare activists for those in its ranks had a clear stake in making a class (and in some cases racial) analysis of poverty. Progressive urban ministries such as the United Church of Christ and the nationwide Interreligious Foundation for Community Organization

(IFCO) often provided WROs with the funding, in-kind resources, and bases of operation necessary for their activities. Liberation theology and Black liberation theology provided ministers and congregants with concrete rationales for Christian social action such as Welfare Rights activism.[18]

Additionally, the student movement was an initial contributor to the Welfare Rights efforts of the 1960s and early 1970s. Whether it was through direct participation in welfare auxiliaries or involvement in brief alliances, student activists from many walks joined the Welfare Rights cause due to their emerging "New Left" critique of the American state.[19] The mainstream labor and feminist movements were not closely aligned until later.

What were the NWRO's specific ideals, goals, and tactics? At its 1967 founding convention in Washington, D.C., delegates resolved to promote the imperatives of "decent jobs with adequate pay for those who can work, and adequate income for those who cannot." A thirteen-point statement called the "Welfare Bill of Rights" undergirded these assertions, expressing values such as an "adequate [guaranteed] income," "dignity," "justice," and "democracy," or "a system which guarantees recipients direct participation in the decision[s] under which they must live."[20] Between 1966 and 1969 NWRO mobilized an expansive network of eight hundred local groups in fifty states in which literally thousands of Aid to Dependent Children (ADC) recipients in more than one hundred cities protested, demonstrated, and joined lawsuits. Activists used various forms of disruptive politics to oppose welfare cuts and insensitive bureaucracies; diminished stipends for school clothes, dietary needs, and utility bills; exclusion from school lunch programs; inadequate public housing accommodations; infringements upon the rights of recipients to join local WROs; and a myriad of other related issues. For example, during this four-year period the WROs of Detroit waged more than two dozen separate campaigns, and activists from other Michigan cities such as Highland Park, Ann Arbor, Benton Harbor, Flint, Pontiac, and Lansing, who also aggressively lobbied county and state officials for increased benefit levels, joined them. Marian Kramer reflected, "We did mobilization here [in Detroit] which sprung a hell of a movement at that time."[21] The pre–1975 period clearly fit Sidney Tarrow's protest cycle definition, for it was a moment of greater than "normal" protest activity by poor Black women and others. It came in the wake of the Civil Rights Movement.

The Civil Rights Master Frame

To be sure, the central goals of the Welfare Rights Movement were unique from those of the early Civil Rights Movement. Whereas the former began with a specific focus upon Black poverty entitlements, the latter was initiated around the broad issues of voting rights, public accommodations, and fair employment. Yet no other movement had a more pronounced effect upon the first cycle of Welfare Rights protest and how it was framed. From the Civil Rights Movement and its activists the NWRO inherited a complex master frame including a belief in the empowerment of the racially oppressed, a belief in inter-racial organizing, and the ideal of allied struggles.

For instance, early in her activist career Fannie Lou Hamer joined Civil Rights workers as they founded a Black independent party called the Missis-sippi Freedom Democratic Party (MFDP). After she left the movement, she became an ardent Welfare Rights organizer in her home county of Sunflower, Mississippi. In 1965 George Wiley was forced to leave the Congress of Racial Equality (CORE) because he was considered too integrationist and bourgeois for its increasingly ghetto-centered Black Nationalism. He later founded the interracial Poverty/Rights Action Center (P/RAC), with the help of the Citizen's Crusade against Poverty, before becoming NWRO's first and best-known ex-ecutive director. To leave no ambiguity about the connection between the two movements, NWRO adopted two linked circles as its logo. Whereas the first circle represented the Civil Rights Movement, the second represented the anti-poverty movement. It was an emblem that was displayed on the literature of WROs across the country alongside the NWRO motto of "Bread and Justice."[22] So, one activist framework mutually informed the other. For example, at a Janu-ary 1966 meeting preceding NWRO's founding, young Civil Rights workers such as Kramer were initially drawn into the Welfare Rights Movement by meeting veterans such as Beulah Sanders.[23]

Since the NWRO emerged during the Black Power era, the Civil Rights mas-ter frame was clearly not the only set of ideals which appealed to its low-income, African American leaders and constituents. Like other Civil Rights–inspired organizations (e.g., CORE, SNCC), the insistence of NWRO's theore-ticians that the group remain largely nonideological actually drove NWRO away from its founding tenets of interracialism and subtle gender equity. Instead, its early 1970s leadership embraced Black Nationalist principles, while it oc-casionally dueled with White feminists. There arose the concern that too many of Wiley-selected NWRO staffers were White and male. Added to these racial and gender conflicts were class conflicts between the welfare mothers who held the organization's elected offices and the middle-class support staff. Tillmon challenged the Alinsky-inspired "Boston model"—which centered organizing around the efforts of professional staffers and external funding—with a model that argued welfare recipients should lead. She believed that the organization should primarily rely upon the membership dues of welfare recipients no mat-ter how meager.[24]

Therefore, NWRO was not merely a product of the Civil Rights Movement. It became a contemporary that borrowed from the Civil Rights master frame, contrasted it against other frames, wrestled with several other frames, and constructed its own. These clashes had a bearing upon the activist networks, protest repertoire, and collective identity veterans preserved during the post–Civil Rights and Welfare Rights period.

Struggles with the Civil Rights Master Frame

Differences over leadership style emerged during a late 1960s antipoverty campaign. Martin Luther King Jr. sought to move the Civil Rights Movement from questions of political disenfranchisement to questions of economic inequality. While militant elements turned toward "Black Power," the more conservative elements, especially the NAACP and National Urban League (NUL), openly opposed King criticizing the Johnson Administration on its conduct of the Vietnam War and the War on Poverty. In an effort to bridge these widening chasms, King proposed a new campaign to recapture previous activist energies. The effort was dubbed the "Poor People's Campaign."[25]

King and the SCLC announced a push for thousands of poor Americans and their allies to encamp in Washington, D.C., until Congress agreed to enact a guaranteed annual income. To mobilize such numbers King needed foot soldiers. In February 1968 he agreed to the demands of NWRO leaders to meet them in Chicago. By then NWRO was about ten thousand members strong and had one hundred active chapters. Flanked by his lieutenants, King walked into the downtown YMCA expecting to gain the NWRO's immediate support without having to make any real commitments. The reception he received was quite different.[26] Tillmon, Sanders, and other WRO leaders admonished King for circumventing the national leadership by only contacting local organizers for support. Then they subtly interrogated him on his position regarding various pieces of proposed welfare reform legislation such as the 1967 Work Incentive Program. When King looked bewildered and a bit peeved, an exasperated Tillmon finally admonished him, "You know, Dr. King, if you don't know about these questions, you should say you don't know, and then we could go on with the meeting." King humbly agreed to the history lesson these Black women presented on welfare reform legislation. Yet Andrew Young, one of King's chief aides, later conceded that the southern ministerial patriarchy he and King embraced made them fearful of "domineering" women as leaders.[27]

After King's assassination on April 4, Coretta Scott King, Ralph Abernathy, and the SCLC continued the formal alliance with NWRO in the hope of fulfilling King's well-intentioned but ill-fated Poor People's Campaign in the spring and summer of 1968. The campaign gathered steam and recruited marchers for the Washington encampment by sponsoring various poor people's caravans to key cities and locales. Indicative of the campaign, in which a disorganized and dispirited "Resurrection City" was erected in the rainy mire and muck of the Washington mall, the nation answered the appeals of poor people for guaranteed income and job opportunities with harassment by the police and arrests. A meaningful alliance between the SCLC and NWRO was forged, but they also were competitors. Both claimed to speak on behalf of the economically disenfranchised.[28]

The bittersweet struggle around President Richard Nixon's proposed Family Assistance Program (FAP) revealed just how much disagreement existed about what goal should frame the antipoverty movement. Because of a dramatically changing political opportunity structure, it spelled the beginning of NWRO's decline. In 1969 Nixon proposed abolishing the AFDC program and replacing it with a guaranteed annual income for poor working families and children under eighteen according to family size. He also wanted to supplement this income with a Negative Income Tax (NIT) as opposed to mandatory work requirements that were determined by a formula. On April 16, 1970, the FAP passed the House by a margin of 243 to 155 and was likely to be approved by a more liberal Senate; however, it never made it out of the Senate Finance Committee.[29]

Initially, many Civil Rights leaders, such as Whitney Young of the NUL, publicly lent their support to a proposal they considered quite forward-looking for a Republican president. Yet once the NWRO persisted in its criticism of the low, proposed benefit levels—$1,600 to $3,920—the NUL and other Civil Rights organizations followed NWRO's lead in opposing the measure.[30] Embedded in the FAP scheme was a subtle gender bias in which the administration claimed it wanted to increase the workforce participation of AFDC mothers but created no program to reach this objective. There also were gender and class differences between Wiley and the Black women in leadership (whom he deeply respected) over the question of whether welfare entitlements or the employment of Black men should be their policy priority. For three years Wiley, Tillmon, and a network of WRO activists organized "Zap FAP" campaigns to support more generous proposals. They initiated a "$5,500 or fight" campaign, appeared before congressional committees, and attempted to garner the support of liberal allies.[31] FAP eventually died from political attrition, but so too did NWRO's effective use of disruptive politics. NWRO won the battle but soon lost the war. The 1970s represented a period of retrenchment and regrouping.

During Abeyance: The Decline of the First Protest Cycle, 1975–1987

Having discussed how the Welfare Rights Movement was and was not framed, I now turn to a formal examination of this movement in abeyance. To recap, my central question is how did the veterans of this movement survive given a very hostile political climate? My thesis is that they were able to maintain certain ideals, alliances, and protest forms for the benefit of new generations of protest. In this section I discuss the context and responses of WROs to the more conservative policy and ideological environments of the 1970s and 1980s.

The Changed Opportunity Structure of the 1970s
Attacks on the Poor

Much of the organizational dynamism of NWRO had dissipated by 1973 due to the resignation and tragic death of George Wiley (from a boating accident), internecine conflicts, and diminished financial support. In 1975 NWRO formally closed its doors. While the early 1970s represented a high-water mark for the Black Power Movement, it also was a period of intense, political repression in which police agencies orchestrated overt attacks on all factions of the Left, especially many of the NWRO's radical allies. The racial, gender, and class stereotypes that accompanied public welfare had not abated since the mid- to late 1960s, when a conservative countermovement pushed for stringent work guidelines. Now conservatives argued the need for a host of public policy prescriptions to the perceived excesses of the 1960s, including welfare dependency, inherent deficiencies in the (matriarchal) female-headed household, and the pathology of Black poverty. The so-called Black welfare queen, or Black matriarch, became a racist and sexist fixture in litanies about the sloth and indolence of underclass Black women. This further fed beliefs about the necessity for workfare. On the fiscal side activists in Michigan, Illinois, and other rustbelt states had to combat belt-tightening measures that governors and state houses imposed to address stagnant economics, declining tax revenues, and burgeoning welfare administration costs.[32]

Workfare, Full Employment, and Welfare Reform

In addition to the disintegration of the national Welfare Rights Movement, the chief bane of the movement, workfare, gained more ground by the late 1970s. Thanks to antipoverty lawyers who were allies, NWRO won a series of court challenges in the late 1960s which helped to remove several legal barriers to AFDC eligibility. Nevertheless, Ronald Reagan, then governor of California, anticipated the turning tide when, in his 1967 inaugural address, he asserted, "We are not going to perpetuate poverty by substituting a permanent dole for a paycheck."[33] Ten years later President Jimmy Carter launched the Program for Better Jobs and Income (PBJI). His administration hoped to make a major foray into welfare reform by replacing AFDC, supplemental security income (SSI), and the food stamp programs with direct cash payments as well as the creation of more than a million public service jobs.

At this point most Welfare Rights and antipoverty networks were centered at state and local levels as opposed to the national level. Therefore, the strongest protests were locally focused. For instance, one hundred members of the Unemployed Workers Organizing Committee (UWOC) of Chicago expressed their ire with Carter's restructuring of unemployment insurance and the slated requirement that unemployed persons had to take minimum-wage jobs.[34] Civil Rights advocates such as Clarence Mitchell of the NAACP and Marian Wright Edelman of the Children's Defense Fund opposed Carter's proposal, partly because it provided few to no additional subsidies to states. Thus, in some cases it actually would mean a reduction in benefit levels. The more important reason Civil Rights leaders disagreed with this welfare reform proposal, however, is because they were more interested in the prospects of Congressman Augustus Hawkins's (D-CA) Full Employment and Balanced Growth Act of 1979. Although it was a very interesting policy statement, this bill only set nonbinding, full employment targets. Unlike the PBJI, the Humphrey-Hawkins Bill passed, but it was largely a paper tiger.[35] From the angle of both Welfare Rights and Civil Rights leaders, the mid- to late 1970s constituted a period of local regrouping before the entrenched battles of the 1980s.

Abeyance and WROs after 1975

Activists such as Tillmon, Smart, and Kramer had seen the NWRO's 1966 germination. More than ten years later they were still active, despite the disbanded national organization. In short, the movement returned to its pre–1966 fragmented, or decentralized, configuration. Tillmon carried on her work with the ANC Mothers in California as Smart continued to lead statewide and local efforts in Louisiana.[36] In Michigan Kramer recruited Yvette Linebarger to work as a comrade on the Welfare Rights front. Prior to then, Linebarger had chaired Detroit's Westside Mothers WRO for five years. By the mid- to late 1970s the two of them reactivated a large umbrella WRO for Detroit's home county of Wayne. Along with its membership in the Michigan Welfare Reform Coalition, the Wayne County WRO helped to organize ten additional WROs. It also challenged many punitive welfare proposals and regulations of county and state welfare administrations. As my 1994 interviews with Kramer and

Linebarger confirmed, they had been active in Welfare Rights for nearly thirty and twenty years, respectively. Such longevity with a cause likely stems from a fundamental dedication to group empowerment despite personal costs. Kramer noted: "We have learned [with] welfare rights, we don't base our thing on the individual. We have to base it on the struggle and the collectivity, and the leaders that come out of that." Dedication of this kind is an example of what Hill Collins refers to as Black women's activist ethic of communal uplift.[37] Such dedication was not an anomaly. In another instance Jacqueline Pope reports in her research that many activists of the Brooklyn Downtown Welfare Advocate Center (B-WAC) still organized low- and moderate-income communities twenty years after the height of the first protest cycle. As a testament to this activism's gravity and the values it inspired, Theresa Funiciello simply conceded, "People who spent time with B-WAC became transformed."[38] My argument, however, is not that the actions of all veterans or students of the first protest cycle positively ensured the movement's survival while in abeyance. Next, I examine the attributes that this abeyance activism safeguarded for the next protest cycle by exploring the activists ties, protest repertoire, and collective identity these veterans preserved.

Activist Networks

Although the movement was decentralized, it remained nominally connected through the activist ties of veterans and newcomers. Two different trajectories of grassroots activism ensured that the diffuse antipoverty movement remained afloat. One trajectory was the continued efforts of local and state WROs and their allies as inspired and joined by antihunger and antihomelessness groups. Among the many enduring WROs were the Massachusetts Welfare Rights Organization; Parents for Justice in New Hampshire; the Welfare Warriors in Milwaukee; Empower in Rochester, New York; the Reform Organization of Welfare in St. Louis; Women for Economic Security in Chicago; the Women's Union in Vermont; Arise in Springfield, Massachusetts; the Downtown Welfare Advocate Center in New York; the Michigan Welfare Rights Organization; Westside Mothers in Detroit; as well as the Wayne County WRO.[39] In 1980 Tillmon admonished her detractors: "I hear people saying that the welfare rights movement is dead. It is not dead. It has changed since those early days of agitating and protesting in the streets. The movement is different but still alive in many parts of the country." Speaking about these activist ties, Kramer agreed: "NWRO disbanded; but each state chapter continued to organize around poverty issues: hunger, childcare, and the new issues of homelessness and workfare. Many of us still communicated with each other on a regular basis."[40]

The other important product of the first Welfare Rights protest cycle evolved into what Harry Boyte (1980) calls the "New Citizen Movements" of the late 1970s. In 1970 George Wiley sent his deputy director, Wade Rathke, to Little Rock, Arkansas, to organize a statewide WRO. What resulted was the Arkansas Community Organizations for Reform Now (ACORN). At one point there was a split in the organization. Whereas one faction wanted a purely Welfare Rights group, the winning faction wanted a group that appealed to all low-income constituents regardless of recipient status. Throughout the 1970s ACORN organized strikes against utility companies as well as ran candidates for municipal and county offices. In 1976 it became a national, multistate organization that renamed itself the Association of Community Organizations for Reform Now. This was the same year ACORN held its first national convention and agreed to march on the Democratic Party's National Convention in Memphis, Tennessee, with its "People's Platform." In this platform were planks on issues ranging from energy to health care to taxes to housing. Despite ACORN's split from the Welfare Rights Movement, it was still a very important conduit through which low-income advocacy strategies were transferred to the 1980s.[41]

Protest Repertoires

WROs were much less successful in capturing the public's attention with protest activities after 1975. But the essential result of their diversionary tactics was to keep the spirit of insurgency alive while they gleaned victories at the margins. True to the examples of the 1960s protest repertoire, these organizations continued to protest at welfare offices; litigate administrative/procedural changes; inform and organize food stamp recipients; enroll new General Assistance and AFDC clients; organize public housing and other subsidized housing tenants; press for equitable utility rate agreements; as well as initiate various educational and community-oriented activities. They even made innovations in this repertoire by running welfare recipients for public office to garner protest votes.[42] Key to this insurgency was still guaranteeing that welfare was respected as a right and that welfare grants provided a livable income. Among the continued problems, however, were difficulties in locating funds to keep their doors open and keeping members involved. But small strides were made in attaining the goals of Welfare Rights. For instance, a Massachusetts statewide group, the Coalition for Basic Human Needs, at least temporarily defeated conservative Governor Edward King's plans to implement austere workfare requirements.[43] Again, these diversionary politics did not permanently rebuff welfare retrenchment. But they conditioned some women in poverty to resist the popular characterization of welfare recipients as the lazy and undeserving poor.

Collective Identity

Movements of marginalized groups often have ideals and political symbols that inspire an oppositional consciousness and serve as public assertions of the movement's creed. Tillmon had long established the rationale for why welfare should be seen as a "woman's issue." Black feminists groups such as the National Black Feminist Organization and the Coalition of 100 Black Women had "established loose ties with the NWRO" in seeing the issues of welfare recipients as important to all women. By the late 1970s the National Council of Women, Work, and Welfare even "attempted to mobilize political support for welfare as a women's issue." The problem, however, was that mainstream feminist organizations such as the National Organization for Women (NOW) were preoccupied with the Equal Rights Amendment and thus did not make explicit political alliances with the now shrunken ranks of the Welfare Rights Movement.[44] The collective identity of Welfare Rights activism continued to embrace the ideals of economic, racial, and gender justice, but the organizational manifestation of these principles were not realized until the 1980s and 1990s.

The Constrained Opportunity Structure of the 1980s: Reagan's New Federalism and Diversionary Politics

Welfare reform was not a central concern of Ronald Reagan's 1980 campaign for the White House. Yet the Reagan Administration made it abundantly clear once in office that its promotion of "New Federalism," which challenged the very existence of the welfare state, meant greater restrictions upon AFDC and other welfare programs. Mimi Abramovitz explains that the 1981 Omnibus Budget Reconciliation Act (OBRA) "tightened eligibility requirements, introduced work requirements, lowered benefits, re-introduced mandatory workfare, and otherwise restructured the program's rules to shrink the rolls. Between 1981 and 1983, over 400,000 working households lost AFDC eligibility altogether, another 300,000 experienced benefit reductions."[45] Throughout the early 1980s a coalition of antipoverty groups attempted to mobilize public sentiment against the Reagan cuts. Again, diversionary politics sought to induce greater insurgency, cushion the poor against the full impact of sanctions, and/or buy time. These groups highlighted the potential impact of these proposals, as is characteristic of diversionary politics. But they were unable to prevent their passage partly due to a Republican and conservative Democratic alliance in Congress.[46] Quite simply, the political opportunity structure had become even more restrictive in comparison to the 1970s. But new or renewed anti-retrenchment coalitions emerged as influenced by previous 1960s movements.

In September 1981, for instance, the AFL-CIO mobilized 250,000 of its members to attend a "Solidarity Day" march on Washington, where Benjamin Hooks of the NAACP and Vernon Jordan of the NUL spoke. And the following May, in 1982, roughly 2,000 people participated in an "All People's Congress," where they observed a "National Day of Resistance" whose objective was to "Roll Back Reaganism." These Washington-centered protests were coupled with the vigorous challenges Welfare Rights and community activists made to the implementation of these cuts in cities and states from Chicago, Illinois, to Los Angeles, California.[47] Activists used a range of diversionary tactics.

Moreover, Reagan's New Federalism shaped the nature and contour of diversionary activism in three principal ways. Drastic decreases in welfare rolls and grant levels left many welfare recipients and former recipients afraid and dispirited after previous gains. Second, along with cuts in several other areas of social welfare spending, the Reagan Administration reduced federal support for legal services grants and made conservative appointments to the federal bench. Slowly, these moves limited the ability of Welfare Rights groups to retain legal counsel and to receive equitable redress from the courts.[48] Lastly, the administration compelled states to experiment with their own workfare initiatives by cutting the WIN program and granting program waivers from federal regulations.[49] New Federalism meant that even more of the fight welfare activists had to wage to maintain minimal grant levels and numbers of recipients was centered not in Washington but in fifty state capitals and a myriad of county and local jurisdictions. This was the effect of welfare devolution upon the diversionary activism of Welfare Rights.

State Welfare Initiatives and Diversionary Politics

For years federal welfare policy innovation had been driven by state experimentation. In effect, the states were so ahead of the federal government in devising workfare programs that it is no exaggeration to assert that the 1996 Welfare Reform Act was in large part an amalgamation of initiatives states had already taken. Wisconsin welfare reforms, as led by its Republican Governor Tommy Thompson, provide a prime example. Near the end of Reagan's second term, in 1987, forty-two states operated optional workfare programs that were permitted under the 1981 OBRA. States tried a number of programs, including a panoply of job training, job search, education, as well as paid and unpaid work combinations. Workfare opponents attempted to be just as creative in countering what they saw as the odious features of these initiatives. They wanted recipients to move off welfare by receiving good-paying jobs with benefits, not increased exploitation. To them workfare models such as Illinois's Project Chance or Massachusetts's Employment and Training Choices (ET) program were not synonymous with greater independence but with involuntary servitude or "slavery."[50]

Cuts in AFDC and state-funded public aid programs commonly known as General Assistance were also of primary concern to public welfare defenders. To compensate for diminished federal support, governors and legislatures reasoned that General Assistance either had to be eliminated, grant levels had to be reduced, or, at the very least, grants could not be increased despite high inflation and joblessness. Activists employed two interrelated tactics to delay, obstruct, or reverse attempts to reduce grants. They sought injunctions and reversals in the courts and lobbied and protested state officials.

On the legal front groups found it increasingly difficult to make gains. The Baltimore WRO filed a class-action suit against the state of Maryland in 1981, charging that the state had failed to give proper and legal notice before terminating the public assistance of thirty-five thousand recipients. More than a month later a state court agreed with the group and ordered the state to restore benefits to all thirty-five thousand households. This differed from the 1988 experience of the Boston-based Coalition for Basic Human Needs, which sued Governor Michael Dukakis for violating a 1986 court order when he bypassed a legislative agreement mandating AFDC increases in his proposed budget. Despite the group's previous ability to demand and win average grant increases of 9 percent for three consecutive years, 1987 was the last year they garnered a victory or won such a suit.[51]

On the lobbying and protest front, there was a similar pattern of progress and setback. In the early 1980s the Redistribute American Movement (RAM) and the Downtown Welfare Advocates Center were able to mobilize three thousand demonstrators to march on New York's state capitol of Albany. They sang "We Shall Overcome" and demanded public assistance grants be indexed to 1980 as opposed to 1972 cost of living formulas. A year later they managed to convince a Republican majority in the state senate to increase grants by 15 percent. By the early 1990s, however, activists of the Michigan Up and Out of Poverty, Now! Coalition were not as successful. They set up a "Tent City" (one of four) to squat on the state capitol lawn and vigorously protest Governor John Engler's elimination of General Assistance. This action left ninety thousand low-income persons with no immediate income and quite possibly homeless. Despite their best efforts, including a loose alliance with Jesse Jackson and a handful of Black church leaders, they failed to move the legislature (or state courts) to rescind the decision.[52]

While substantive coalitions were formed at the state and local levels, Welfare Rights activists sometimes clashed with Civil Rights leaders such as Mayor Andrew Young in Atlanta, the Rev. Jesse Jackson, or Marian Wright Edelman of the Children's Defense Fund. Activists felt these leaders were ignoring grassroots perspectives on welfare reform proposals such as the 1988 federal Family Support Act.[53] To be sure, this was reminiscent of the late 1960s period when Welfare Rights activists felt it necessary to upbraid King and other Civil Right leaders for overlooking their grassroots work. What had partly emboldened these activists to challenge mainstream Black leaders was the formation of a new national Welfare Rights organization—in short, a second protest cycle.

After Abeyance: The Rise of the Second Protest Cycle, 1987–1996

Although twice before state and local activists attempted to re-establish the NWRO, success was not to come until the summer of 1987. On June 30, 1987, the twenty-first anniversary of NWRO's founding, the National Welfare Rights Union (NWRU) was founded at a Georgetown University conference. Paying homage to the ideals of the NWRO, the NWRU declared it was dedicated "to the pursuit of social justice for all members of our society, particularly those who have been excluded from the benefits of this nation." Highland Park and Detroit, Michigan, became the NWRU's base of operation, and *Survival Notes* became its national organ, distributed in thirty-eight states and six nations. Kramer was elected NWRU's president. What made this gathering pivotal was that longtime activists such as Smart, Kramer, and Maureen Taylor of Michigan had the opportunity to convey their preserved ties, tactics, and ideals to a new generation of young, women activists. The movement was again coordinated by a national organization.[54]

Moreover, this second protest cycle was not new because it generated a disruptive politics powerful enough to check significantly retrenchment across the welfare system. Rather, it was a "new cycle" in that it fits Tarrow's definition of being a greater-than-"normal" level of sustained protest activity. This second cycle differs from the first in that it was limited to the use of diversionary politics. But its diversionary politics brought a new awareness to the Welfare Rights cause. An analogy can be drawn between this second phase of the Welfare Rights Movement and the second (or 1970s and 1980s) phase of the movement for an Equal Rights Amendment, whose organizers also did not see their desired reform materialize, but their mobilization brought a greater awareness of the legal status of women.[55] My evidence that the NWRU represented a second protest cycle (after an abeyance period) stems from the strides NWRU made in reinvigorating past activist ties, protest repertoires, and ideals of collective identity between 1987 and 1996.

Activist Networks

The first annual convention of the NWRU in September 1988 drew one hundred people from eighteen states to Detroit after Labor Day. This activist network inspired the formation of the National Union of the Homeless (NUH), led in part by Chris Sprowell of Philadelphia. NWRU organizers in Detroit were also instrumental in helping to found Detroit's chapter of the NUH. In July 1989 over 350 people attended a National Survival Summit in Philadelphia which was sponsored by the NWRU, the NUH, the National Anti-Hunger Coalition, and the United Church of Christ. Several other survival summits were sponsored to bring into focus problems with youth, hunger, homelessness, poor women, welfare reform, and the media blackouts of poor people's activism.[56]

Overall, NWRU became a vital member of a broader antipoverty front. In 1987 Massachusetts activists associated with Advocacy for Resources for Modern Survival (ARMS), the CBHN, as well as the Massachusetts Law Reform Institute launched a 1987 campaign they entitled "Up to Poverty," demanding benefits that were up to the poverty line. It later became "Up and Out of Poverty" and then "Up and Out of Poverty, Now!" They approached the newly selected board of the National Welfare Rights Union to cosponsor this campaign, and the NWRU eagerly agreed to an alliance. Yvette Linebarger of Detroit became its national chair. The NWRU was impressed that this campaign had grown from five to ninety Welfare Rights groups and had been extremely successful in lobbying the Massachusetts General Assembly.[57]

Furthermore, in 1992 Patricia Ireland, president of NOW, invited Marian Kramer to Boston to address the group's annual convention. Since the theme of the convention was the poverty of women, Kramer and Boston Welfare Rights activists participated in a town hall meeting. Due to this contact, NOW joined the Up and Out of Poverty, Now! Coalition and directed its local chapters to support anti–welfare retrenchment activism in every state and city. This alliance was facilitated by the work of a NOW Black staffer, Faith Evans—the only man to have ever served on the board of the NWRO. Shortly thereafter, Ireland and Marian Kramer were arrested together as they attempted to gain entry into a congressional hearing on welfare reform. In 1994 NOW launched its emergency campaign entitled "As if Women Mattered" as well as its "100 Days of Action" in opposition to the Republican Contract with America. NOW broadened the welfare focus to form a Children Exclusion Coalition, including the Center for Reproductive Law and Policy, the National Black Women's Health Project, the American Civil Liberties Union, and the very powerful American Association for Retired Persons. The NOW Legal and Defense Education Fund in 1995 also convened a summit entitled "The Link between Violence and the Poverty in the Lives of Women and Their Children," at which NWRU leaders made presentations.[58]

Protest Repertoires

Innovating upon old protest repertoires for renewed battles, NWRU and its affiliates took on a bevy of issues. They squatted and appropriated abandoned public or private housing in Detroit and Philadelphia; lobbied against welfare polices in Oakland, California; held a "Who Speaks for the Poor?" conference in July 1994 to announce a new four-part organizing strategy; and generally closed the ranks of the antipoverty front in opposition to welfare measures emanating from the White House and Congress. Many current local and state WROs in states such as New York, Utah, California, Pennsylvania, Louisiana, and Washington as well as welfare activists on college campuses were established during this second protest cycle.[59]

Although press coverage of the 1996 welfare reform act was dominated by congressional deliberations, a wide range of protest activity occurred. Thousands participated in rallies in front of federal buildings, marches to state capitols and in front of the White House, petition drives, teach-ins, sit-ins, pray-ins, and a myriad of other campaigns before the passage of the 1996 Personal Responsibility and Work Opportunity Reconciliation Act.[60] On one occasion in New York, months before the 1996 November presidential election, about one hundred activists confronted Clinton and Gore at the opening of their New York campaign office and yelled "Shame! Shame!" at them and other Democrat loyalists, thus compelling some loyalists tacitly to admit their disapproval of the proposed bill.[61] In the wake of the PRA's passage, a national resistance campaign took off with calls for "fight back campaigns," a "National Day of Action for Welfare/Workfare Justice," mass rallies in Washington, D.C., and even walkouts by welfare department employees.[62]

Collective Identity

Lastly, this new phase of the Welfare Rights Movement clearly drew upon and recreated a collective identity based upon recurring movement themes. One of the NWRU's most outspoken affiliates was the Philadelphia-based Kensington Welfare Rights Union (KWRU), led by Cheri Honokola. Founded in 1991, it vigorously worked to frame itself as the cross-section of many movements for economic and social justice. Along with squatting in abandoned housing to combat homelessness, it established in 1995 what it called the "Underground Railroad Project" to symbolize the fight for all poor people to be free from the "slavery" of workfare. In August 1996 its members marched

125 miles to the Pennsylvania state capitol in Harrisburg to set up "Ridgeville" named after Republican governor Tom Ridge. Its aim was to protest the state's enactment of PRA guidelines. In June and July 1997 KRWU donned black-and-white fatigues, organized one hundred poor people of various cultural backgrounds, and marched for ten days from the Liberty Bell in Philadelphia to the United Nations Building in New York City. Once there, it accused the United States and the PRA of violating the Universal Declaration of Human Rights. And in 1997 it allied with the American Federation of State, County, and Municipal Employees (AFSCME) and the National Union of Hospital and Healthcare Employees to organize workfare workers into unions.[63] The KRWU represents the recombination of many movement themes within the Welfare Rights frame including those of feminism, antiracism, antipoverty, unionism, and human rights.

The Persistence of Welfare Rights Activism

Why was the Welfare Rights Movement able to survive in an era hostile to its chief goal? The reason the Welfare Rights Movement has persisted against the odds is that during the 1970s and 1980s it underwent a painful but successful abeyance process. It was able to preserve and transmit its activist networks, protest repertoires, and collective identity. Each of these elements is essential to any successful social movement. One of the central influences or master frames for the Welfare Rights Movement was the Civil Rights Movement. Although there definitely were differences between them, the two movements and their successors benefited from each other. These movements broadly shared a common set of ideals about redistributive justice and employed a common set of tactics grounded in nonviolent, direct action. Welfare Rights clearly also contributed to and borrowed from antipoverty activists, the Black and White Left, community organizers, feminists, students, and union organizers.

Second, how well has the Welfare Rights Movement been able to use diversionary politics, as I call them? This chapter has demonstrated that precisely because the resources for organizing have decreased and public support for welfare entitlements has nearly evaporated, Welfare Rights activism has had to regroup and reconfigure itself. To push for a national guaranteed income or a massive public works program in this conservative era, as NWRU leaders did at a 1994 congressional hearing, is, of course, a Herculean task. But, clearly, Welfare Rights activists have not simply tried to coincide with public opinion but, rather, have tried to induce a shift in it. Obviously, the diversionary politics of the current Welfare Rights Movement have not diverted or blunted some of the most austere features of what is now the welfare law of the land. The second protest cycle is technically a new protest cycle, but it has not yet generated a disruptive politics or true social change. Unlike the politics around the Family Assistance Program, it has not yet compelled those in power to set or reverse a prescribed course of action. Yet, if these protests are prologue, Welfare Rights and other antipoverty activists may help to generate the oppositional climate needed for progressive reform. In fact, the public battle over welfare came in 2002, when TANF faced reauthorization under a reluctant Bush Administration. To paraphrase Piven and Cloward, Welfare Rights activism, during a lagging economy, could eventually spark the recognition of a new welfare crisis thus inducing at least modest social change.

Lastly, Welfare Rights activism may be on the rise due to increasing alliances, but the jury is still out. Like pro–affirmative action activism, Welfare Rights may enjoy a new appeal among young women, African Americans, Latinos, and other activists who are frustrated with the current antiminority and antipoor climate of the United States. In the summer of 1998 the first meeting of the Black Radical Congress was convened in Chicago with about two thousand persons in attendance. Welfare rights spokeswoman Marian Kramer made appeals to the many youth and college students who assembled to commit themselves to a struggle that is an outgrowth of the 1960s activism many of them venerated. Their ability to convince the younger generation of this ongoing imperative will be another important test of the movement's persistence. Yet for any of us to understand the broad legacy of the Civil Rights Movement requires much more than an analysis of what the mainstream movement organizations have done and are doing. It requires us to reevaluate those whom we consider the key participants of that movement and the ways they have carried the tradition of grassroots activism—the spears if you will—forward.

Ten

Akwasi B. Assensoh and Yvette Alex-Assensoh

Black Political Leadership in the Post–Civil Rights Era

An examination of the history of Black people in America invokes more than 350 years of slavery, overt discrimination, segregation, and institutional racism.[1] It also reveals the indefatigable strength of Black people and their enduring political leadership.[2] At the same time, poverty statistics demonstrate a widening gulf between middle-class and poor Blacks, most of whom are falling daily into a chasm of economic despair and social isolation.[3] Moreover, despite the U.S. Supreme Court's *Brown v. Board of Education* ruling of May 17, 1954, which rendered the tainted notion of separate but equal educational facilities unconstitutional, Black children still languish in educational facilities that are racially homogeneous but desperately unequal to those of Whites.[4] What, in fact, baffles Blacks in twenty-first-century America is that it was the Court's chief justice Earl Warren, in speaking for a unanimous Court, who underscored, among other things, that "separate educational facilities are inherently unequal."[5] The racial situation is more alarming because these poverty and educational trends have worsened despite an ever-increasing number of Black elected officials.[6] These problems, as well as the pervasive conservative tone of the American political scene, have led many Americans to question the efficacy of Black political leadership in the post–Civil Rights era. In the axiomatic title of a recent book, the overwhelming notion in some quarters is that Blacks "have no leaders."[7]

Indeed, current research on Black political leadership, which includes elected officials as well as civil rights and community leaders, has focused on three different types of explanations of the waning efficacy of Black political leadership in the post–Civil Rights era. The first explanation focuses on a host of such external factors as racism, municipal reform structures, and other institutional arrangements that constrain the ability of Black elected officials to govern.[8] The second explanation stresses the failure of political incorporation and coalition building with groups outside the Black community.[9] The third explanation underscores the demobilizing effects of Black political incorporation and incumbency.[10]

Building on the foundations of these three theories of Black political leadership, this chapter offers a fourth explanation for the current state of Black political leadership in the United States. In contrast to the foregoing explanations, this theory focuses on the internal dynamics among Blacks in the United States. We contend that the limitations of Black political leadership are due in part to the lack of resource mobilization and intraracial coalition building on the part of Black political officials. The chapter is divided into four sections. The first three provide a review of extant theories, while the final section specifies how Black political leadership has consistently underutilized various internal community resources and has thereby generally reduced the effectiveness of Black politics in the United States.

Institutional Constraints to Black Political Leadership

The most enduring strands of research on Black elected officials delineate the role of several institutional factors in constraining the ability of Black leaders to affect policies that would benefit the Black masses. Some aspects of the literature have focused on the late suffrage, whereby Blacks were delayed in their ability to participate fully in electoral politics.[11] Others highlighted the issues of post-reform structures in municipal elections, which made it difficult for African Americans mayors to govern.[12] Others have emphasized the machinations as well as the manipulation of the party system, which screen Black candidates from the process and make it difficult for Black elected officials to pass legislation that is beneficial to their constituents.[13] With the passage of the 1965 Voting Rights Act as well as the increasing number of Black elected officials, the prevailing scholarship on Black politicians has moved from a focus on institutional impediments to an assessment of the role of political incorporation in elevating the political as well as socioeconomic status of Blacks.

Black Elected Leadership: The Failure of Political Incorporation and Coalition Building

Although votes are needed to elect Blacks to public office, the ability of elected officials to become politically incorporated—to become an integral part of the policy-making coalition—is most important. For example, the first term of the late mayor Harold Washington of Chicago was deemed virtually ineffective by both critics and even some of his supporters because of the lack of political incorporation.[14] During his second term majority support from the city council and some bureaucratic agencies provided him with the resources necessary to win crucial policy battles that mattered to his constituents. As members of such policy-making coalitions, incorporated African American leaders at the municipal, state, and national levels are able to influence the policy-making agenda.

Students of Black political leadership have noted that, while political incorporation and coalition building have some symbolic benefits, the tangible and substantive benefits of such political strategies are minimal at best. Robert C. Smith, in his analysis of Black politics since 1965, has argued that Black leaders and their organizations have become ineffective in improving the socioeconomic status of the masses of Black people in the United States. Furthermore, Smith contends that Black political leadership has become irrelevant to the structure of the larger political system. Instead of emphasizing strategies of political incorporation and coalition building, he argues, Black leadership should have focused on nationalist strategies that emphasized the importance of self-help and group solidarity.[15]

Black Political Leadership: The Failure of Incumbency and the Need for Mobilization

According to David Mayhew, all politicians are motivated by the desire to win elections.[16] Therefore, elected political actors legislate, govern, and interact with constituents in ways that maximize the likelihood of winning their respective reelections. Some scholars of Black politics have also argued that the desire to win subsequent elections forces Black elected officials to forsake their agenda in support of issues that appeal to middle-class and White voters. Some students of urban politics have noted that Black mayors have abandoned a reform agenda in search of a color-blind politics that is more appealing to White, middle-class voters. In this sense incumbency does not represent the crystallization of a reformist agenda but, rather, capitulation to mainstream interests. In fact, much of the recent scholarship on Black mayors has emphasized the impact of de-racialization as well as coalition building in demobilizing the Black reformist agenda.[17] In contrast to Smith, who has promoted self-help/self-reliance tactics as the best route to reform, these scholars have argued that Black political officials should make better use of the American political system and its structures instead of totally abandoning it.[18] For these intellectuals the possibility of a meaningful inclusion exists.

The foregoing theories of Black elected leadership—which emphasize structural impediments, the failure of political incorporation, and demobilization—have improved our understanding of external factors. At the same time, there has been inadequate attention to internal factors. It is our contention that the ineffectiveness of Black leaders in dealing with a host of social, economic, and political problems stems from two-related factors. First, Black elected officials erroneously conceive of the Black community as having homogeneous interest and policy dispositions. Second, Black leaders underutilize the disparate resources among Blacks.

The Myth of Homogeneity and the Underutilization of Political Resources

It is, indeed, undeniable that Black political officials continue to define the Black community in ways that limit and mask the heterogeneity and different interests within its ranks. Such definitions were acceptable prior to the 1960s, when Blacks of all socioeconomic and religious backgrounds felt that they faced a common enemy and that they were involved in the struggle against overt racial discrimination in the United States. Liberal housing laws, affirmative action policies, and increases in education among Blacks have led, however, to an expansion of the Black middle class.

No longer inhibited by the strict moral codes and norms of the Black church, many Blacks are joining the ranks of other Americans in loudly proclaiming their sexual preference. Homosexual Blacks have clamored for their rights through the work of intellectuals and advocacy organizations. Additionally, while the southern Black Belt was once viewed as the geographic home of Black America, Blacks have dispersed and settled in the West, Midwest, and Northeast as well. Moreover, immigration laws have led to the emigration of Blacks from African and Caribbean countries who tend to be ideologically diverse. Blacks from foreign countries may sometimes give up their original citizenship for naturalization in the United States, yet they nevertheless constitute a group that is different culturally and linguistically from mainstream Black America. Therefore, their interests, as diverse as they may be, must be addressed.

Increasingly, diversity is also apparent in the American political party system. Although Blacks initially aligned themselves with the Republican Party, the Hayes Compromise of 1877 as well as subsequent racially hostile treatment by the Republican Party, coupled with the political enticement of the Democratic Party, led the majority of Blacks to identify with the Democrats. Several proscriptions of the 1800s made it very difficult for Blacks to make a living. Between 1805 and 1831 such states as Maryland, Georgia, and North Carolina had passed a variety of prohibiting laws, including outright political disenfranchisement of Blacks under conservative Republican leadership.[19] There has been a resurgence, however, of very influential Blacks who have recently aligned themselves with the Republican Party.

Rarely do Black elected and nonelected leaders reach out to minority groups within the Black community. Instead, immigrants, homosexuals, Republicans, and Black immigrants are marginalized. By failing to incorporate these "minorities" into the so-called mainstream Black agenda, Black political leaders have missed an opportunity to tap the political, economic, and social resources of these groups for the larger quest of Black political empowerment. Consequently, while Reed notes the structural factors that facilitate diversity, we contend that many Blacks have been demobilized by the lack of attention and policy representation on the part of Black elected leaders. In this context Black political leaders have made ineffective use of important resources within the Black community which could buttress their respective individual political agendas.

Furthermore, the Black community has undergone several important changes over the last two decades. Consequently, theories of Black political leadership must stress not only the importance of external factors but also internal forces that limit the effectiveness of Black political leaders. Today's Blacks are compelled by a variety of centrifugal forces that challenge the notion that racial factors supersede every other factor in determining political allegiance and ideology.[20] Specifically, diversity has occurred most prominently along social, economic, and political fronts.

Social Heterogeneity

Social heterogeneity among Blacks is evident in religious identification, sexual orientation, and ethnicity.[21] In the midst of the hectic years of the American Civil Rights Movement, the Black Protestant church assumed a major role in mobilizing and organizing resources for the advancement of the Black political agenda. Most prominent among them was the Baptist church, which also stressed the importance of family values and leveled strict admonishments against sexual immorality. As the Civil Rights Movement was transformed from the protest to the electoral politics phase, the role of the church was eclipsed by the role of politicians and political institutions. Subsequent challenges against the overarching role of religion in educational and governmental affairs led Americans of all racial backgrounds to reassess the role of the church in their lives.

Meanwhile, the diminishing role of the Black Protestant church has been accompanied by an increase in the popularity of Islam, especially among working-class and poor urban Blacks. The growing prominence of Islam as well as the increasing acceptance of the leadership of Minister Louis Farrakhan in the

Black community was highlighted in 1995 when Farrakhan's Nation of Islam called for and led an overwhelmingly successful day of atonement for Black men, which was dubbed the "Million Man March," in Washington, D.C.[22] The popularity of Islam as well as the rise of other types of religious affiliations of Blacks has led to greater religious heterogeneity. This heterogeneity will likely have two results. First, since the Black Baptist church has served as a direct source of Black political leadership—producing leaders such as the Rev. Dr. Martin Luther King Jr., Rev. Adam Clayton Powell, Rev. Al Sharpton, and Rev. Jesse Jackson—the emergence of different types of religious institutions might facilitate the rise of leaders with more radical political ideologies such as Minister Farrakhan.

Second, the influence of the Black church has also decreased in terms of the ability of the church to set the moral standard for the Black community. With an increasing number of Blacks proclaiming their homosexuality, for example, many Black political officials have found themselves in a precarious situation. The religious affiliation of Black leaders, on the one hand, coupled with their commitment to civil liberties, on the other hand, has frequently resulted in vague and ambiguous positions by Black leaders on issues of homosexual rights as they affect Blacks, at a time when major Black leaders—including Dr. King, Ralph Abernathy, and Rev. Henry Lyons—have been accused of sexual indiscretions.[23] To many people this is a double standard that does not augur well for the credibility of Black political leadership in the United States.

In addition to the diversity within the Black community on issues of religion and sexual orientation, there is also increasing ethnic diversity. As already stated, the liberal immigration laws of the late 1960s enabled Blacks from many African and Caribbean nations to come to the United States and subsequently become citizens through naturalization. Compared with Blacks who were born in the United States, Africans and their Caribbean counterparts (often referred to as West Indians) are noted for their business acumen and high academic attainment as well as professional productivity. In fact, a recent article in the *Economist* noted that, among both White and nonwhite immigrants, Africans often hold the highest educational credentials of any immigrant group in the United States. Yet very little attention is devoted to African-related issues on the part of Black elected leaders in the United States, even though, by doing so, they are ignoring a possible base of individuals who could contribute money and other resources to their political campaigns in a way that economically successful Asian and Latino immigrants are doing for other candidates.

This lack of representation by Black political leaders of the African and West Indian communities is especially visible in the current debate about immigration laws. By defining Black interests in terms of poor Blacks in urban areas and, therefore, attempting to restrict it and protect the so-called jobs of urban Blacks, Black political officials have alienated the growing African and West Indian populations, for which immigration is an important issue.

Finally, the social heterogeneity of the Black community is also evident in terms of gender differences. The political participation literature has consistently demonstrated that Black women participate in politics more than Black men. Yet social statistical figures have noted that Black women are more likely to receive governmental welfare benefits and become impoverished, while Black men are more likely to be jobless and connected with the criminal justice system. The differences are important and salient, but political leaders have failed to address gender differences, choosing instead to focus on the so-called larger issue of race.

When racial and gender factors conflict, Black political leaders have notoriously chosen to ignore the concerns of women as evinced by the Clarence Thomas–Anita Hill hearing debacle as well as the Mike Tyson rape case, in which many Black leaders gathered and prayed for Mike Tyson. Without understanding the gender dynamics of these problems, Black political leaders will continue to demobilize and alienate precious gender resources, which are critical to the overall equation of Black political leadership and the subsequent empowerment of the poor.

Economic Heterogeneity

Critics of political incorporation and coalition-building strategies have often argued that Black political officials have become irrelevant in dealing with the economic problems of the Black community. Proponents of this view, however, have regularly failed to take into account the fact that Blacks fall into a variety of economic categories, especially since there has been a steady and increasing middle class among Blacks.[24] Researchers have commented on the adept use of affirmative action requirements by Black mayors to benefit and expand the Black middle class in various municipal areas.[25] At the same time, many more Blacks in the United States have been beleaguered by economic marginalization that is compounded by the globalization of the urban economy, the bifurcation of the service economy, and the suburbanization of low-skilled jobs.[26] These factors have led to the growth of concentrated poverty neighborhoods, in which a minimum of 40 percent of the residents fall below the poverty line. Residence in such neighborhoods exacerbates the problems of individual poverty by making it impossible for the affected poor to access job networks, which are necessary for socioeconomic mobility. Moreover, the concentration of impoverishment very often leads to crime and other forms of social deviance which, in turn, intensify the problems of social and spatial isolation experienced by neighborhood residents.

Black political leadership has been ineffective in addressing the economic agenda, and this is particularly so as it has not stressed the bimodal economic experiences of Blacks in the United States. When addressing economic issues, Black political leaders frequently emphasize concerns of the middle class. The perennial debate about affirmative action as well as the recent boycotts of some American corporations by rank-and-file Blacks have helped direct the focus on the middle class. After all, most poor Blacks lack the skills and educational credentials either to qualify for affirmative action positions and benefits or to gain entry into many well-paying corporate jobs. Sadly, by abandoning the agenda of economic reform, Black political leaders would invariably facilitate the growth of a widening gap between the poor and middle-class Blacks in the United States.

Political Heterogeneity

Black politics has always been characterized by a diversity of approaches to political power. Even before Blacks were granted the franchise, Booker T. Washington of Tuskegee Normal School for Colored Teachers and W. E. B. Du Bois of the NAACP debated the efficacy of various strategies of Black upliftment. The differences have remained in today's era of Black politics, but the medium for those differences have changed. In many respects political heterogeneity among Blacks is most evident along lines of partisan identification. A majority of Blacks identify themselves as Democrats, although the level of commitment to that party varies widely among Blacks as a whole.[27] In addition, a small but increasing proportion of Blacks have aligned themselves with the Republican Party. While there are differences among many Black Republicans, they continue to argue that Blacks should utilize self-help and self-reliant strategies and thereby cease to rely on governmental programs and benefits, which they feel have induced perpetual dependence.

In large measure the Black political leadership has looked askance at other Black leaders who continue to identify as Republicans. The nomination of Clarence Thomas as a Supreme Court justice, for example, caused great dissension within the Black community. Many Blacks argued that Justice Thomas's appointment, coming from conservative President George Bush, would not be beneficial to the Black community. These issues, within the context of conservative politics, were recently revisited when Congressman J. C. Watts, a rising star in ranks of the Republican Party, who is also a Black minister from Oklahoma, was quoted in *Jet* magazine as calling the Rev. Jesse Jackson "a poverty pimp."[28] Other disputes between Black Republican and

Democratic leaders have occurred at the congressional level, as when Connecticut Black Republican congressman Gary Franks was initially denied membership in the Congressional Black Caucus, which assembles and often coordinates the activities of Black members of Congress.

Conclusion

This discussion suggests that students of Black politics in general, and Black political leaders in particular, need to focus on a concept of Black political interest which is more inclusive than the current definition, which either alienates or outrightly excludes homosexuals, non-Protestants, Black immigrants, Republicans, and women. Such an inclusive definition of Black aspirations and political interests may allow Black leaders to mobilize resources among all Blacks, instead of focusing on a few interests while alienating and demobilizing others.

Heretofore, Black political leadership—elected as well as unelected—in the United States has relied heavily on narrowly constructed racial appeals to mobilize Blacks. Recent critiques have contended that Black political leaders have become ineffective in addressing the needs of an increasingly diverse and complex Black community. We have argued that current Black political leadership, as it is constituted, suffers from an inability to mobilize the diverse aspects of the post–1960s Black community effectively. By defining itself too narrowly, Black political leadership has alienated and demobilized segments of the African American population.

Coalition building with groups outside the Black community will not be effective until Black political leaders see the wisdom of addressing the internal factions that exist among African Americans. In our opinion, no brand of radical politics would pay off without proper organization and deliberate efforts to facilitate an inclusive politics for all Blacks in America.

Eleven

Valerie C. Johnson

Where Do We Go from Here?

Facing the Challenges of the Post–Civil Rights Era

Answering those who asked him to help Cleveland's poor in the first decade of the twentieth century, the mayor, Tom Johnson, said that while it was a noble thing to help drowning people out of the river, it might be more useful to "go upstream . . . to see who is pushing the people in."
—William W. Goldsmith

As a critique of Black politics in the post–Civil Rights era, the preceding chapters address numerous factors that challenge the effectiveness of Black political organizations. Key to this assessment is the general acknowledgment that Black political organizations and institutions have been constrained in their ability to promote lasting solutions to the problems affecting Black people, particularly the urban poor. As a result, despite the major successes of the Civil Rights Movement (the Civil Rights Act of 1964 and the Voting Rights Act of 1965), many Blacks face serious difficulties. An examination of any socioeconomic indicator would confirm this conclusion.

In 1967 the ratio of Black to White median family income was 0.59. In 1990, despite the growth of the Black middle class, the ratio had declined to 0.58. In 1998, 28 percent of Black families had incomes over $50,000, compared to 52 percent of White families. The median home value for Blacks was $50,700 in 1990, compared to $80,200 for Whites. In 1999 the poverty rate of Blacks was 23.6 percent and 7.7 percent for Whites. Although 12.3 percent of the population, Blacks accounted for 26.5 percent of those in poverty in 1996. The Black infant mortality rate is 15.2 deaths per 1,000 live births and 6.3 for Whites. In 1998, 37 percent of Black children lived in poverty, compared to 11 percent of

White children. On the opposite end of the spectrum, 26.4 percent of the Black elderly lived below the poverty line, compared to 8 percent of White elderly people. Twenty-one percent of Blacks do not have health insurance, compared to 11.6 percent of Whites. Fifty-one percent of U.S. prison and jail inmates are Black. There is a 10.3 percent disparity between Black and White high school graduation rates and a 10.7 percent disparity between Black and White college graduation rates. And, even when holding for region and job experience, academic degrees do not pay as well for Blacks and other minorities as they do for Whites. The differential between the average incomes of Black and White males with a bachelor's degree is $19,295. For professional degrees the disparity increases to $32,606. Although life chances have increased for all Americans, Blacks continue to lag behind, particularly the Black poor.

Although the primary objective of the Civil Rights Movement was to eliminate racial discrimination and socioeconomic inequality, solutions appear elusive at best. While Black political organizations in the post–Civil Rights Era face a number of obstacles, their limited success in addressing these issues may be more the result of their unwillingness to go upstream—to attack the more resistant and root causes of racial and class inequality. This chapter examines Black issue articulation in the post–Civil Rights era by contrasting the strategies of mainstream Black political organizations and Black nationalists and radical organizations and leaders, the dominance of strategies promoted by mainstream Black political organizations, and the effect of these strategies on the lives of Blacks. Lastly, this chapter sets forth some suggestions on how Black political organizations and institutions may revive and renew their commitment to eliminating racial and socioeconomic inequality. The basic argument is that the mainstream (moderate reformist) Black political organizations presented in the preceding chapters have largely promoted the agenda of the Black middle class and in the process have demobilized its largest constituency—the Black poor—by failing to address the fundamental factors associated with racial and socioeconomic inequality. Chief among these factors is the nexus between racism and capitalism.

Black Issue Articulation in the Post–Civil Rights Era

The National Black Political Assembly (the Gary Convention), held in Gary, Indiana, March 10–11, 1972, stands as the earliest post–Civil Rights era attempt at Black unity and reconciliation nationally. Prior to the Gary Convention Black nationalist leaders and organizations had long soured on the efficacy of integration as a solution to the problems besieging Blacks. On the opposite end of the spectrum from the mainstream Black political organizations, Black nationalists "stressed the nexus of racism and capitalism, advocated coalitions with other oppressed peoples, and attacked U.S. imperialism abroad."[1]

The main goals of the convention were to develop a strategy for mobilizing Black political power nationally, agree on an outline for a national Black political agenda, and unify previously disunified factions within the Black electorate. Three thousand delegates and six thousand participants attended the convention from forty-four states, representing a cross-section of Black America which included members of the Congressional Black Caucus (CBC), state and local elected officials, leaders of the mainstream Black political organizations, and grassroots and Black nationalist leaders. Of all the diverse ideas and strategies represented at the convention, the basic agreement of delegates and participants can be summed up in the following excerpts of the Gary Declaration:

> The crises we face as Black people are the crises of the entire society. They go deep, to the very bones and marrow, to the essential nature of America's economic, political and cultural systems. They are the natural end product of a society built on the twin foundations of white racism and white capitalism.
>
> A Black political convention, indeed all truly Black politics must begin from this truth: The American system does not work for the masses of our people, and it cannot be made to work without radical fundamental change. (Indeed, this system does not really work in favor of the humanity of anyone in America.) [2]

Although chiefly aimed at Blacks, the convention sought to become a vanguard of other oppressed and disenchanted groups. This sentiment is best expressed in the remarks of Gary, Indiana, mayor, Richard Hatcher, a chief organizer of the convention: "And when, and if, we form a third political movement, we shall take with us Chicanos, Puerto Ricans, Orientals, a wonderful kaleidoscope of colors. And that is not all. We shall also take with us the best of white America. We shall take with us many a white youth nauseated by the corrupt values rotting the innards of this society, many a white intellectual . . . many of the white poor, and many of the white working class, too."[3]

Before the convention adjourned, the level of unity present at the beginning of the conference had begun to fall apart. As Lucius Barker, Mack H. Jones, and Katherine Tate note, participants had three fundamental differences—ideological, strategic, and tactical—and differences in their bases of support. Thus, the failure to establish the National Black Assembly can be found in the incompatible tendencies of three forces: (1) nationalist and integrationist; (2) those who advocated working within the two-party system (members of the Congressional Black Caucus) and those desiring an independent

Black political party; and (3) those committed to reformist strategies (NAACP) and revolutionary ideas (the Congress of African People). As Barker, Jones, and Tate argue, "in the absence of such a national organization, efforts toward national Black political empowerment continued to evolve around the politics of presidential elections."[4]

In the period following the Gary Convention the dominance of mainstream Black political organizations became exceedingly clear as the nationalist agenda began to diminish as a visible and viable option.[5] The first manifestations were Representative William Clay, Walter Fauntroy, and Rev. Jesse Jackson's endorsement of George McGovern; Charles Evers and Cleveland politician Arnold Pickney's endorsement of Hubert Humphrey as Democratic Party presidential nominees; and the quick distancing of the nation's Black elected officials from then Black nationalist Amiri Baraka.[6] Another manifestation was the salience of increasing Black political representation and integration as strategies within the Black community. Without unity among the Black leadership, strategies focusing on the structure of the American economy and its convergence with racism were lost in the mix of politics as usual.

In 1972 McGovern received 87 percent of the Black vote in the general election, which constituted 21 percent of the total Democratic Party vote. Although Black support for McGovern was considerably lower than for Humphrey in 1968 (97 percent), it was a greater share of the total Democratic vote, which was 18 percent in 1968 and 12 percent in 1964, when Johnson won 99 percent of the Black vote. Thus, despite discussion about the need to develop alternatives to the two-party system at the Gary Convention, Blacks, led by mainstream Black political organizations and leaders, continued to provide support to the existing parties, particularly for the Democratic Party. The next major attempt at a national Black political agenda arose on the heels of growing disenchantment among Blacks over the policies of Ronald Reagan's presidential administrations. Reagan's policies had practically turned Black communities across the nation into Black poverty zones. The poverty rate among Blacks rose from 32.5 percent to 35.7 percent, representing an addition of 1.3 million people to the poverty rolls.[7]

Amid all the pain the "Cosby Show" became a popular hit among Blacks and Whites alike, promoting the view that racial inequality had vanished; Jesse Jackson ran twice for the presidency; and the number of Black elected officials increased from 4,900 in 1980 to 7,226 in 1989. Against this backdrop the Black rank-and-file met in New Orleans in April 1989 for the African American Summit.

In a matter of seventeen years the predominant theme among Blacks had changed from "Unity without Uniformity" (at the Gary Convention) to "Self

Help" (at the African American Summit). Although it was not as well attended as the Gary Convention, the one thousand Summit participants represented a diverse group. Key Black leaders in attendance included Rev. Jesse Jackson, Minister Louis Farrakhan, Communist Party leader Angela Davis, Coretta Scott King, Democratic Party chairman Ron Brown, and former Gary, Indiana, mayor Richard Hatcher. Visibly absent were twenty-one of twenty-four Black members of Congress, Washington mayor Marion Barry, Atlanta mayor Andrew Young, Philadelphia mayor W. Wilson Goode, NAACP executive director Benjamin Hooks, and Republican leader Fred Brown of New York, who boycotted the event.

Chief among the proposals presented were calls for reparations, a requirement that Black history be taught in public schools, creation of minority joint ventures to build capital in Black communities, and the establishment of a national think-tank to guide a national war on drugs. If the Gary Convention was a failed but clear denunciation of American institutions and capitalism, the summit represented the dominion of Black reformist and inclusionist politics, despite the absence of the majority of the Congressional Black Caucus, whose members had largely avoided the event as a result of Farrakhan's leading role.

The resonance of the self-help theme is troubling at best. Amid consistent appeals for governmental support on a range of issues affecting the Black poor, Black self-help is a clear enunciation of the government's inability to accommodate them through the routine mechanisms of government—something that all Americans, rich and middle class alike, have become dependent upon. As Reed argues, endorsement of the self-help agenda by Black elected officials "amounts to an admission of failure, an acknowledgement that the problems afflicting their constituents are indeed beyond the scope of the institutional apparatus under their control, that Black officials are in fact powerless to provide services to inner-city citizens effectively through those institutions."[8] The salience of the Black self-help theme can be seen in President George W. Bush's proposals to channel community resources to Black churches and its wide embrace by key Black ministers across the country. To any other organized interest in the country—for example, the Israeli lobby or the corporate class—self-help proposals would be summarily dismissed as ludicrous.

Similar to the period after the Gary Convention, the postconference strategies of Black political organizations and leaders at the African American Summit focused on the politics of presidential elections, with Blacks giving Democratic Party nominee Bill Clinton 82 percent of their vote in 1992 (which represented 15 percent of the 43 percent of the electorate that elected Clinton). In 1996 Blacks gave Clinton 84 percent and in 2000 gave Gore 86 percent of their vote.

The establishment of the Black Radical Congress (BRC), June 19–21, 1998, in Chicago on the campus of the University of Illinois at Chicago, was the last major, but by no means only, call for unified Black political action. Preconference literature issued a call to convene in order to establish a "center without walls for transformative politics that will focus on the conditions of Black working and poor people."[9] Similar to the 1972 Gary Convention manifesto, the Black Radical Congress's Agenda for the 21st Century states: "Black people face a deep crisis. Finding a way out of this mess requires new thinking, new vision, and a deep spirit of resistance. We need a new movement of Black radicalism. . . . We know that America's capitalist economy has completely failed us. Every day more of us are unemployed and imprisoned, homeless and hungry."[10] Nearly thirty years later, Black radical leaders are revisiting the nexus of racism and capitalism as a focal point of the struggle toward racial and economic equality—a nexus that had not been adequately addressed among mainstream Black political organizations. The Black Radical Congress called on diverse tendencies within Black radicalism—including socialism, revolutionary nationalism, and feminism—in opposition to all forms of oppression, "including class exploitation, racism, patriarchy, homophobia, anti-immigration prejudice and imperialism."[11] Some common concerns set forth in the BRC's Principles of Unity include:

—The technological revolution and capitalist globalization have changed the economy, labor force and class formations that need to inform our analysis and strategies. The increased class polarization created by these developments demand that we, as Black radicals, ally ourselves with the most oppressed sectors of our communities and society.
—Gender and sexuality can no longer be viewed solely as personal issues but must be a basic part of our analyses, politics and struggles.
—We reject racial and biological determinism, Black patriarchy and Black capitalism as solutions to problems facing Black people.
—We cannot limit ourselves to electoral politics—we must identify multiple sites of struggle.

Although the BRC maintains that its agenda is not an intention to replace or displace existing organizations, parties, or campaigns, it was a clear rejection of business as usual and the strategies and tactics of mainstream Black political organizations. One major difference between the BRC's agenda and previous calls for unified Black political action was the inclusion of gays and feminists. As Todd Shaw's chapter on the welfare movement notes, the impasse between the largely female-dominated welfare movement and Martin Luther King and the SCLC was "that the southern ministerial patriarchy . . . made them fearful of domineering women as leaders." The exclusion of feminists and gays amounts to what Assensoh and Assensoh refer to as demobilization of key elements in the Black community.

The problems besieging Black women—the feminization of poverty and the rise in single female–headed households—cry out for attention, now more than ever before. Currently, 70 percent of Black children are born out of wedlock (compared to 19 percent in 1940), and only 36 percent of Black children live in two-parent households. Although slavery has often been advanced as the source of Black family dissolution, from 1840 to 1940 Blacks had a marriage rate slightly higher than Whites. In 1950, 64 percent of Black males fifteen years of age and older were married, compared to 41 percent today.[12] As a result of the large proportion of out of wedlock births, poverty is highest among Black single female–headed households. In 1999, 41 percent of Black female–headed households lived in poverty, compared to 19.8 percent of White female–headed households.

The historical exclusion of significant gender-related issues speaks to the sexist orientations of Black political organizations in both the pre- and post–Civil Rights Era. It also addresses the extent to which Black political organizations and leaders purport to represent a phantom monolithic Black community in order to promote their own agenda. As Reed argues, the "Black community" "is a reification that at most expresses the success of some interest networks in articulating their interpretations and programs and asserting them in the name of the group."[13] Therefore, what are often presented as "Black interests" are often the distinct interests of a segment of the African American community—those who have been most successful in articulating their claims, namely, the Black middle class.

Thus far, while promising, the BRC has more generally followed the tactics of other radical and mainstream Black political organizations—chasing the fire truck—speaking out against egregious acts while not offering substantive strategies. Like the mainstream Black political organizations, the BRC has faced criticism for excluding sectors of the Black community, in this case moderate Black leaders who have worked within the Democratic Party apparatus. Noted scholar Ronald Walters, for example, criticized the BRC for its inability to transcend "the petty ideological disputes of the 1960s and 1970s that have kept [the Black] community divided." He argues that the test of the BRC's effectiveness will be in its ability to influence the grassroots level.[14]

An example of the growing challenge in reaching the grassroots is the BRC's use of the Internet as its main channel of communication. Given the digital divide in the Black community, BRC discussion and mobilization efforts may in fact be akin to preaching to the choir. Another challenge facing the BRC, as in the case of the mainstream organizations, is the lack of a "clear chain of command or a well-defined operating structure . . . and its paltry revenue flow."[15] To its credit the BRC has, since its inception, effectively organized local chapters in New York, Pittsburgh, Baltimore, Chicago, St. Louis, and Minneapolis and has been vocal on issues facing Blacks in other cities.

The Efficacy of Strategies Promoted by Mainstream Black Political Organizations

By far the two most salient issues promoted by mainstream Black political organizations in the post–Civil Rights Era have been increased Black representation and integration. In the area of representation Blacks have made considerable progress in electing Black candidates. In 1970 there were 1,469 Black elected officials; by 1998 that figure had grown to 8,868.[16] Nonetheless, this figure represented only 1.7 percent of all elected officials, most of whom were elected to county and municipal offices.[17] The largest increase in Black representation, ironically, followed the major call for unity and creation of a Black political agenda. In the four years after the Gary Convention (1972–1976) the number of Black officials increased by 115 percent, compared to 24 percent during the 1976–1980 period. The increase attests to the preeminence of the Black political organizational shift from protest to politics and the weakness of the nationalist trend.

Strategies that have promoted integration have largely been a failure. The reported decline of racist attitudes among Whites is overrated, considering that their proximity to Blacks has widened during the post–Civil Rights Era. Whites have indicated their real views with their hats—they have put them on and fled to the suburbs. As a result Blacks, more than any other minority group, are likely to live in segregated communities, so much so that Black living patterns have been referred to as "hyper-segregation."[18]

Segregated living has had a tremendous impact on the life chances of Blacks as jobs have followed the White middle class to the suburbs. In the 1990s, for example, 87 percent of new entry-level unskilled jobs were created in the suburbs.[19] Added to the resegregation of public schools, the integration experiment has largely spelled doom for Blacks. According to a July 2001 study by Gary Orfield, codirector of the Civil Rights Project at Harvard University, 70 percent of Black children nationwide attended predominantly minority schools during the 1998–99 school year. This figure marks an increase from 66 percent in the 1991–92 school year and 63 percent in the 1980–81 school year.[20]

Integration, like other strategies supported by mainstream Black political organizations, address a tendency to seek Band-Aid solutions to the problems facing a diverse Black community. Other salient issues during the post–Civil Rights Era include economic integration and affirmative action and welfare policies. These policies also point to the limited focus of mainstream Black political organizations. Karin Stanford's chapter on Reverend Jackson and the Rainbow/PUSH Coalition highlights the dominance of the Black middle-class agenda. In many respects the justification for Black inclusion into the corporate economy resembles Reagan's trickle-down policies of the 1980s. Again, the poor must wait for the ascension of the affluent and middle classes before their needs are met.

As in the general population, considerable class inequality exists within the Black community. According to Harvard professor William Julius Wilson, the richest one-fifth of African Americans now earn a record 50 percent of the total income of the Black community. The gap between rich and poor is widening faster in the Black community than in the White community, where it is also at record levels.[21]

Needless to say, Black capitalism does little to resolve capitalism's failure to provide economic opportunity to all Americans. In 1987 Black men between the ages of twenty-five and thirty-four were the first to experience a lower median income than their fathers' generation. By 1997 their income was still less than their fathers' generation. Conversely, the income of Black women in this age group has been consistently higher than that of their mothers.[22] Further, the unprecedented growth of the Black middle class has done little to abate racial inequality in corporate America, particularly for Black men. In 1999, 19 percent of Black men were employed in managerial and professional specialty occupations, compared to 32 percent of White men. And, despite Jesse Jackson's thirty-year battle to increase the proportion of Blacks in professional positions, Blacks represent 3.2 percent of all people occupying positions in the marketing, advertising, and public relations fields, compared to 94 percent of Whites. The proportions were slightly higher between Blacks and Whites in the financial manager category, at 4.7 and 91 percent, respectively.[23]

Economic disparity also extended to the business arena. In 1997, the latest year for which data are available, Black businesses totaled 823,500, employed 718,300 people, and generated $71.2 billion in revenues. Although seemingly impressive, businesses owned by Blacks made up 4 percent of the 20.8 million businesses in the nation and 0.4 percent of the $18.6 trillion in receipts for all businesses. Sole proprietorships—unincorporated businesses owned by individuals—made up the largest proportion of Black-owned firms, at 90 percent. About half of all Black businesses (49 percent) had receipts under $10,000, 23 percent had receipts between $10,000 and $25,000, and about 1 percent had receipts of $1 million or more. African American firms averaged $86,500 in receipts, compared to $410,600 for all U.S. firms.[24] What is most striking about these figures, however, is the disparity between the proportions of businesses to receipts (4 to 0.4 percent). Black businesses are clearly not capturing their fair share of the market.

The salience of affirmative action and welfare policy points to a critical problem in the alliance between mainstream Black political organizations and the Democratic Party. Despite the fact that Blacks have on average given Democrats more than 90 percent of their vote since the 1960s, the largest erosion in affirmative action and the total revamping of welfare occurred during the Clinton Administration. As the chapters by Shaw and Smith illustrate, Black political organizations and leaders mobilized heavily for Clinton in 1996, the year that he signed welfare legislation limiting welfare to a total of five years. Welfare reform, and by extension workfare, coupled with limited potential to obtain a job with a living wage, has turned the poor into the working poor. The Democratic Party as the party of the little guy is a thing of a bygone era.

The fact that Clinton could get elected with strong Black support (15 percent of the total Democratic Party vote) again speaks to Black political organizations and leaders' limited leverage on issues facing a large proportion of the Black population. As it regards affirmative action, Clinton's "mend it, don't end it" policy, illuminates the paucity of support for issues high on the Black community's agenda, despite continuing racial inequality in the business and economic realm. It also highlights the extent to which Black political organizations and leaders seemingly lack an insult level. The Black community has been consistently pushed in the river, as the numbers of Black elected officials have increased and Black leaders have increasingly assumed insider positions within Democratic Party ranks.

In the post–Civil Rights era there has been a growing divide between the positions that Black political organizations take and the needs of the Black community, particularly the needs of the poor. As Barker, Jones, and Tate note, while the historical relationship between Blacks and the Republican Party can be described as "freedom, betrayal, and abandonment," Blacks' relationship with the Democratic Party can nonetheless be described as "loyalty and neglect."[25]

Black association with the Democratic Party has been antithetical to the interests of Black people. Although representing the lesser of two evils, the Democratic Party does not and will never be fundamentally different from the Republican Party. Both support representative democracy and capitalism. When one considers the increase of Black political representation amid the hostile effects of de-industrialization and globalization on the life chances of Blacks, neither is a friend to the Black community. Electoral politics in the post–Civil

Rights era is centrist politics. Both parties converge toward the middle in the hopes of increasing their chance of winning and, in the case of the Democratic Party, shifting their constituency as the country has moved further to the right. Despite the fact that Black political organizations and leaders have shifted their strategy from protest to politics, it is clear that they have met with little success. And given the growing socioeconomic divide within the Black community, neither does the strategic shift from politics to economics hold much promise of success.

The key to economic and racial equality in the twenty-first century will no doubt rest in Black political organizations' ability to do something different. They might begin by going upstream to determine what is pushing Black people in the water. Until the realities of institutionalized racism and economic inequality are crystal clear, the Black community will likely receive more of the same. At least, if nothing more, Black political organizations can promote a nationwide dialogue about capitalism and class inequality, an issue that impacts the lives of the majority of Americans.

Where Do We Go from Here?

The Herculean task of attacking the forces of capitalism has been a challenge to mainstream and radical Black political organizations alike. The implementation of a bottom-up strategy has been largely elusive. As the preceding chapters have illustrated, Black political organizations have been challenged by a number of constraints. The chief constraint of the mainstream organizations has been their lack of will to embrace the needs of a diverse Black population.

Other constraints, as the chapters by Robert Smith and Charles Jones on the NAACP and CORE illustrate, include resource mobilization, a lack of salience on the issue of race within the general population, the ambiguous quality of racism, and Republican Party control of the presidency and the Congress. Despite constraints, the condition of Blacks necessitates that Black political organizations begin the process of carving out a new direction. The first step in this process may be to mend broken relationships between Black political organizations and leaders.

Can We All Just Get Along?

The preceding examination of Black issue articulation illuminates the tendency toward internecine warfare among Black political organizations and leaders. This in turn has demobilized significant forces within the Black community and diminished the potential leverage that Blacks have within the political system. The key to solving this dilemma is a clear enunciation of the factors that negatively impact the lives of Blacks. Racial and socioeconomic inequality impacts all sectors of the Black community, albeit to different degrees. Once a common enemy is recognized, all forces within the community must be galvanized to do that which it is best equipped to do. Needless to say, given the gravity of the problem, there is a role for all sectors of the Black community. The chief objective is to utilize the resources that are available to educate the demobilized and disconnected on the problems affecting the Black community at large. This is where the real work must begin.

Brown's chapter on the political involvement of the Black church illustrates a shift away from the liberation theology that was prevalent in the Civil Rights era. Nonetheless, there are Black religious leaders who have managed to retain and build large congregations based on their ability to relate to the needs of people. The examples are numerous. Mobilizing such leaders with the express purpose of reaching out to and training other ministers on the utility of a liberation theology, while difficult, must be done. Despite declining membership, churches nonetheless have the largest and most consistent audiences within the Black community. Reverend Jackson's model of reaching out to ministers in the early days of Operation Breadbasket, as described in Karin Stanford's chapter, is instructive. In large and small congregations alike, the benefits to this strategy will at least begin to address the demobilization problem.

There are several caveats to this tactic, namely the problems associated with charismatic leadership and the need to channel energies toward productive uses. Although there is a continuing need to chase fire trucks—to call attention to prevalent problems that arise—energies must be channeled toward sustained protest and policy articulation. The most significant point is that, once a common enemy has been defined, it matters less that one group throws sticks and the other chooses to negotiate. What matters most is that all energies are turned toward defeating a common foe.

The Black community and its leaders must begin to hold one another accountable. Challenging and withdrawing support is the only effective way to discipline leaders, whether they are Black or White. The Black community cannot afford to condone unconscionable and undisciplined behavior. This may be a more difficult challenge for Black clergy and the Black media, given their predilection to support Black male leaders who are attacked.

Other channels of community education can and must be realized through the numerous community organizations that provide social services. Hungry people make a captive audience when there is a chance they will have their needs met. Here the key is obtaining support in exchange for assistance—a principle that has been lost on the Black community during the post–Civil Rights era.

The first step toward identifying a common enemy has in many respects already been accomplished. The next, and perhaps most important, step is toward community education. The hardest challenge will be to eschew all forms of divisions and petty rivalries based on ideologies, tactics, gender, and sexuality. Again, accountability is the key. There is a need to disassociate from all individuals and sectors of the community which are unable to arrest counterproductive tendencies.

Mobilizing Resources

As Jones's chapter illustrates in the case of CORE, one of the enduring challenges for Black organizations in the post–Civil Rights era is resource mobilization. Again, churches are the key. Allison Calhoun-Brown notes in her chapter on the Black church that "90 percent of all Black giving is channeled through the church . . . amounting to approximately two billion dollars per year." This figure is a significant resource. The key, however, is channeling it toward community purposes. While building larger and more ornamental churches has its place, unless churches are utilized on behalf of community purposes—for example, as places to meet and organize—they have a diminished purpose and must be held accountable. Many Black churches have already established community-related programs and offer social services. The problem however, is that their activities are not directed toward substantive purposes such as political and social education.

Another resource currently available to many churches is the capacity to broadcast their services on the radio and on television. In cities with large Black populations such as Chicago, the program lineup of several cable television and radio stations is solely oriented toward religious programming. This resource, too, must be channeled toward community purposes.

The Lack of Salience on the Race Question

Education must begin within the Black community and spread outward. One of the chief impediments to a dialogue about race is the effectiveness of propaganda that erroneously communicates racial socioeconomic parity. Once Blacks themselves are educated about their own socioeconomic condition they can begin to counter and attack incorrect information. In many cases Black leaders and elected officials themselves do not have access to accurate information. This is where the skills of scholars can be most effective.

The catalyst for White support generated during the Civil Rights era was based on broad recognition of the problem. Continued alliances with organizations that have a history of support of Black-related causes are key. In many instances these alliances are based on common problems related to labor, education, health care, gender, class, or sexual orientation. The key is to promote and exploit commonalities wherever they occur. Alliances with other organizations and groups that are affected by the same problems can also begin to address some of the resource limitations facing Black political organizations. All alliances, however, must be based on trust and reciprocity.

There is nothing ambiguous about the realities of racial and class inequality. The real culprit is misinformation and a lack of information. The effectiveness of race-baiting propaganda is largely the cause of shifting views on race and the escalation of racial violence. There is enormous potential for alliances. These opportunities must be courted and pursued, but they must begin with internal efforts, mobilizing forces within the Black community.

Republican Party Control of the Presidency and Congress

The fact that a primary focus on electoral politics yields little in the way of fundamental change has not been lost on even the least politically savvy, namely nonvoters. What should be clear is that the largest beneficiaries of electoral politics are the richest 20 percent of the American population, a group with few Black members. The largest resource available to the remaining 80 percent is one that is often acquiesced, and that is their strength in numbers. Supporting the least of two evils does not and will not work. Blacks' involvement in the electoral politics game should make this exceedingly obvious.

The degree of difference between Republican and Democratic administrations is miniscule at best—in both, Blacks have occupied a disadvantaged position. And there are no signs that centrist trends within the Democratic Party are going to abate. The development of a third party that loses at first is a far more effective strategy for progressive groups than continuously supporting parties that have the potential to win but will not support their agenda. As the adage goes: to continue to do the same thing expecting different results is insane. It is high time that progressives establish their own bandwagon rather than jumping onto one that is not going their way. Third party development must begin with a withdrawal of support for Republican and Democratic Party candidates alike, giving support, instead, to candidates who are committed to a progressive agenda.

Success, like change, is always incremental and will not occur overnight. Yet the contributions made by the first generation can promote a dialogue about alternatives which may speak to the interests of the bottom 80 percent of the population. Jesse Jackson's candidacy held promise, but, unfortunately, his vision did not extend beyond an unresponsive Democratic Party.

Although these proposals may be overly optimistic, the Black community must begin where it is. The first step is to utilize more effectively the institutions and resources that already exist. Needless to say, whatever strategy is followed, there will be detractors, yet, once an effective plan is implemented, renegades can be pulled in. The key is to promote a coherent agenda, to begin the process of mobilizing support around it, and to move beyond reformist politics and begin the process of going upstream.

Notes

Introduction

1. William Julius Wilson, *The Truly Disadvantaged: The Inner City, the Underclass, and Public Policy* (Chicago: University of Chicago Press, 1987); and *When Work Disappears: The World of the New Urban Poor* (New York: Alfred A. Knopf, 1997).
2. Melvin L. Oliver and Thomas M. Shapiro, *Black Wealth / White Wealth: A New Perspective on Racial Inequality* (New York: Routledge, 1995); Dalton Conley, *Being Black, Living in the Red: Race, Wealth, and Social Policy in America* (Berkeley: University of California Press, 1999).
3. For historical overviews of Black life and politics, see John Hope Franklin and Alfred Moss Jr., *From Slavery to Freedom: A History of African Americans* (New York: Alfred A. Knopf, 1994); Darlene Clark Hine and Kathleen Thompson, *A Shining Thread of Hope: The History of Black Women in America* (New York: Broadway Books, 1998); Robin D. G. Kelley, *Race Rebels* (New York: Free Press, 1998); Michael Goldfield, *The Color of Politics: Race and the Mainsprings of American Politics* (New York: New Press, 1997). For good discussions of the origins, development, and consequences of the Civil Rights Movement, see Aldon Morris, *Origins of the Civil Rights Movement* (New York: Free Press, 1983); Doug McAdam, *Political Process and the Development of Black Insurgency, 1930–1970* (Chicago: University of Chicago Press, 1982); and Peter B. Levy, *The Civil Rights Movement* (Westport, Conn.: Greenwood Press, 1998). For analyses of Black politics in the post–Civil Rights era, see Hanes Walton Jr. and Robert C. Smith, *American Politics and the African American Quest for Universal Freedom* (New York: Longman, 2000); Lucius Barker, Mack Jones, and Katherine Tate, *African Americans and the American Political System* (Englewood Cliffs, N.J.: Prentice-Hall, 1999); Marcus D. Pohlmann, *Black Politics in Conservative America,* 2d ed. (New York: Longman, 1999); and Huey L. Perry and Wayne Parent, eds., *Blacks and the American Political System* (Gainesville: University Press of Florida, 1995).
4. Ronald J. Hrebenar, *Interest Group Politics in America* (New York: M. E. Sharpe, 1997); Paul S. Herrnson, Ronald G. Shaiko, and Clyde Wilcox, eds., *The Interest*

Group Connection: Electioneering, Lobbying, and Policymaking in Washington (Chatham, N.J.: Chatham House, 1998); Mark P. Petracca, ed., *The Politics of Interests: Interest Groups Transformed* (Boulder, Colo.: Westview Press, 1992).

5. Robert C. Smith, *We Have No Leaders: African Americans in the Post–Civil Rights Era* (Albany: State University of New York Press, 1996).

6. Dona Cooper Hamilton and Charles V. Hamilton, *The Dual Agenda: Race and Social Welfare Policies of Civil Rights Organizations* (New York: Columbia University Press, 1997).

7. James Q. Wilson, *Political Organizations* (Princeton, N.J.: Princeton University Press, 1995).

8. Robert Michels, *Political Parties: A Sociological Study of the Oligarchical Tendencies of Modern Democracy* (New York: Free Press, 1962).

9. For an application of elite theory to the Black Panther Party, see Ollie A. Johnson III, "Explaining the Demise of the Black Panther Party: The Role of Internal Factors," in *The Black Panther Party Reconsidered,* ed. Charles E. Jones (Baltimore, Md.: Black Classic Press, 1998).

10. Sondra Kathryn Wilson, ed., *In Search of Democracy: The NAACP Writings of James Weldon Johnson, Walter White, and Roy Wilkins (1920–1977)* (New York: Oxford University Press, 1999).

11. *St. Petersburg Times* and *Tampa Tribune,* February–March 1999; Black Entertainment Television (BET), "Lead Story," 1999.

12. Joanne Grant, *Ella Baker: Freedom Bound* (New York: John Wiley and Sons, 1998); see chap. 6, esp. 121.

13. Karen McGill Arrington and William L. Taylor, eds., *Voting Rights in America: Continuing the Quest for Full Participation* (Washington, D.C.: Leadership Conference Education Fund and the Joint Center for Political and Economic Studies, 1992).

14. David J. Garrow, *Bearing the Cross: Martin Luther King, Jr., and the Southern Christian Leadership Conference* (New York: William Morrow, 1986).

15. Bayard Rustin, "From Protest to Politics," *Commentary* (February 1965); Jervis Anderson, *Bayard Rustin: Troubles I've Seen: A Biography* (Berkeley: University of California Press, 1997), 284–286.

16. Roy Wilkins with Tom Mathews, *Standing Fast: The Autobiography of Roy Wilkins* (New York: Da Capo Press, 1994), 331.

17. Ibid, 312–326; Charles E. Jones, ed., *The Black Panther Party Reconsidered* (Baltimore, Md.: Black Classic Press, 1998); William L. Van Deburg, ed., *Modern Black Nationalism: From Marcus Garvey to Louis Farrakhan* (New York: New York University Press, 1997).

18. Alphonso Pinkney, *Red, Black, and Green: Black Nationalism in the United States* (Cambridge, U.K.: Cambridge University Press, 1976); William L. Van Deburg, *New Day in Babylon: The Black Power Movement and American Culture, 1965–1975* (Chicago: University of Chicago Press, 1992).

19. Wilkins, *Standing Fast,* 314–326.

20. William L. Clay, *Just Permanent Interests: Black Americans in Congress, 1870–1992,* rev. ed. (New York: Amistad, 1993); Carol M. Swain, *Black Faces, Black Interests: The Representation of African Americans in Congress* (Cambridge, Mass.: Harvard University Press, 1993).

21. Hanes Walton Jr. and Robert C. Smith, *American Politics and the African American*

Quest for Universal Freedom (New York: Longman, 2000); Marcus D. Pohlmann, *Black Politics in Conservative America,* 2d ed. (New York: Longman, 1999).

22. David O. Sears, John J. Hetts, Jim Sidanius, and Lawrence Bobo, "Race in American Politics: Framing the Debates," in *Racialized Politics: The Debate about Racism in America,* ed. David O. Sears, Jim Sidanius, and Lawrence Bobo (Chicago: University of Chicago Press, 2000), 9–16.
23. Paul M. Sniderman and Edward G. Carmines, *Reaching beyond Race* (Cambridge, Mass.: Harvard University Press, 1997); Paul M. Sniderman and Thomas Piazza, *The Scar of Race* (Cambridge, Mass.: Harvard University Press, 1993).
24. George M. Fredrickson, *White Supremacy: A Comparative Study in American and South African History* (Oxford, U.K.: Oxford University Press, 1981), xi.
25. Joe R. Feagin and Hernan Vera, *White Racism: The Basics* (New York: Routledge, 1995), 7.
26. Katheryn Russell, *Racial Hoaxes* (New York: New York University Press, 1997).
27. Joe R. Feagin, *Racist America: Roots, Current Realities, and Future Reparations* (New York: Routledge, 2000).
28. Robert C. Smith, *Racism in the Post–Civil Rights Era: Now You See It, Now You Don't* (Albany: State University of New York Press, 1995).

One   Will the Circle Be Unbroken?

1. Aldon Morris, *The Origins of the Civil Rights Movement* (New York: Free Press, 1984).
2. W. E. B. Du Bois, *The Souls of Black Folk* (New York: Avalon, 1903), 343.
3. E. Franklin Frazier, *The Negro Church in America* (New York: Schocken Books, 1964).
4. Gayraud Wilmore, *Black Religion and Black Radicalism* (Maryknoll, N.Y.: Orbis, 1983); Benjamin E. Mays and Joseph Nicholson, *The Negro's Church* (New York: Institute for Social and Religious Research, 1933).
5. Gunnar Myrdal, *An American Dilemma* (New York: Harper and Row, 1944), 936.
6. Mays and Nicholson, *Negro's Church,* 11.
7. Eric C. Lincoln and Lawrence Mamiya, *The Black Church in the African American Experience* (Durham, N.C.: Duke University Press, 1990), 8.
8. Frazier, *Negro Church in America,* 49.
9. Morris, *Origins of the Civil Rights Movement,* 77.
10. Robert C. Smith, "Politics Is Not Enough," in *From Exclusion to Inclusion,* ed. Ralph C. Gomes and Linda F. Williams (Westport, Conn.: Praeger, 1992).
11. John Brown Childs, *The Political Black Minister* (Boston: G. R. Hall and Co., 1980); Frazier, *Negro Church in America,* 1964; Myrdal, *American Dilemma;* Anthony Orum, "A Reappraisal of the Social and Political Participation of Negroes," *American Journal of Sociology* 72:32–46.
12. Hart Nelsen and Anne K. Nelsen, *The Black Church in the Sixties* (Lexington: University Press of Kentucky, 1975); Allison Calhoun-Brown, "African American Churches and Political Mobilization," *Journal of Politics* 58:935–953; Fredrick Harris, "Something Within: Religion as a Mobilizer of African American Political Activism," *Journal of Politics* 56:42–68; Arthur Miller, Patricia Gurin, Gerald Gurin, and Oksana Malanchuk, "Group Consciousness and Political Participation,"

American Journal of Political Science 25:494–511; B. Jackson, "The Effects of Racial Group Consciousness on Political Mobilization in America," *National Journal of Sociology* 8:149–159; and Robert Shingles, "Black Consciousness and Political Participation: The Missing Link," *American Political Science Review* 75:76–91.

13. Lincoln and Mamiya, *Black Church.*

14. Wilmore, *Black Religion;* Gary Marx, "Religion: Opiate or Inspiration of Civil Rights Militancy among Negroes?" in *Racial Conflict,* ed. Gary Marx (Boston: Little, Brown, 1971); Adolph Reed Jr., *The Jesse Jackson Phenomenon* (New Haven, Conn.: Yale University Press, 1986).

15. Anthony Oberschall, *Social Conflict and Social Movement* (Englewood Cliffs, N.J.: Prentice-Hall, 1973); Douglas McAdam, *Political Progress and the Development of Black Insurgency* (Chicago: University of Chicago Press, 1982); Morris, *Origins of the Civil Rights Movement.*

16. Robert Putnam, *Making Democracy Work: Civic Tradition in Modern Italy* (Princeton, N.J.: Princeton University Press, 1993); Harris, "Something Within."

17. Lincoln and Mamiya, *Black Church,* 15.

18. Peter Eisinger, "The Condition of Protest Behavior in American Cities," *American Political Science Review* 67:11–28.

19. McAdam, *Political Progress,* 43, 45.

20. Michael Preston, Lenneal Henderson Jr., and Paul Puryear, eds., *The New Black Politics* (New York: Longman, 1982).

21. William E. Nelson, "Cleveland: The Rise and Fall of New Black Politics," in *The New Black Politics,* ed. Michael Preston, Lenneal Henderson, and Paul Puryear (New York: Longman, 1982).

22. Smith, "Politics Is Not Enough," 105.

23. Ibid.

24. Marcus Pohlman, *Black Politics in Conservative America* (New York: Longman, 1990).

25. For statistics on and analyses of Black elected officials, see *Black Elected Officials: A National Roster* (Washington, D.C.: Joint Center for Political and Economic Studies Press, 1993); and Theresa Chambliss, "The Growth and Significance of African American Elected Officials," in *From Exclusion to Inclusion,* ed. Ralph Gomes and Linda Williams (Westport, Conn.: Praeger, 1992); Smith, "Black Appointed Officials: A Neglected Category of Political Participation Research," *Journal of Black Studies* 14:369–388; Frances Fox Piven and Richard Cloward, *Why Americans Don't Vote* (New York: Pantheon Press, 1988).

26. Katherine Tate, *From Protest to Politics* (New York: Russell Sage, 1993), 166.

27. For example, Charles Hamilton argued that in the 1970s the post–Civil Rights era should focus activity toward full employment. In his words, it was advantageous because "it applies to the total society, not only to Blacks and other traditionally stigmatized minorities, who are seen as wanting only hand-outs. It would, in other words, recognize the critical factor of race and racism, but offers a deracialized solution" ("Full Employment as a Viable Issue," in *When the Marching Stopped: An Analysis of Black Issues in the 1970s,* ed. Hanes Walton [New York: National Urban League, 1973]).

28. McAdam, *Political Progress,* 43.

29. Oberschall, *Social Conflict;* James Freeman, "Resource Mobilization and Strategy,"

in *The Dynamics of Social Movement,* ed. M. Zald and J. McCarthy (Cambridge, U.K.: Winthrop Publishers, 1979); J. C. Jenkins, "Resource Mobilization: Theory and Study of Social Movements," *Annual Review of Sociology* 9:527–533.

30. Morris, *Origins of the Civil Rights Movement,* 4.

31. Lincoln and Mamiya (*Black Church*) include among Black denominations the African Methodist Episcopal Church; the African Methodist Episcopal Zion Church; the National Baptist Convention USA, Incorporated; the National Baptist Convention of America, Unincorporated; the Christian Methodist Episcopal Church; the Progressive National Baptist Convention of America, Unincorporated; and the Church of God in Christ.

32. Emmett Carson, *A Hand Up: Black Philanthropy and Self Help in America* (Washington, D.C.: Joint Center for Political and Economic Studies Press, 1993).

33. Robert Hill, "The Role of the Black Church in Community and Economic Development Activities," *National Journal of Sociology* 8:149–159.

34. Lincoln and Mamiya, *Black Church,* 259.

35. Andres Tapia, "Soul Searching: How Is the Black Church Responding to the Urban Crisis?" *Christianity Today,* March 4, 1996, 26–30.

36. *Christian Century,* April 27, 1994, 440.

37. Richard B. Freeman, "Who Escapes: The Relation of Churchgoing and Other Background Factors to the Socioeconomic Performance of Black Male Youths from Inner City Tracts," in *The Black Youth Employment Crisis,* ed. Richard B. Freeman and Harry Holzer (Chicago: University of Chicago Press, 1986).

38. Tapia, "Soul Searching."

39. Lincoln and Mamiya, *Black Church,* 326.

40. Henry Duvall, "Youth Demanding Change in Black Church," *Crisis* 89:9.

41. Lawrence Jones, "The Black Church New Agenda," *Christian Century,* April 1–8, 1979, 434–438.

42. Jack Bloom, *Class, Race and the Civil Rights Movement* (Bloomington: Indiana University Press, 1987).

43. Ida R. Mukenge, *The Black Church in Urban America* (Lanham, Md.: University Press of America, 1983).

44. F. Smothers, "Atlanta Still on a Roll but New Doubts Arise," *New York Times,* July 14, 1988, A21.

45. Tapia, "Soul Searching," 30.

46. Ibid.

47. James Q. Wilson, *Political Organizations* (New York: Basic Books, 1974), 297–300.

48. Reed, *Jesse Jackson Phenomenon,* 44.

49. *Christian Century,* October 18, 1995, 952.

50. *St. Petersburg Times,* February 28, 1999, March 18, 1999; *Tampa Tribune,* February 28, 1999, March 18, 1999.

51. Morris, *Origins of the Civil Rights Movement,* 6.

52. McAdam, *Political Progress,* 48, 51.

53. Miller et al., "Group Consciousness and Political Participation," 48; Walton, *When the Marching Stopped,* 48.

54. Lincoln and Mamiya, *Black Church,* 195.

55. James Cone, *My Soul Looks Back* (Nashville, Tenn.: Abingdon, 1982), 79; Patrick Bascio, *The Failure of White Theology: A Black Theological Perspective* (New York:

Peter Long, 1994); James Cone, *Black Theology and Black Power* (New York: Seabury Press, 1969).

56. Bernice King, *Hard Questions, Heart Answers: Speeches and Sermons* (New York: Broadway Books, 1996), 62.

57. Clyde Wilcox, *God's Warriors* (Baltimore, Md.: Johns Hopkins University Press, 1992); Allison Calhoun-Brown, "Still Seeing in Black and White: Racial Challenges for the Christian Right," *Sojourners in the Wilderness: The Christian Right in Comparative Perspective* (Lanham, Md.: Rowman and Littlefield, 1997).

58. Vashti McKenzie, *Not without a Struggle: Leadership Development for African American Women in Ministry* (Cleveland, Ohio: United Church Press, 1996), 45.

59. *Christian Century,* April 27, 1994, 440.

60. See Lincoln and Mamiya, *Black Church,* for a history of these denominations.

Two   The NAACP in the Twenty-first Century

This chapter was originally prepared for presentation at a symposium sponsored by the Academy of Leadership, University of Maryland, College Park, and the Smithsonian Institution, American Museum of History, July 8, 1997. I would like to thank Ronald Walters for his comments on the earlier draft.

1. Kenneth Clark, "The Civil Rights Movement: Momentum and Organization," in *The Negro American,* ed. Talcott Parsons and Kenneth Clark (Boston: Beacon Press, 1966), 623. See also his article "The NAACP: Verging on Irrelevance," *New York Times,* July 14, 1985; Harold Cruse, *Plural but Equal: Blacks and Minorities in America's Plural Society* (New York: William Morrow, 1987); Lucius Barker and Mack Jones, *African Americans and the American Political System* (Englewood Cliffs, N.J.: Prentice-Hall, 1995), 201–205; Clarence Lusane and James Steele, "A Fatal Attraction: The Firing of Ben Chavis by the NAACP," *Black Political Agenda* 2 (1994): 10–13.

2. Ralph Bunche, "The Programs of Organizations Devoted to the Improvement of the Status of the Negro," *Journal of Negro Education* 8 (1939): 542–565; and Louis Lomax, *The Negro Revolt* (New York: Signet, 1963).

3. W. E. B. Du Bois, *Dusk of Dawn: An Essay toward an Autobiography of a Race Concept* (1940; rpt., New York: Schocken Books, 1968), 288–297.

4. Clark, *Civil Rights Movement,* 623.

5. See Robert C. Smith, *We Have No Leaders: African Americans in the Post Civil Rights Era* (Albany: State University of New York, 1996), 88–98.

6. See Louis Harris, *A Study of Attitudes toward Racial and Religious Minorities and Women* (New York: National Conference of Christians and Jews, 1978); Howard Schuman, Charlotte Steeh, and Lawrence Bobo, *Racial Attitudes in America: Trends and Interpretations* (Cambridge, Mass.: Harvard University Press, 1985).

7. Harris, *Study of Attitudes,* 68.

8. Schuman, Steeh and Bobo, *Racial Attitudes in America;* Paul Sniderman and Michael Hagan, *Race and Inequality: A Study in American Values* (Chatham, N.J.: Chatham House, 1985) .

9. David Sears, "Symbolic Racism," in *Eliminating Racism,* ed. P. Katz and D. Taylor (New York: Plenum, 1988); Paul Sniderman, T. Piazza, P. Tetlock, and A. Kendrick,

"The New Racism," *American Journal of Political Science* 35 (1991): 423–447; and Lawrence Bobo, J. Klugel, and R. Smith, "Laissez Faire Racism: The Crystallization of a Kinder, Gentler Anti-Black Ideology," *Racial Attitudes in the 1990s: Continuity and Change,* ed. S. Tuchand J. Martin (Westport, Conn.: Praeger, 1997).

10. Paul Sniderman, "The New Look of Public Opinion Research," in *The State of the Discipline,* ed. A. Finifter (Washington, D.C.: American Political Science Association, 1993), 231–232.

11. Sears, "Symbolic Racism," 54.

12. See Lee Seligman and Susan Welch, *Black Americans' Views of Inequality* (Cambridge, U.K.: Cambridge University Press, 1991).

13. Donald Kinder and Lynn Sanders, *Divided by Color: Racial Politics in American Democracy* (Chicago: University of Chicago Press, 1996), 287.

14. Daniel Walden, *W. E. B. Du Bois: The Crisis Writings* (Greenwich, Conn.: Fawcett Books, 1972).

15. For a detailed discussion of Blacks and the welfare debate, see chapter 9 in this volume (by Todd Shaw).

16. Robert C. Smith, *Racism in the Post Civil Rights Era* (Albany: State University of New York Press, 1995); Andrew Hacker, *Two Nations: Black, White, Separate, Hostile, Unequal* (New York: Scribners, 1992); Joe Feagin and Herman Vera, *White Racism* (New York: Routledge, 1995).

17. See Smith, *Racism,* chap. 4.

18. Ibid., 66.

19. Ibid., 142.

20. Robert C. Smith, *We Have No Leaders: African Americans in the Post–Civil Rights Era* (Albany: State University of New York, 1996), chap. 6.

21. Matthew Holden, "The President, Congress and Race Relations" (Ernest Patterson Memorial Lecture, University of Colorado at Boulder, 1986).

22. Clement Vose, "Litigation as a Form of Pressure Group Activity," *Annals of the American Academy of Political and Social Sciences* 319 (1958): 20–31; Genna Rae MacNeil, "Justifiable Cause: Howard University Law School and the Struggle for Civil Rights," *Howard Law Journal* 22 (1979): 108–132.

23. Robert Dahl, "Decision Making in a Democracy: The Supreme Court as a National Policy Maker," *Journal of Public Law* 6 (1957): 257–288; Giraradeau Spann, *Race against the Court: The Supreme Court and Minorities in Contemporary America* (New York: New York University Press, 1993).

24. Cruse, *Plural but Equal,* 385.

25. Ethan Bronner, *Battle for Justice: How the Bork Nomination Shook America* (New York: W. W. Norton, 1983).

26. Quoted in Linda Greenhouse, "Marshall Says Court's Ruling Imperils Rights," *New York Times,* September 9, 1989.

27. Smith, *We Have No Leaders,* 175–185; see, for example, *St. Mary's Honors Center v. Hicks,* 92–602, 1993 (slip opinion), esp. Justice Souter's dissent.

28. *J. A. Croson v. City of Richmond,* 44, US 469 (1989).

29. *Adarand Contractors v. Pena,* 903, 1841, 1995 (slip opinion).

30. The precedents overturned are *Fullilove v. Klutznik,* 448, US 448 (1980); and *Metro Broadcasting v. Federal Communications Commission,* 110 S.Ct. 1997 (1990).

31. Augustus Jones and Clyde Brown, "State Response to *Richmond v. Croson:* A Sur-

vey of Equal Employment Opportunity Officers," *National Political Science Review* 3 (1992): 40–61.

32. *Shaw et al. v. Reno,* 92–357, 1993 (slip opinion).
33. J. Morgan Kouser, *Dead End: The Development of Nineteenth Century Litigation on Discrimination* (New York: Oxford University Press, 1986).
34. Dianne Pinderhughes, "Racial Interest Groups and Incremental Politics" (MS, University of Illinois at Urbana, 1980), 36.
35. Pinderhughes, personal communications, 1994.
36. David Levering Lewis, *W. E. B. Du Bois: Biography of a Race* (New York: Henry Holt, 1993), 409–410.
37. David Levering Lewis, *W. E. B. Du Bois: A Reader* (New York: Henry Holt, 1995), 112.
38. John Dittmer, *Local People: The Struggle for Civil Rights in Mississippi* (Urbana: University of Illinois Press, 1995); Charles Payne, *I've Got the Light of Freedom: The Organizing Tradition and the Mississippi Freedom Struggle* (Berkeley: University of California Press, 1995).
39. One thing we can probably safely conclude is that there are too many local chapters in many communities competing for limited human and financial resources. For example, in my locale there are three chapters in three small cities within a five-mile radius of one another.
40. Robert C. Smith, "NAACP Special Project Panels." Paper prepared for presentation at the Twenty-seventh Annual Meeting of the National Conference of Black Political Scientists, Savannah, Ga., 1996.
41. Thus far six chapters in various parts of the country have been studied, including a suburban county chapter, two northern big city chapters, and two small city southern chapters.

Three   The National Urban League

1. See <*http://www.nul.org*>.
2. Interview with Hugh B. Price, president and CEO of the National Urban League, September 5, 2001.
3. See <*http://www.nul.org.com*>.
4. Guichard Parris and Lester Brooks, *Blacks in the City: A History of the National Urban League* (Boston: Little, Brown , 1971), 4–25.
5. Nancy J. Weiss, *The National Urban League, 1910–1940* (New York: Oxford University Press, 1974).
6. Dennis Dickerson, *Militant Mediator: Whitney M. Young, Jr.* (Lexington: University Press of Kentucky, 1998).
7. Nancy J. Weiss, *Whitney M. Young, Jr. and the Struggle for Civil Rights* (Princeton, N.J.: Princeton University Press, 1989), 102.
8. Ibid., 105.
9. See <*http://www.gale.com/index.htm*>.
10. National Urban League, "Playing to Win: A Marshall Plan for America," report, July 1991.
11. "The New Mission Statement: An Action Strategy for Implementation by the Affiliate Network," report prepared by National Planning and Evaluation Department of the National Urban League, July 1991.

12. Frank Lomax, speech given at the 1992 Western Regional Assembly in Anaheim, Calif.
13. Ibid.
14. Hugh B. Price, "Public Discourse: Our Very Fate as a Civil Society Is at Stake" in *Vital Speeches* 61, no. 7 (1995): 213.
15. *Black Enterprise,* 1997.
16. Price, "Public Discourse," 216–296.
17. Interview with Hugh Price, September 5, 2001.
18. Interview with Price September 15, 2001.
19. Ibid.
20. Ibid.
21. Ibid.
22. Ibid.

Four   A Layin' On of Hands

1. Bernice McNair Barnett provides a discussion and critique on existing treatments of African American women's political behavior, especially within the context of Civil Rights protest in "Invisible Southern Black Women Leaders in the Civil Rights Movement: The Triple Constraints of Gender, Race, and Class," *Gender and Society* 7, no. 2 (June 1993): 162–182. Vicki L. Crawford, Jacqueline Anne Rouse and Barbara Woods, eds., *Women in the Civil Rights Movement: Trailblazers and Torchbearers 1941–1965* (Bloomington: Indiana University Press, 1993), provide a detailed investigation into the leadership strategies and obstacles faced by African American women while developing a gender- and race-sensitive perspective from which to evaluate this activity during the 1950s and 1960s. In her book Belinda Robnett provides a critical discussion of social movement literature, particularly as it relates to the concept of micromobilization and the role of race, gender, and leadership. Part of her intent is to reexamine the impact of race and gender on the types of leadership strategies employed by Black women in the Civil Rights Movement within organizational hierarchies. For further discussion, see *How Long How Long? African American Women in the Struggle for Civil Rights* (New York: Oxford University Press, 1997).

2. *Micromobilization* has been understood to refer to the process of building social movements at a more intimate community level. In order for large-scale social movements to occur, activists and organizational intellectuals have to build successful relationships and institutions at the grassroots level which include everyday citizens and build a dynamic relationship between movement ideals and individual political identity. For further discussion, see Doug McAdam, "Conceptual Origins, Current Problems, Future Directions," in *Comparative Perspectives on Social Movements: Political Opportunities, Mobilizing Structures, and Cultural Framings,* ed. Doug McAdam, John D. McCarthy, and Mayer N. Zald(New York: Cambridge University Press, 1996), 23–40. This chapter applies the concept in the realm of daily politics and defines *micromobilization* from the perspective of process and participants in this activity.

3. Deborah King presents a thorough critique of additive approaches to considering race and gender as factors influencing political behavior in "Multiple Jeopardy,

Multiple Consciousness: The Context of a Black Feminist Ideology," *Signs* 14, no. 1 (1988): 42–72.

4. R. Darcy and Charles D. Hadley, "Black Women in Politics: The Puzzle of Success," *Social Science Quarterly* (1988): 627–645. Githens and Prestage provide a detailed discussion of the double disadvantage hypothesis in their treatment of the development of African American women's politics, in Marianne Githens and Jewel L. Prestage, eds., *A Portrait of Marginality: The Political Behavior of American Women* (New York: Longman, 1977). Also see Sandra Baxter and Marjorie Lansing, eds., *Women and Politics: The Invisible Majority* (Ann Arbor: University of Michigan Press, 1980), who present discussion on the gender gap in politics.

5. King, "Multiple Jeopardy, Multiple Consciousness"; Patricia Hill Collins, *Black Feminist Thought: Knowledge, Consciousness, and the Politics of Empowerment* (Boston: Unwin Hyman, 1991).

6. Joan Scott, *Gender and the Politics of History* (New York: Columbia University Press, 1988). Scott's discussion of gender as an analytic category provides the framework for my understanding of race and gender as analytic categories.

7. Linda Gordon, ed., "Introduction"; and Paula Baker, "The Domestication of Politics: Women and American Political Society, 1780–1920," both in *Women, the State, and Welfare,* ed. Linda Gordon (Madison: University of Wisconsin Press, 1990); Gwendolyn Mink, *The Wages of Motherhood: Inequality in the Welfare State, 1917–1942* (Ithaca, N.Y.: Cornell University Press, 1995); Nancy Fraser and Linda Gordon, "A Genealogy of Dependency: Tracing a Keyword of the U.S. Welfare State," *Signs* 19, no. 2 (1994): 303–337.

8. Cheryl Townsend Gilkes, "'If It Wasn't for the Women . . .': African American Women, Community Work and Social Change," *Women of Color in U.S. Society,* ed. Maxine Baca Zinn and Bonnie Thorton Dill (Philadelphia, Pa.: Temple University Press, 1994), 230.

9. Ibid.

10. Patricia Hill Collins, *Black Feminist Thought: Knowledge, Consciousness and the Politics of Empowerment* (Boston: Unwin Hyman, 1990), 21–30.

11. For a discussion of the strategies and goals of Black women's community work, see Paula Giddings, *When and Where I Enter* (New York: Bantam Books, 1984), chaps. 5 and 15. Deborah Gray White provides an extensive discussion of a range of national Black women's organizations and their subsequent community activism from 1884–1984 in her book *Too Heavy a Load: Black Women in Defense of Themselves: 1894–1994* (New York: W. W. Norton, 1999). Also see Stephanie J. Shaw, "Black Club Women and the Creation of the National Association of Colored Women," *Journal of Women's History* 3, no. 2 (Fall 1991): 10–23. Marjorie H. Parker provides a discussion of community work during the 1920s and the Depression era as performed through Black women's sororities in *Alpha Kappa Alpha through the Years* (Chicago: Mobium Press, 1990), 181–196.

12. Gilkes, "'If It Wasn't for the Women'"; Collins, *Black Feminist Thought;* Giddings, *When and Where I Enter.*

13. Giddings, *When and Where I Enter;* Elsa Barkley Brown, "Negotiating and Transforming the Public Sphere: African American Political Life in the Transition from Slavery," *Women Transforming Politics,* ed. Cathy J. Cohen, Kathleen B. Jones, and Joan C. Tronto (New York: New York University Press, 1997), 343–376; Kevin K.

Gaines, *Uplifting the Race: Black Leadership, Politics and Culture in the Twentieth Century* (Chapel Hill: University of North Carolina Press, 1997); Glenda Gilmore, *Gender and Jim Crow* (Chapel Hill: University of North Carolina Press, 1996).

14. Gray White, *Too Heavy a Load;* Giddings, *When and Where I Enter;* Shaw, "Black Club Women."

15. See Aldon D. Morris, *The Origins of the Civil Rights Movement: Black Communities Organizing for Change* (New York: Free Press, 1984); Vicki L. Crawford, Jacqueline Anne Rouse, and Barbara Woods, eds., *Women in the Civil Rights Movement: Trailblazers and Torchbearers, 1941–1965* (Bloomington: Indiana University Press, 1993); Giddings, *When and Where I Enter;* Charles Payne, "Men Led, but the Women Organized: Movement Participation of Women in the Mississippi Delta,'" in Crawford, Rouse, and Woods, *Women in the Civil Rights Movement,* 1–12.

16. Giddings, *When and Where I Enter;* Crawford, Rouse, and Woods, *Women in the Civil Rights Movement.*

17. Giddings, *When and Where I Enter;* Shaw, "Black Club Women."

18. Giddings, *When and Where I Enter;* Gilmore, *Gender and Jim Crow;* Barkley Brown, "Negotiating and Transforming the Public Sphere."

19. Mark T. Carleton, *Politics and Punishment: the History of the Louisiana State Penal System* (Baton Rouge: Louisiana State University Press, 1971); W. E. B. Du Bois, *The Souls of Black Folk* (1903; rpt., New York: Penguin Books, 1989).

20. Barkley Brown, "Negotiating and Transforming the Public Sphere," 361.

21. Joy James, *Transcending the Talented Tenth: Black Leaders and American Intellectuals* (New York: Routledge, 1997); Rhonda M. Williams, "Beyond Human Capital: Black Women, Work, and Wages," Working Paper 183 (Wellesley, Mass.: Wellesley College Center for Research on Women, 1988); William Julius Wilson, *The Truly Disadvantaged: The Inner City, the Underclass, and Public Policy* (Chicago: University of Chicago Press, 1987).

22. For a discussion of theoretical advances in the discussion of politics from a feminist perspective, see Ann Bookman, and Sandra Morgen, eds., "Introduction," *The Politics of Empowerment* (Philadelphia: Temple University Press, 1988); Cathy J. Cohen, Kathleen B. Jones, and Joan C. Tronto, eds., "Introduction," *Women Transforming Politics* (New York: New York University Press, 1997); Iva Ellen Deutchman. "The Politics of Empowerment," *Women and Politics* 11, no. 2 (1991): 1–17. Louise A. Tilly and Patricia Gurin, eds., *Women, Politics, and Change* (New York: Russell Sage Foundation, 1990).

23. Ann Bookman and Sandra Morgen, eds., *The Politics of Empowerment* (Philadelphia: Temple University Press, 1988).

24. Carol Fanta-Hardy, *Latina Politics, Latino Politics: Gender, Culture, and Political Participation in Boston* (Philadelphia: Temple University Press, 1993), intro., chap. 1.

25. Ibid.

26. Gray White, *Too Heavy a Load;* Giddings, *When and Where I Enter.*

27. Gray White, *Too Heavy a Load,* 150–151: Giddings, *When and Where I Enter.*

28. Gray White, *Too Heavy a Load;* Giddings, *When and Where I Enter.*

29. Gray White, *Too Heavy a Load,* 157.

30. Gray White, *Too Heavy a Load,* 150–151; *When and Where I Enter.*

31. Gray White, *Too Heavy a Load; When and Where I Enter.*

32. Ibid.
33. *NCNW National Newsletter,* NCNW National Headquarters, Washington, D.C., 1999.
34. NCNW membership information packet, 2000.
35. Ibid.
36. For this case study the Washington, D.C., metropolitan region includes Washington, D.C., Prince Georges County, and the southern portion of Montgomery County. The PVS was selected for this case study because its membership reflected a wide range of ages and backgrounds, in contrast to the Washington, D.C., millennium section or two of the older sections, where the membership was primarily over fifty-five. Age of the interviewees was an important characteristic in assessing the relevancy of community work as a political practice among African American women.
37. Interview with the PVS NCNW steering board, March 2000.
38. The Personal Responsibility and Work Opportunity Act of 1996, title 1, sec. 103 (Public Law 104–193).

Five   From Protest to Black Conservatism

1. Bob Dart, "Tributes Paid to Civil Rights Giant," *Atlanta Journal-Constitution,* September 11, 1999, A6; Richard Severo, "James Farmer, Civil Rights Giant in the 50's and 60's, Is Dead at 79," *New York Times,* July 10, 1999, A1 and A11; and "What James Farmer Leaves Behind," *New York Times,* July 12, 1999, A18.
2. August Meier and Elliott Rudwick, *CORE* (Urbana: University of Illinois Press, 1975). Meier and Rudwick's study represents an excellent scholarly examination of CORE upon which this essay draws heavily when discussing CORE activities from 1942 to 1965. For a general history of the Civil Rights Movement, see Juan Williams, *Eyes on the Prize: America's Civil Rights Years, 1954–1965* (New York: Viking Press, 1987).
3. Manning Marable, "CORE: Demise of an Ideal," *New York Amsterdam News,* February 12, 1983, 36.
4. For a more detailed discussion of the political process model, see Doug McAdam, *Political Process and the Development of Black Insurgency, 1930–1970* (Chicago: University of Chicago Press, 1982); also see Neil Smelser, *Theory of Collective Behavior* (New York: Free Press, 1962); John D. McCarthy and Mayer Zaid, "Resource Mobilization and Social Movements: A Partial Theory," *American Journal of Sociology* (1977): 1212–41; and Talcott Parsons, ed., *The Theory of Social and Economic Organization* (New York: Free Press, 1947), for an overview of Max Weber's theory of charismatic movements.
5. Adolph Reed Jr., *The Jesse Jackson Phenomenon: The Crisis of Purpose in Afro-American Politics* (New Haven, Conn.: Yale University Press, 1986), 9.
6. Manning Marable, "The Fire This Time: The Miami Rebellion, May 1980," *Black Scholar,* 11 (July–August 1980): 6–7.
7. Matthew Holden Jr., *The Politics of the Black Nation* (New York: Chandler Publishing Co., 1973), 42.
8. Ibid., 43.

9. August Meier and Elliott Rudwick, "How CORE Began," *Social Science Quarterly* 49 (March 1969): 799.
10. Elliot Rudwick, "CORE: The Road from Interracialism to Black Power," *Journal of Voluntary Action Research* 4 (1972): 12.
11. Ibid., 14.
12. Elliot Rudwick and August Meier, "Organizational Structural and Goal Succession: A Comparative Analysis of NAACP and CORE, 1964–1968," *Social Science Quarterly* 12.
13. Aldon D. Morris, *The Origins of the Civil Rights Movement: Black Communities Organizing for Change* (New York: Free Press, 1984), 128–130.
14. Meier and Rudwick, "How CORE Began," 796–799; Meier and Rudwick, *CORE,* 3–30; and James Farmer, *Lay Bare the Heart* (New York: Amsterdam Library, 1985).
15. Farmer, *Lay Bare the Heart,* 165; also see Meier and Rudwick, *CORE,* 33–39. *Morgan v. Freeman* 328 U.S. 373 (1976).
16. Meier and Rudwick, *CORE,* 39.
17. Ibid., 40–71.
18. Herbert Haines, *Black Radicals and the Civil Rights Mainstream, 1954–1970* (Knoxville: University of Tennessee Press, 1988), 25.
19. Morris, *Origins of the Civil Rights Movement,* 131.
20. Meier and Rudwick, *CORE,* 159; *Boynton v. Virginia* 364 U.S. 454 (1960).
21. Ibid., 282–328.
22. "Harlem 1964, Leaders, Leaders Everywhere," *Rights and Views* 1 (1964): 2.
23. See Meier and Rudwick, *CORE,* 374–395; and Rudwick, "CORE: The Road from Interracialism to Black Power," 12–19.
24. Meier and Rudwick, *CORE,* 381, 406–407.
25. Ibid., 415.
26. Akinyele O. Umoja, "The Ballot and the Bullet: A Comparative Analysis of Armed Resistance in the Civil Rights Movement," *Journal of Black Studies* 29, no. 4: 558–578; also see Meier and Rudwick, *CORE,* 296–298.
27. Robert Allen, *Black Awakening in Capitalistic America* (Garden City, N.Y.: Doubleday, 1969), 70.
28. Meier and Rudwick, *CORE,* 409–410.
29. Ibid., 420–421.
30. Earl Caldwell, "CORE Picks Harlem Militant for Its No. 2 National Position," *New York Times,* December 28, 1967 (Schomburg clipping files); Roy Innis, interview by author, June 18, 1999, New York; Meier and Rudwick, *CORE,* 380.
31. Roy Innis, "Separate Economics: A New Social Contract," in *Black Economic Development,* ed. William F. Haddad and G. Douglas Pugh (Englewood Cliffs, N.J.: Prentice-Hall, 1969), 50–59.
32. Ibid., 51.
33. Rudwick and Meier, "How CORE Began," 802.
34. Warren Weaver, "Civil Rights Unit Fights Bus Plan," *New York Times,* April 29, 1973, A26; Doris Innis, "Black Power in Education: A Proposal for Change in Harlem Schools" 3, no. 2 (Winter 1968): 3; "Core Urges City to Let Harlem Run Own Schools," *New York Times,* March 4, 1969, 28; "Black Leader's Idea for South's Schools: Interview with Roy Innis, National Director, Congress of Racial Equality,"

U.S. News and World Report, March 2, 1970, 2; "CORE Planning to Fight Richmond Busing Order," *New York Times,* January 27, 1972, 40; "CORE Opposes Order Merging Virginia School," *New York Times,* January 16, 1972, 60; "CORE Chief Tours the South Urging Black School Districts," *Washington Post,* February 5, 1970, A4.

35. "James Farmer Quits CORE in Angola Feud," *New York Times,* February 20, 1976, A6; "Black Congressman Calls for Federal Probe of C.O.R.E.," *Black Panther,* February 28, 1976, 11 and 22; "Threatened Black Boycott Forces Cancellation of Roy Innis Speech," *Black Panther,* February 21, 1976, 5.

36. "Threatened Black Boycott Forces Cancellation of Roy Innis Speech," 5.

37. "Black Congressman Calls for Federal Probe of C.O.R.E.," 22.

38. Greg Harris, "State Probes CORE's Funds," *New York Amsterdam News,* June 16, 1979, 1–2; also see Harry Zehner, "How Roy Innis Ravaged CORE," *Saturday Review,* April 28, 1979, 21–24; Marable, "CORE: Demise of an Ideal," 36.

39. Zehner, "How Roy Innis Ravaged CORE," 22.

40. Annette Samuels, "McKissick, Farmer Seek CORE's Roy Innis Ouster," *New York Amsterdam News,* August 1978, A1–2. Thomas A. Johnson, "Dissidents in CORE Tell of a Lawsuit to Unseat Innis," *New York Times,* November 21, 1978, A8; Dennis A. Williams and Elliot D. Lee, "Civil Rights: CORE War," *Newsweek,* August 28, 1978, 29.

41. Ronald Smothers, "Court Finds Innis to Be Legitimate Head of CORE," *New York Times,* July 29, 1983, A3.

42. Lucius J. Barker and Jesse McCorry, *Black Americans and the Political System* (Cambridge, Mass.: Winthrop Publishers, 1980), 195.

43. Dennis Duggan, "Innis Found Innocent of Assault," *Newsday,* April 8, 1982. For further discussion of Innis's legal difficulties during this period, see "Citibank Sues CORE's Innis," *New York Post,* February 21, 1980. These and other articles on CORE can be found in the Clipping File, Schomburg Center for Research in Black Culture, New York Public Library.

44. "CORE Members Dismiss Innis," *New York Times,* November 2, 1980, A26.

45. Smothers, "Court Finds Innis to Be Legitimate Head of CORE," A3.

46. Mack Jones, "The Political Thought of the New Black Conservatives: An Analysis, Explanation and Interpretation," in *Readings in American Political Issues,* ed. Franklin D. Jones (Dubuque, Iowa: Kendall Hunt Publishing Co., 1987), 27; also see Lewis A. Randolph, "A Historical Analysis and Critique of Contemporary Black Conservatism," *Western Journal of Black Studies* 19 (1995): 149–163.

47. Jones, "Political Thought of New Black Conservatives," 28–31.

48. Kenneth Noble, "Bork Panel Ends Hearings; Vote Scheduled on Tuesday," *New York Times,* October 1, 1987, B59.

49. Ross Anderson, "Most Blacks Back Thomas, CORE Leader Says," *Seattle Times,* August 29, 1991, B4.

50. Roy Innis, "A Call for Black Americans to Develop Bold New Political Tactics and Strategies," MS, 1984.

51. Frank Borzellieri, "Arming Citizens to Fight Crime," *USA Today,* July 1985, 57. For additional information on CORE's freedom patrols, see Meier and Rudwick, *CORE,* 367.

52. Roy Innis, interview by author, New York, June 18, 1999.

53. Ibid.

54. Ibid.

55. "We Are Brothers under the Skin—Imperiale and Innis," *New York Post,* September 8, 1983, Schomburg Collection. For additional information on Anthony Imperiale's relationship with the Black community in Newark, N.J., see Komozi Woodard, *A Nation within a Nation: Amiri Baraka (Leroi Jones) and Black Power Politics* (Chapel Hill: University of North Carolina Press, 1999), 97–100 and 231–236.

56. "Rights Groups Says Gun Ban Hurts Blacks," *St. Petersburg Times,* January 6, 1990, 6A; also see "N.R.A. Joins CORE Drive," *New York Times,* May 30, 1986; Borsellier, "Arming Citizens to Fight Crime," 56–57.

57. Joe Conason, "The Strange Career of Roy Innis," *Village Voice,* July 30, 1985, 16.

58. Michael Oreakes, "Innis Surprises Republicans," *New York Times,* November 25, 1988, B8; "Innis Plans Primary Bid," *New York Times,* February 19, 1994, A22.

59. George Holmes, interview by author, June 18, 1999, New York; also see Congress of Racial Equality, "Project Independence: A Unique Welfare Reform and Job Training Program," pamphlet, n.d.

60. Jim Dwyer, "Debt at CORE of Woes," *Daily News* (N.Y.), January 17, 1999, 8; "CORE $2 Million in Debt, Record Shows," *Atlanta Journal-Constitution,* February 27, 1994, C7; Jim Dwyer, "This King Fete Rotten to CORE," *Daily News* (N.Y.), January 18, 1998, 8.

61. James C. McKinley Jr., "Praise of Innis Wins Rebuke for Giuliani," *New York Times,* January 22, 1994, 24.

Six "You're Not Ready for Farrakhan"

1. The title of this essay is from a 1984 Louis Farrakhan speech quoted in "Farrakhan on Race, Politics and the News Media," *New York Times,* April 17, 1984, A16. For biographical information on Jesse Jackson, see Marshall Frady, *Jesse: The Life and Pilgrimage of Jesse Jackson* (New York: Random House, 1996); Tom Landess, *Jesse Jackson and the Politics of Race* (Ottawa, Ill.: Jameson Books, 1985); Ernest R. House, *Jesse Jackson and the Politics of Charisma* (Boulder, Colo.: Westview Press, 1988); Arnold Gibbons, *Race, Politics and the White Media: The Jesse Jackson Campaigns* (Lanham, Md.: University Press of America, 1993); Lorenzo Morris, ed., *The Social and Political Implications of the 1984 Jesse Jackson Presidential Campaign* (New York: Praeger, 1990); and Jesse Jackson, *Straight from the Heart* (Philadelphia, Pa.: Fortress Press, 1987).

2. The use of the term *Muslim* in this essay will refer to the Nation of Islam and its membership unless otherwise specified.

3. For works on Louis Farrakhan and the Nation of Islam, see Mattias Gardell, *In the Name of Elijah Muhammad: Louis Farrakhan and the Nation of Isla*m (Durham, N.C.: Duke University Press, 1996); Arthur J. Magida, *Prophet of Rage: A Life of Louis Farrakhan and His Nation* (New York: Basic Books, 1996); Amy Alexander, ed., *The Farrakhan Factor* (New York: Grove Press, 1998); Florence H. Levinsohn, *Looking for Farrakhan* (Chicago, Ill.: Ivan R. Dee, 1997); and Louis Farrakhan, *Seven Speeches by Minister Louis Farrakhan* (Newport News, Va.: Ramza Associates and United Brothers Communications Systems, n.d.). For Elijah Muhammad,

Malcolm X, and the first Nation of Islam, see C. Eric Lincoln, *The Black Muslims in America* (Boston: Beacon Press, 1961); E. U. Essien-Udom, *Black Nationalism* (Chicago, Ill.: University of Chicago Press, 1962); Elijah Muhammad, *Message to the Blackman in America* (Chicago, Ill.: Muhammad Mosque of Islam No. 2, 1965); Malcolm X (with Alex Haley), *The Autobiography of Malcolm X* (1965; rpt., New York: Ballantine Books, 1998); Claude A. Clegg III, *An Original Man: The Life and Times of Elijah Muhammad* (New York: St. Martin's Press, 1997); and Karl Evanzz, *The Messenger: The Rise and Fall of Elijah Muhammad* (New York: Pantheon, 1999).

4. Susan C. Cowley and Martin Weston, "'Yesterday's Message,'" *Newsweek,* June 30, 1975, 71; "'White Muslims?'" *Time,* June 30, 1975, 52; Wallace D. Muhammad, "Special Announcement," *Muhammad Speaks,* October 31, 1975, 1; Wallace D. Muhammad, "The Lost-Found Nation of Islam in the West," *Bilalian News,* November 14, 1975, 20; Barbara Reynolds, "Changes in Black Muslims: Why the Surprise?" *Chicago Tribune,* March 7, 1976, 38; Dennis A. Williams and Elaine Sciolino, "Rebirth of the Nation," *Newsweek,* March 15, 1976, 33; "Nation of Islam Changes Name to Fight Black Separatist Image," *New York Times,* October 19, 1976, 33; "Conversion of the Muslims," *Time,* March 14, 1977, 59; "Black Muslims Revise View of Former Leader," *Washington Post,* May 3, 1977, Nathaniel Sheppard Jr., "Black Muslim Movement Divided in Dispute over Doctrinal Changes," *New York Times,* March 7, 1978, 18; A4; Paul Delaney, "Radical Changes by New Leader Leave Many Muslims Disaffected," *New York Times,* December 25, 1978, 16; Bruce M. Ganns and Walter L. Lowe, "The Islamic Connection," *Playboy,* May 1980, 203; and Nathaniel Sheppard Jr., "Nationalist Faction of Black Muslim Movement Gains Strength," *New York Times,* March 8, 1982, A12.

5. George E. Curry, "Farrakhan, Jesse and Jews," *Emerge* (July–August 1994): 31; Frady, *Jesse,* 349.

6. Ibid., 349; E. R. Shipp, "Candidacy of Jackson Highlights Split among Black Muslims," *New York Times,* February 27, 1984, A10.

7. Muhammad, *Message to the Blackman,* 172–173; "The Honorable Elijah Muhammad Tells Why We Must Elect Our Own Candidates," *Muhammad Speaks,* March 18, 1963, 3; and "Quotations from the Messenger," *Muhammad Speaks,* August 2, 1963, 9.

8. According to one investigator of this mass registration of voters, only 167 people registered to vote during Farrakhan's trek to the Election Commission (Shipp, "Candidacy of Jackson Highlights," A10; Chinta Strausberg, "Muslims Get into Politics; Hundred Register to Vote," *Chicago Defender,* February 11, 1984, 3.

9. "Minister Farrakhan Speaks at Princeton: What Is the Need of Black History?" in Louis Farrakhan, *Back Where We Belong,* ed. Joseph D. Eure and Richard M. Jerome (Philadelphia: PC International Press, 1989), 71–78.

10. Rick Atkinson, "Peace with American Jews Eludes Jackson," *Washington Post,* February 13, 1984, A1, A4; Rick Atkinson, "Jackson Denounces 'Hounding' from Jewish Community," *Washington Post,* February 22, 1984, A12; and Curry, "Farrakhan, Jesse and Jews," 36–37.

11. Shipp, "Candidacy of Jackson Highlights," A10; Chinta Strausberg and Henry Locke, "Muslim Faithful Honor Jackson," *Chicago Defender,* daily edition, February 27, 1984, 1; William A. Henry III, "Pride and Prejudice," *Time,* February 28, 1994, 25; and Atkinson, "Jackson Denounces Hounding," A12.

12. Malcolm Galdwell, "The Roots of Farrakhan's Apparent Obsession with Jews," *Washington Post,* national weekly edition, January 22–28, 1996, 8; Bill Turque, "Playing a Different Tune," *Newsweek,* June 28, 1993, 30–31.

13. "Farrakhan on Race," A16; "Minister Farrakhan Speaks at Morgan State University," in Farrakhan, *Back Where We Belong,* 120–121; Susan Schmidt, "Farrakhan Flays Black Critics, Jews, the Press," *Washington Post,* September 27, 1985, C1, C6; "Nation of Islam Leader Warns Black Reporter," *New York Times,* April 3, 1984, B4; and "Muslim Accuses Press of Twisting His Comments," *New York Times,* April 12, 1984, B12.

14. Landess and Quinn, *Jesse Jackson,* 127, 222–224.

15. Ibid., 224; Frady, *Jesse,* 350–351; and Curry, "Farrakhan, Jesse and Jews," 39–40.

16. Landess and Quinn, *Jesse Jackson,* 221.

17. "Jackson Delegates Favor Farrakhan, Survey Finds," *Los Angeles Times,* July 16, 1984, 7; Chinta Strausberg, "Jesse Rebukes Min. Farrakhan," *Chicago Defender,* June 30, 1984, 46.

18. Ibid.

19. Howard Fineman and Vern E. Smith, "An Angry Charmer," *Newsweek,* October 30, 1995, 33; Curry, "Farrakhan, Jesse and Jews," 40–41.

20. Juan Williams, "Desert Military, Blacks Urged," *Washington Post,* February 25, 1985, A3.

21. Lee May, "Farrakhan Reports Load from Kadafi," *Los Angeles Times,* May 3, 1985, 4.

22. Ibid., 4.

23. Henry, "Pride and Prejudice," 26.

24. Arthur S. Brisbane, "Barry Criticizes Farrakhan Speech Vilifying Jews," *Washington Post,* 10 September 10, 1985, C1; "Minister Farrakhan Speaks at Morgan State," 122–123.

25. Ibid.; Joe Pichirallo, "Black Leaders Criticize Farrakhan Stab at Barry," *Washington Post,* September 28, 1985, B3; and Chinta Strausberg, "Anti-Farrakhan Resolution Passed," *Chicago Defender,* November 27, 1985, 3–4.

26. "Minister Farrakhan Speaks at Morgan State," 126; Schmidt, "Farrakhan Flays Black Critics," C1; and Curry, "Farrakhan, Jesse and Jews," 34.

27. For Farrakhan's comments regarding Malcolm X, see Louis X, "Boston Minister Tells of Malcolm—Muhammad's Biggest Hypocrite," *Muhammad Speaks,* December 4, 1964, 11–15.

28. "Politics without Economics Is Symbol without Substance," in Farrakhan, *Back Where We Belong,* 201–214; Louis Farrakhan, speech at the Closing Plenary Session of Blacks in Government, Washington, D.C., August 20, 1989; Robert Shogan, "Jackson Says He Will Not Accept Farrakhan's Support," *Los Angeles Times,* June 6, 1987, 29; "Ducking Politics, Leader Talks Business," *Christian Science Monitor,* November 13, 1987, 3; William K. Stevens, "Farrakhan Restates His Support of Jackson in Criticizing the Press," *New York Times,* April 14, 1988; and Gardell, *In the Name of Elijah Muhammad,* 313.

29. Thomas B. Edsall and Gwen Hill, "Farrakhan Accuses U.S. of Acting to Hurt Blacks," *Washington Post,* April 24, 1989, A3; Nathan McCall, "D.C. Council Votes to Praise Farrakhan's Anti-Drug Work," *Washington Post,* October 25, 1989, A1, A10; George E. Curry, "Farrakhan," *Emerge* (August 1990): 34; Nathan McCall,

"Farrakhan Hits Local Leadership," *Washington Post,* May 6, 1990, D1, D11; and Michele L. Norris, "Glendening, Hoyer Sail to Victory," *Washington Post,* September 12, 1990, A21, A27.

30. By 1993 Farrakhan had concluded that efforts to secure reparations for Blacks, while justified, were at the time less important than addressing other problems. Kenneth B. Noble, "U.S. Blacks and Africans Seek Stronger Ties," *New York Times,* May 27, 1993, A10; "The Minister Speaks," *Newsweek,* June 28, 1993, 31; Lynne Duke, "Farrakhan Defends Clinton, Asks Critics to 'Get to Know Me Better,'" *Washington Post,* May 5, 1993, A22; Louis Farrakhan, *A Torchlight for America* (Chicago: FCN Publishing Co., 1993), 34, 38–41; and Don Terry, "Farrakhan: Fiery Separatist in a Sober Suit," *New York Times,* March 3, 1994, A1, B9.

31. Farrakhan, *Torchlight,* 36–37, 40–41; Lynne Duke, "Congressional Black Caucus and Nation of Islam Agree on Alliance," *Washington Post,* September 17, 1993, A3.

32. Henry, "Pride and Prejudice," 22, 27; Lynne Duke, "Black Caucus Sits between Farrakhan, Jews," *Washington Post,* October 12, 1993, A11.

33. Bernard Holland, "Sending a Message, Louis Farrakhan Plays Mendelssohn," *New York Times,* April 19, 1993, C16.

34. By 1996 Nation of Islam businesses were in substantial debt. Taxes due to the Internal Revenue Service alone totaled more than one million dollars. Lorraine Adams, "A Dream Past Due," *Washington Post,* national weekly edition, September 9–15, 1996, 6; "Los Angeles Complex Calls in Muslims Guards," *New York Times,* October 11, 1992; Steven A. Holmes, "As Farrakhan Groups Land Jobs from Government, Debate Grows," *New York Times,* March 4, 1994, A18; and Farrakhan, *Torchlight,* 41.

35. Jon Nordheimer, "Divided by a Diatribe," *New York Times,* December 29, 1993, B1, B6; Jon Nordheimer, "Angry Echoes of Campus Speech," *New York Times,* January 26, 1994, B4.

36. Steven A. Holmes, "Farrakhan Is Warned over Aide's Invective," *New York Times,* January 25, 1994, A12; Alan Finder, "Muslim Gave Racist Speech, Jackson Says," *New York Times,* January 23, 1994, 21, 24; Nathan McCall, "Farrakhan Strikes a Nerve," *Washington Post,* May 7, 1990, D1; and Kevin Merida, "Black Leaders Call on Farrakhan to Repudiate Controversial Remarks by Aide," *Washington Post,* January 26, 1994, A3

37. Ibid., A3.

38. Steven A Holmes, "Farrakhan Repudiates Speech for Tone, Not Anti-Semitism," *New York Times,* February 4, 1994, A1; Steven A. Holmes, "Congressional Black Caucus Backs Away from Farrakhan," *New York Times,* February 3, 1994, A14; Kevin Merida, "Black Caucus Says It Has No Official Working Ties with Nation of Islam," *Washington Post,* February 3, 1994, 16; Congressional Record, 103d Cong., 2d sess., 1994, House Resolution 343, vol. 140, H567; Rene Sanchez, "Ex-Aide Says Farrakhan Still One against 'Enemies,'" *Washington Post,* February 24, 1994, B3; Lynne Duke, "Farrakhan Rebukes Key Aide," *Washington Post,* February 4, 1994, A14.

39. Thirty-four percent of Black respondents in the *Time*/CNN poll viewed Farrakhan as "a bigot and a racist." "They Suck the Life from You," *Time,* February 28, 1994, 25; "The Fallout from Khalid Abdul Muhammad's Speech at Kean College," *Jour-*

nal of Blacks in Higher Education 3 (Spring 1994): 84; and Henry, "Pride and Prejudice," 22.

40. Louis Farrakhan, interview by Barbara Walters, "20/20," ABC, April 22, 1994; Louis Farrakhan, interview by Mike Wallace, "60 Minutes," CBS, April 14, 1996.

41. Sandra Skowron, "NAACP Leadership Summit Opens Today," *Charlotte Observer,* June 12, 1994, 13A; George E. Curry, "Unity in the Community," *Emerge* (September 1994): 36.

42. Skowron, "NAACP Leadership Summit," 13A; Don Terry, "Director of N.A.A.C.P. Is Fighting for Survival," *New York Times,* August 17, 1994, A14; and Curry, "Unity in the Community," 36, 38.

43. Louis Farrakhan, speech at the Million Man March, Washington, D.C., October 16, 1995; Maulana Karenga, "The Million Man March / Day of Absence Mission Statement," *Black Scholar* 25, no. 4 (Fall 1995): 2–11.

44. Farrakhan, speech at the Million Man March.

45. According to the Cable News Network (CNN), more people watched Farrakhan's televised speech at the Million Man March than viewed President Clinton's January State of the Union address. Steven A. Holmes, "After March, Lawmakers Seek Commission on Race Relations," *New York Times,* October 18, 1995, B9.

46. Vern E. Smith and Steven Waldman, "Farrakhan on the March," *Newsweek,* October 9, 1995, 42; Erin L. Clarke, "Brothers in Arms: The Million Man March," *Crisis* (December 1995): 10–11; Dionne 2X Flewellen, "Rosa Parks Endorses Million Man March," *Final Call,* September 27, 1995, 3; and D'Vera Cohn and Debbi Wilgoren, "March Foes Assail Leader, Not Aims," *Washington Post,* October 14, 1995, A11.

47. Henry L. Gates Jr., "The Charmer," *New Yorker,* April 29 and May 6, 1996, 129; Jesse Jackson, speech at the Million Man March, Washington, D.C., October 16, 1995.

48. Tom Raum, "Clinton Appeals for End to Racism," *Times-News* (Burlington, N.C.), October 17, 1995, A1; Steven A. Holmes, "After March, Lawmakers Seek Commission on Race Relations," *New York Times,* October 18, 1995, B9; George E. Curry, "After the Million Man March," *Emerge* (February 1996): 40; and Gates, "Charmer," 129.

49. "'My Duty Is to Point Out the Wrong and the Evil,'" *Newsweek,* October 30, 1995, 36; Louis Farrakhan, speech at Saviour's Day convention, University of Illinois, Chicago, February 25, 1996.

50. "Farrakhan Registers to Vote, Kicks Off National Drive," *Jet,* July 1, 1996, 31.

51. Ferman M. Beckless, "Farrakhan, Mohammad to Reunite," *Chicago Defender,* February 26, 2000, 1; Dirk Johnson, "Farrakhan Ends Longtime Rivalry with Orthodox Muslims," *New York Times,* February 28, 2000, A8; Steve Kloehn, "Farrakhan Points to New Path," *Chicago Tribune,* February 28, 2000, 7; Michael Paulson, "Farrakhan's Nation of Islam Softening Stance," *Boston Globe,* March 4, 2000, B1; B4; Louis Farrakhan, interviewed by Mike Wallace, "60 Minutes," CBS, May 14, 2000; "Farrakhan Admits Role in Slaying of Malcolm X," *Chicago Tribune,* May 11, 2000, 5; "Farrakhan Responds to Media," *Carolina Peacemaker,* May 25, 2000; 8; Ferman M. Beckless, "Nation of Islam, Orthodox Jews Announce Accord," *Chicago Tribune,* February 29, 2000; 3; Paul Shepard, "Farrakhan Trades Divisive

Rhetoric for Populist Message," *Indianapolis Star,* October 15, 2000, D6; "Thousand Celebrate Role of American Family," *Herald-Times* (Bloomington, Ind.), October 17, 2000, A5; and Darryl Fears and Hamil R. Harris, "A Family Celebration," *Washington Post,* October 17, 2000, A14.

52. "Farrakhan on Race, Politics," A16.

Seven   The Southern Christian Leadership Conference

Epigraph: Vern E. Smith, "Dialogue [with Martin Luther King III]: His Own Dream," *Emerge* 9, no. 4 (February 1998): 42.

1. James Q. Wilson, *Political Organizations* (Princeton, N.J.: Princeton University Press, 1995), 13.
2. Aldon Morris, *The Origins of the Civil Rights Movement* (New York: Free Press, 1984), 85.
3. Ibid., 86–90.
4. Ibid., 87, 93, 96.
5. Ibid., 99, 106–108, 113.
6. Walton, *Invisible Politics* (Albany: State University of New York Press, 1985), 261.
7. David J. Garrow, *Bearing the Cross* (New York: William Morrow, 1986), 820.
8. Ralph D. Abernathy, *And the Walls Came Tumbling Down* (New York: Harper and Row, 1989), 477.
9. Ibid., 495–498.
10. Adam Fairclough, *To Redeem the Soul of America* (Athens: University of Georgia Press, 1987), 390–391.
11. Abernathy, *And the Walls Came Tumbling Down,* 512.
12. Ibid., 527.
13. Ibid., 517.
14. Ibid., 539.
15. Fairclough, *To Redeem the Soul of America,* 388.
16. Abernathy, *And the Walls Came Tumbling Down,* 542–544.
17. Ibid., 548.
18. Ibid., 550.
19. Ibid., 555.
20. Ibid., 568.
21. Ibid., 574–575.
22. Ibid., 575.
23. SCLC, Official Program, 38th Annual Convention, New Orleans, La.
24. Fairclough, *To Redeem the Soul of America,* 396–397.
25. Abernathy, *And the Walls Came Tumbling Down,* 580.
26. Ibid., 581.
27. Ibid., 585.
28. Ibid., 590.
29. Vern E. Smith, "Standing at the Crossroads," *Emerge* 9, no. 4 (February 1998): 56.
30. Maynard Eaton, "The Struggles of Today's Civil Rights Organizations," *Atlanta Tribune,* 8, no. 22, February 22, 1995.
31. John Blake, "Outrage at SCLC Meeting," *Atlanta Journal-Constitution,* August 2, 1995.

32. Smith, "Standing at the Crossroads," 58.
33. Hollis R. Towns, "Martin Luther King, Jr.'s Sons Continue the Dreams," *Atlanta Journal-Constitution,* January 19, 1998.
34. Clarence Lusane, *African Americans at the Crossroads* (Boston: South End Press, 1994), 77.
35. Maria Lameiras, *Atlanta Journal-Constitution,* November 2, 1997.
36. Smith, "Dialogue," 43.
37. *SCLC Magazine,* January–February 1999.
38. Ernie Suggs, "Showdown Looms over Leadership of MLK III," *Atlanta Journal Constitution,* July 29, 2001
39. Ibid.
40. Suggs, "SCLC Keeps Leaders in Place, Preaches Unity," *Atlanta Constitution,* August 9, 2001.
41. Ibid.
42. Ibid.
43. Abernathy, *And the Walls Came Tumbling Down,* 556–557.

Eight   Reverend Jesse Jackson and the Rainbow/PUSH Coalition

1. *Trading Partners Brochure,* Rainbow/PUSH Coalition, n.d.
2. Jesse L. Jackson, *Straight from the Heart* (Philadelphia: Fortress Press, 1987), xiii and xvii.
3. Barbara A. Reynolds, *Jesse Jackson: The Man, the Movement, the Myth* (Chicago: Nelson Hall, 1975), 169–183.
4. Digital Equipment Corporation, *Trading Partners* 1, no. 3 (September 1997): 2. *Trading Partners* is the official newsletter and information source of the Rainbow/PUSH Coalition Wall Street Project.
5. See "Victory at Texaco," *Trading Partners* 1, no. 1 (April 1997): 2; and "Mitsubishi Motors," *Trading Partners* 1, no. 1 (April 1997): 2; also see Charles R. Babcock, "A Deal with Unsettling Dissent," *Washington Post,* July 28, 1999, E1.
6. Under the GTE/Georgetown Venture, Chester Davenport, became chairman of the GTE subsidiary, Cellular Communications, which was created for this venture. Georgetown Partners also owns a portion of the new company. See "Big Business Makes Mega-Minority Deals," *Trading Partners* 3, no. 4 (April 1999): 1.
7. "Wall Street Project Members Strike Telecom Deals," *Trading Partners* 3, no. 7 (September 1999): 1.
8. Manning Marable, *Race, Reform and Rebellion: The Second Reconstruction in Black America, 1945–1990,* 2d ed. (Jackson: University of Mississippi Press, 1991), 83; Frances Fox Pivens and Richard A. Cloward, *Poor People's Movements: Why They Succeed, How They Fail* (New York: Vintage Books, 1979), 255.
9. Herbert H. Haines, *Black Radicals and the Civil Rights Mainstream, 1954–1970* (Knoxville: University of Tennessee Press, 1988), 51.
10. Ibid., 61.
11. See Aldon Morris, *The Origins of the Civil Rights Movement: Black Communities Organizing for Change* (New York: Free Press, 1984).
12. Lyndon B. Johnson, *The Vantage Point* (New York: Holt, Rinehart and Winston, 1971); and "Kennedy, Johnson and the War on Poverty," *Journal of American History* 69 (June 1982).

13. Stephen Oates, *Let the Trumpet Sound: The Life of Martin Luther King, Jr.* (New York: Mentor Books, 1982), 434.
14. Adam Fairclough, *To Redeem the Soul of America* (Athens: University of Georgia Press, 1987), 370–382.
15. Martin Luther King Jr., *Where Do We Go from Here?: Chaos of Community* (Boston: Beacon Press, 1967).
16. Reynolds, *Jesse Jackson,* 104.
17. Leon H. Sullivan, *Moving Mountains: The Principles and Purpose of Leon Sullivan* (Valley Forge, Pa.: Judson Press, 1998), 12.
18. Ibid., 13.
19. Ibid., 14.
20. Fairclough, *To Redeem the Soul of America,* 285.
21. Ibid., 349.
22. David Llorens, "Apostle of Economics: Youthful Rev. Jesse Jackson Guides Chicago Negroes to $15 Million Additional Income," *Ebony* (1967): 78–86.
23. Ibid.
24. "Black Pocketbook Power," *Time,* March 1, 1968, 17.
25. Roger D. Hatch, *Beyond Opportunity: Jesse Jackson's Vision for America* (Philadelphia: Fortress Press, 1988), 11.
26. Patricia C. McKissack, *Jesse Jackson: A Biography* (New York: Scholastic, Inc., 1989), 47.
27. Reynolds, *Jesse Jackson,* 169.
28. For more discussion of Operation Breadbasket's boycott of A&P, see Patricia McKissack, *Jesse Jackson: A Biography* (New York: Scholastic, Inc., 1989), 37; Eddie Stone, *Jesse Jackson* (Los Angeles: Holloway House, 1979), 75–77; and Barbara A. Reynolds, *Jesse Jackson: The Man, the Movement, the Myth* (Chicago: Nelson Hall, 1975), 130–133.
29. Taken from an interview with Gary Massoni, a minister and staff member of the Rainbow PUSH coalition (Reynolds, *Jesse Jackson,* 140).
30. Ibid.
31. Ibid., 208–218.
32. Ibid., 124.
33. Jesse L. Jackson, *Straight from the Heart* (Philadelphia: Fortress Press, 1987), 277.
34. "The Vision of a New Course, a New Coalition, and a New Leadership," speech given at the Twelfth Annual Operation PUSH Convention, Atlanta, July 27, 1983.
35. Jackson, *Straight from the Heart,* speech entitled, "Black Americans Seek Economic Parity," 277–281.
36. Reynolds, *Jesse Jackson,* 171.
37. Restated Covenant among Operation PUSH, Inc., Burger King Corporation, and the Minority Franchise Association, November 24, 1984.
38. Hatch, *Beyond Opportunity,* 47.
39. Ibid., 45.
40. Ibid.
41. Ibid., 48.
42. Reynolds, *Jesse Jackson,* 177. Reynolds compares Chicago's African American business activity to that of Durham, North Carolina, which held the previous title for having the most African American businesses.

43. Sheila Collins, *The Rainbow Challenge: The Jesse Jackson Campaign and the Future of U.S. Politics* (New York: Monthly Review Press, 1986), 86.
44. Ibid., 246.
45. Rodney D. Green and Finley C. Campbell, "The Jesse Jackson Economic Platform of 1984: A Critique and Analysis," in *The Social and Political Implications of the 1984 Jesse Jackson Presidential Campaign,* ed. Lorenzo Morris (New York: Praeger, 1990), 101; and Collins, *Rainbow Challenge,* 246.
46. Frank Clemente and Frank Watkins, ed., *Keep Hope Alive: Jesse Jackson's 1988 Presidential Campaign* (Boston: South End Press, 1989), 73–92 and 93–94.
47. Ibid., 94.
48. Ibid., 47.
49. Jackson, *Straight from the Heart,* speech entitled "Black Americans Seek Economic Equity and Parity," 277.
50. Ibid.
51. Lucius J. Barker, *Our Time Has Come: A Delegate's Diary of Jesse Jackson's 1984 Presidential Campaign* (Urbana: University of Illinois Press, 1988), 137; and Bob Faw and Nancy Skelton, *Thunder in America* (Austin: Texas Monthly Press, 1986), 190.
52. Greene, "Jesse Jackson's Economic Platform," 121.
53. Organizational Documents of Operation PUSH, 1982–1987.
54. Donald Katz, *Just Do It: The Nike Spirit in the Corporate World* (Holbrook, Mass.: Adams Publishing, 1994), 110.
55. Rainbow Coalition, "Rebuild America: 1992 and Beyond," conference brochure, 1992.
56. Internal Merger Documents of Rainbow/PUSH Coalition, 1995–1996.
57. International Trade Bureau Membership Directory, Rainbow/PUSH Coalition, 1999.
58. U.S. Bureau of the Census, *Poverty in the United States: 2000,* ser. P–60, no. 214; and *1998 Green Book,* app. H; and U.S. Bureau of the Census, *Housing Vacancies and Homeownership: Annual Statistics, 2000,* table 20.
59. William O'Hare, "Minority Owned Firms in America," *Readings in Black Political Economy,* ed. John Whitehead and Cobie Kwasi Harris (Dubuque, Iowa: Kendall/Hunt Publishing Co.), 196–197.
60. Thomas Boston, "Generating Jobs through African American Business Growth," *Readings in Black Political Economy,* ed. John Whitehead and Cobie Kwasi Harris (Dubuque, Iowa: Kendall/Hunt Publishing Co.), 306.
61. Federal Glass Ceiling Commission, *Good for Business: Making Full Use of the Nation's Human Capital* (Washington, D.C.: U.S. Government Printing Office, March 1995), 65–71.
62. Information on the Wall Street Project—specifically its structure, goals, and accomplishment—was provided by an interview with the director of the Wall Street Project, Chee Chee Williams. Personal knowledge, April 7, 2000 (author was bureau chief of the Washington, D.C., office from 1997 to 1999).
63. Ibid.
64. Ibid.
65. See Thomas Boston, "Generating Jobs through African American Business Growth," 305–310.

66. Ibid., 305.

67. Ibid., 307.

68. Ibid., 308.

69. Interview with Williams, April 7, 2000.

70. Viacom/Evergreen/Chancellor Agreement, internal documents of the Rainbow/ PUSH Coalition, 1997; Federal Communications Commission Approval, 1997.

71. Interview with Williams, April 7, 2000.

72. Robert E. Weems Jr., "Economic Self-Destruction: African American Consumerism in the 1990s," in Whitehead and Kwasi Harris, *Readings in Black Political Economy,* 190–193.

73. "White House Pushes New Markets Initiative," *Trading Partners* 3, no. 4 (April 1999); New Markets Plan, *Trading Partners* 3, no. 6 (July–August 1999).

74. Manning Marable, "Civil Rights or Silver Rights?" *Znet Commentary <http:// www.zena.secureforum.com/zdaily/index.cfm>,* January 2, 2000.

75. Williams Julius Wilson, *The Truly Disadvantaged* (Chicago: University of Chicago Press, 1987).

76. Earl Ofari Hutchinson, "Black Capitalism: Entrepreneurs and Consumers," in *Readings in Black Political Economy,* ed. John Whitehead and Cobie Kwasi Harris (Dubuque, Iowa: Kendall/Hunt Publishing Co.), 201–209, 205n.

77. Manning Marable, "Civil Rights or Silver Rights?" *Znet Commentary,* January 2, 2000.

Nine "We Refused to Lay Down Our Spears"

The title of this chapter is taken from a dialogue with Marian Kramer, interview by author, tape recording, Detroit, Michigan, August 4, 1994. I thank Shawn D. Williams and Swarna Rajagopalan for their invaluable research assistance with this chapter.

Epigraph: Johnnie Tillmon, first chair of the National Welfare Rights Organization, quoted in Guida West, *The National Welfare Rights Movement: The Social Protest of Poor Women* (New York: Praeger, 1981), x.

1. Jeffrey Katz, "Welfare: After 60 Years, Most Control Is Passing to States," *CQ,* August 3, 1996, 2190; for a critique of the assumptions about the racial and gender dynamics of the "underclass," see Adolph Reed, "The Underclass as Myth and Symbol: The Poverty of Poverty Discourse," *Radical America* 24, no. 1 (1991): 33–37.

2. Robert Pear, "Clinton to Sign Welfare Bill That Ends U.S. Aid Guarantee and Gives States Broad Power, *New York Times,* August 1, 1996, A:1, col. 6; online edition, <http://www.nytimes.com>. For an overview of the main elements of the original reform bill, see Katz, "Welfare," 2192. Additional figures are from Illinois Department of Public Aid, *Draft, State of Illinois, Temporary Assistance for Needy Families, State Plan,* February 3, 1997 (Springfield, Ill.), 1–3; Public Law 193, 104th Congress, 2d sess. (August 22, 1996), sec. 1; Katz, "Welfare," 2190.

3. See Margaret Weir, Shola Orloff and Theda Skocpol, eds., *The Politics of Social Policy in the United States* (Princeton, N.J.: Princeton University Press, 1988); also see U.S. House Committee on Ways and Means, *Overview of Entitlement Programs, 1993 Green Book,*103d Congress, 1st sess., July 7,1993. Committee Print 18, 615. Pear details the savings derived from this retrenchment ("Clinton Says He'll Sign Bill Overhauling Welfare System," 2).

4. Pear, "Clinton to Sign Welfare Bill," 1; see also Dona Cooper Hamilton and Charles V. Hamilton, *The Dual Agenda: The African-American Struggle for Civil and Economic Equality* (New York: Columbia University Press, 1997), 1–2.

5. Mark Hornbeck, "Efforts to Weaken Welfare Bills Defeated," *Detroit News,* November 9, 1995, 1; online edition, *<http://www.detroitnews.com/menu/stories/23946.htm>.*

6. Diane Dujon and Ann Withorn, eds., *For Crying Out Loud: Women's Poverty in the United States* (Boston: South End Press, 1996). In 1991 African American women constituted 38.8 percent of the women who received AFDC and all women of color constituted almost 62 percent. See U.S. House Committee on Ways and Means, *Overview of Entitlement Programs, 1993 Green Book,* 697.

7. Sidney Tarrow, *Struggling to Reform: Collective Action, Social Movements, and Cycles of Protest* (Ithaca, N.Y.: Western Societies Program, Cornell University, 1983); Verta Taylor, "Social Movement in Continuity: The Women's Movement in Abeyance," *American Sociological Review* 54 (October 1990): 761–762; Ephraim Mizruchi, *Regulating Society: Marginality and Social Control in Historical Perspective* (New York: Free Press, 1983), 1–7; David Snow and Robert Benford, "Master Frames and Cycles of Protest," in *Frontiers in Social Movement Theory,* ed. Aldon Morris and Carol McClurg Mueller (New Haven, Conn.: Yale University Press, 1992), 133–155.

8. See Piven and Cloward, *Poor People's Movement,* 24–25; also E. E. Schnattschneider, *Semisovereign People* (Hinsdale, Ill.: Dryden Press, 1975), 1–19; also see Doug McAdam, *Political Process and the Development of Black Insurgency, 1930–1970* (Chicago: University of Chicago Press, 1982), 146–180; Payne, *I've Got the Light of Freedom,* 132–179.

9. Frances Fox Piven and Richard A. Cloward, "Normalizing Collective Protest," in *Frontiers in Social Movement Theory,* ed. Aldon Morris and Carol McClurg Mueller (New Haven, Conn.: Yale University Press, 1992), 301–325; Piven and Cloward, *Poor People's Movements,* 276–277.

10. Quotes in paragraphs taken from Piven and Cloward, *Poor People's Movements,* xxi–xxii and 352–353, respectively.

11. Snow and Benford, "Master Frames and Cycles of Protest," 141.

12. Quotes taken from Taylor, "Social Movement Continuity," 761 and 762, respectively.

13. Ibid., 762.

14. For good discussions of the concept of preexisting organizational networks, see Charles Euchner, *Extraordinary Politics: How Protest and Dissent Are Changing American Democracy* (New York: Westview Press, 1996), 29–63; Aldon Morris, *The Origins of the Civil Rights Movement: Black Communities Organizing for Change* (New York: Free Press, 1984); and Anthony Oberschall, *Social Movements: Ideologies, Interests, and Identities* (New Brunswick, N.J.: Transaction, 1993), 24–31.

15. William Gamson, *The Strategy of Social Protest,* 2d ed. (Belmont, Calif.: Wadsworth Publishing, 1990); Oberschall, *Social Movements,* 149–186; Piven and Cloward, *Poor People's Movements,* 23–37; James Scott, *Domination and the Arts of Resistance: Hidden Transcripts* (New Haven, Conn.: Yale University Press, 1990); Robin Kelley, "The Black Poor and the Politics of Opposition in a New South City, 1929–1970," in *The Underclass Debate: Views from History,* ed. Michael Katz (Princeton, N.J.: Princeton University Press, 1993), 293–332.

16. For a discussion of such difficulties, see Betty Reid Mandell and Ann Withorn, "Keep On Keeping On: Organizing for Welfare Rights in Massachusetts," in *Mobilizing the Community: Local Politics in the Era of the Global City,* ed. Robert Fisher and Joseph Kling (Newbury Park, Calif.: Sage, 1994), 135.

17. To understand the founding dynamics of the NWRO, see Nick Kotz and Mary Lynn Kotz, *A Passion for Equality: George A. Wiley and the Movement* (New York: W. W. Norton, 1976), 194–202. Black women in the Welfare Rights Movement have given poignant accounts about the expertise and insights they brought to welfare rights organizing. See Marian Kramer, "Speaking for Ourselves: A Lifetime of Welfare Rights Organizing," in *For Crying Out Loud,* ed. Diane Dujon and Ann Withorn (Boston: South End Press, 1996), 353.

18. Robert Mast ed., *Detroit Lives* (Philadelphia: Temple University Press),103–106; West, *National Welfare Rights Movement,* 219–220, 172–201. For a discussion of the contributions of the IFCO and the United Church of Christ, see West, *National Welfare Rights Organization,* 145–153.

19. West, *National Welfare Rights Organization,* 308; Jackson, "State, the Movement, and the Urban Poor"; Euchner, *Extraordinary Politics,* 36–43.

20. West, *National Welfare Rights Organization,* 39.

21. See Metropolitan Detroit Welfare Reform Coalition, "The Welfare Reform Coalition?"; Kramer, interview by author, August 4, 1994, Detroit, Mich. Information on welfare rights protests in various Michigan cities taken from Kotz and Kotz, *Passion for Equality,* 310–313.

22. Payne, *I've Got the Light of Freedom,* 338. Also see Kotz and Kotz, *Passion for Equality,* 172, 184–188, for details about Wiley's split with CORE. See also Metropolitan Detroit Welfare Reform Coalition, *News and Views,* papers of the Welfare Employees Union Collection of the Archives of Labor and Urban Affairs, Walter Reuther Archive of Labor and Urban Affairs, box 18, folder 4.

23. Kramer, interview by author.

24. West, *National Welfare Rights Organization,* 60–65, 108–113, 115; Mandell and Withorn, "Keeping On Keeping On," 134–135.

25. Martin Luther King Jr., *The Trumpet of Conscience* (New York: Harper and Row, 1968), 21–34; Gerald McKnight, *The Last Crusade: Martin Luther King, Jr., the FBI, and the Poor People's Campaign* (Boulder, Colo.: Westview Press, 1998), chap. 1.

26. Paula Giddings, *When and Where I Enter: The Impact of Black Women on Race and Sex in America* (New York: Bantam Books, 1984), 312–313.

27. Quotations and the account of King and the NWRO meeting were taken from Kotz and Kotz, *Passion for Equality,* 248–249. Andrew Young's comment cited in Giddings, *When and Where I Enter,* 313.

28. Charles Fager, *Uncertain Resurrection: The Poor People's Washington Campaign* (Grand Rapids, Mich.: William B. Eerdmans Publishing, 1969); and McKnight, *Last Crusade.*

29. Jill Quadagno, "Race, Class, and Gender in the U.S. Welfare State: Nixon's Failed Family Assistance Plan," *American Sociological Review* 55 (February 1990): 11–28.

30. "Welfare Mothers Will Seek Recruits," *Detroit Free Press,* August 23,1969, 4A; Quadagno, "Race, Class, and Gender in the U.S. Welfare State"; and Hamilton and Hamilton, *Dual Agenda,* 188–191.

31. Hamilton, *Dual Agenda,* 188–191; Jackson, "State, the Movement, and the Urban Poor," 434–435; Jacqueline Pope, *Biting the Hand That Feeds Them* (Westport, Conn.: Greenwood, 1989), 75–77; Quadagno, "Race, Class, and Gender in the U.S. Welfare State," 25.

32. William J. Wilson, *The Truly Disadvantaged: The Inner City, the Underclass, and Public Policy* (Chicago: University of Chicago Press, 1987), 6–19; Katz, *Undeserving Poor;* Clarence Lusane, "If I Were a Rich Man," *Race in the Global Era: African Americans at the Millennium* (Boston: South End Press, 1997), 35–36.

33. Mimi Abramovitz, *Regulating the Lives of Women: Social Policy from Colonial Times to the Present* (Boston: South End Press, 1988), 335.

34. Gary Bryner, *The Great American Welfare Reform Debate: Politics and Public Morality* (New York: W. W. Norton, 1998), 71–72; Hamilton and Hamilton, *Dual Agenda,* 192–198; Joel Handler, *The Poverty of Welfare Reform* (New Haven, Conn.: Yale University Press, 1995), 60–61; Monroe Anderson, "Protesters Hit Jobless Aid, Carter Welfare Proposal," *Chicago Tribune,* October 30, 1977, sec. 3, 13.

35. Public Law 523, 95th Cong., 1st sess. (October 27, 1978), secs. 101–102; Robert Smith, *We Have No Leaders: African Americans in the Post–Civil Rights Era* (Albany: State University of New York Press, 1996),187–210.

36. West, *National Welfare Rights Organization,* x; Kramer, "Speaking for Ourselves," 366.

37. Quote and information taken from Kramer, interview by author; Patricia Hill Collins, *Black Feminist Thought: Knowledge, Consciousness, and the Politics of Empowerment* (New York: Routledge, 1990).

38. Reference to B-WAC comes from Pope, *Biting the Hand That Feeds Them,* 134. Funiciello quote taken from Mandell and Withorn, "Keeping On Keeping On," 135.

39. Mimi Abramovitz, *Under Attack, Fighting Back: Women and Welfare in the United States* (New York: Monthly Review Press), 132–133; Mandell and Withorn, "For Crying Out Loud."

40. Tillmon quoted in West, *National Welfare Rights Organization,* v; Kramer, "Speaking for Ourselves," 361.

41. Gary Delgado, *Organizing the Movement: The Roots and Growth of ACORN* (Philadelphia: Temple University Press, 1986). See "ACORN's 25-Year History" (1997), *ACORN Home Page, <http://www.acorn.org/community/ACORN_25_history. html#roots>.*

42. See Brian Flanigan, "Coalition Rips Welfare Review," *Michigan Chronicle,* June 14, 1975, 1A; Marie Teasley, "Westside Mothers Launch Food Stamp Info Campaign," *Michigan Chronicle,* March 15, 1975, 1A, 4A; Tom Bergeson of the Michigan Welfare Reform Coalition to Member Organizations Re: Coalition Letter to Dr. John Dempsey, October 18, 1978, Citizens, Papers in Citizens for Welfare Reform Collection, Commission on Community Relations, Walter Reuther Archives of Labor and Urban Affairs, Detroit, Mich., Wayne State University, box 81; see also Dottie Stevens, "Welfare Rights Organizing Saved My Life," in *For Crying Out Loud: Women's Poverty in the United States* (Boston: South End Press, 1996), 313.

43. "CWRO Loses Grant," *Chicago Defender,* March 11, 1978, 5; Mandell and Withorn, "Keep On Keeping On," 131–132; Stevens, "Welfare Rights Organizing Saved My Life," 316–325.

44. Kotz and Kotz, *Passion for Equality,* 189–190; "Welfare Rights Vigil," *Call and Post* (Cleveland), July 8, 1978, 5A; Dujon and Withorn, *For Crying Out Loud,* 157; Abramovitz, *Under Attack, Fighting Back,* 130–131.

45. Abramovitz, *Regulating the Lives of Women,* 358.

46. Manning Marable, *Race, Reform, and Rebellion: The Second Reconstruction in Black America, 1945–1990,* 2d ed. (Jackson: University of Mississippi Press, 1991), 181–184.

47. Edward Sargent, "Marchers Protest against Reagan Policies," *Washington Post,* May 2, 1982, B4; Vincent Taylor, "Two Hundred and Fifty Thousand in Solidarity Day March," *Afro-American* (Baltimore), September 26, 1981, 1, 2; Nick Brown, "Local Citizens Oppose Budget Cuts," *Los Angeles Sentinel,* March 26, 1981, 2A; "Chicago Coalition to Fight Reagan Cuts in Welfare," *Chicago Tribune,* March 16, 1981, sec. 4, 1.

48. R. C. Longworth, "Welfare 'Moving Day' Shows Depth of Fear among Poor," *Chicago Defender,* September 30, 1981, sec. 1, 5; and Michigan Tenants Rights Coalition, "Federal Cutbacks Hurt the Poor," *MTRC Newsletter* (April 1981), Papers of the Commission on Community Relations, Walter Reuther Archives of Labor and Urban Affairs, Detroit, Mich., Wayne State University, box 121, folder 7, 1, 5. Housing also witnessed deep cuts. See Rachel Bratt, "Public Housing: The Controversy and Contribution," in *Critical Perspectives on Housing,* ed. Rachel Bratt, Chester Hartman, and Ann Meyerson (Philadelphia: Temple University Press, 1986), 335–361.

49. Bryner, *Great American Welfare Debate,* 72–73; and Handler, *Poverty of Welfare Reform,* 60–64, discuss the federal prodding of state welfare initiatives.

50. A detailed description of Wisconsin welfare initiatives and those elsewhere can be found in Bryner, *Great American Welfare Debate,* 95–100. Eddie Mae Binion of St. Louis's Southside Welfare Rights Organization compared workfare with slavery. See Donald Thompson, "Grassroots Oppose Workfare as New Slavery," *St. Louis Argus,* February 25, 1982, 2–1.

51. Frank Phillips, "Welfare Budget Violates Court Order, Groups Allege," *Boston Globe,* January 31, 1988, 26; Stevens, "Welfare Rights Organizing Saved My Life," 321–322; Simon Anekwe, "Rally for Public Assistance," *Amsterdam News,* April 5, 1980, 22.

52. Richard Meislin, "New York Senate Votes to Raise Welfare Grants 15%," *New York Times,* February 24, 1981, B6; Kelly Lewis, "Tent City Protest Going to Lansing, Advocates for Needy Will Build 'Englerville,'" *Detroit Free Press,* December 2,1991, 1B; editorial, Charles Adams, "Lansing: Power to the People," *Michigan Chronicle,* January 22, 1992, 7A.

53. Hamilton and Hamilton, *Dual Agenda,* 225–235; see Kramer, interview by author; and Robert Anderson, "March Staged to Protest Policies toward the Poor," *Atlanta Journal and Constitution,* July 25,1988, E(5)1; and Handler, *Poverty of Welfare,* 95.

54. Kramer, interview by author; quotation from Abramovitz, *Under Attack, Fighting Back,* 132–133; Claire Cummings and Betty Reid Mandell, "Finding Voice: Building beyond Community at Survival News," *For Crying Out Loud,* 163–181; Judi Russell, "Welfare Reforms Are Sought," *Times-Picayune* (La.), July 16, 1989, 1, 2.

55. Jane Mansbridge, *Why We Lost the ERA* (Chicago: University of Chicago Press, 1986); Taylor, "Social Movement Continuity," 772–773; Michael McCann, *Rights*

at Work: Pay Equity Reform and the Politics of Legal Mobilization (Chicago: University of Chicago Press, 1987).

56. Abramovitz, *Under Attack, Fighting Back;* Kramer, interview by author.
57. Kramer, interview by author; Maureen Taylor, interview by author, November 14, 1994; Stevens, "Welfare Rights Organizing Saved My Life," 322.
58. Kramer gave the author a detailed interview with regard to the activities between NOW and NWRU. This alliance and the "Committee of 100" were also discussed by Abramovitz, *Under Attack, Fighting Back,* 134–136; Mardi Davis, *"Now Is the Time:* Mainstream Feminism's Statement on Welfare Rights," in *For Crying Out Loud,* 337–340; and Eva Keder Kittay, "Dependency, Equality, and Welfare," *Feminist Studies* 24, no. 1 (Spring 1998): 32–43.
59. Abramovitz, *Under Attack, Fighting Back,* 132–134.
60. J. Zambga Browne, "Rev. Al Sharpton Marches on to Albany: Numbers Swell as Peaceful Rallies Held," *Amsterdam News,* March 18, 1995, 4; Mark Fearer, "Welfare Moms Organize," *Progressive,* February 1996, 60, 18; "Christians Protest Welfare Cutbacks," *Christianity Today,* February 5, 1996.
61. Jonathan Hicks, "At Once of Campaign, a Protest on Welfare," *New York Times,* August 9, 1996, B1, B4.
62. Mare Cooper, "When Push Comes to Shove: Who Is Welfare Reform Really Helping?" *Nation,* June 2, 1997; "Activists Take to Streets to Blast Welfare-to-Work Job Shortage," *Chicago Defender,* December 11, 1997, 1; Chinta Straausberg, "Chicago Joins Nation in National Welfare 'Fight Back' Rally," *Chicago Defender,* December 8, 1997, 1, 8; Rachel Melcer, "March to Protest Federal Welfare Reform," *Chicago Tribune,* March 10, 1997, 2C.
63. Kensingston Welfare Rights Union, "We Refuse to Lose!" *Home Page* (February 22, 1998), <*http://www.libertynet.org/80/~kwru/kwru.htm*>. U.S. House Committee on Government Operations, Human Resources and Intergovernmental Relations Subcommittee, *Ending Welfare as We Know It: Progress or Paralysis?* 103d Congress, 2d sess., March 10, 1994, 42–51.

Ten Black Political Leadership in the Post–Civil Rights Era

1. John Hope Franklin and Alfred A. Moss Jr., *From Slavery to Freedom: A History of African Americans* (New York: Alfred A. Knopf, 2000); Andrew Hacker, *Two Nations: Black, White, Separate, Hostile, Unequal* (New York: Ballantine Books, 1992).
2. Hanes Walton Jr., *Invisible Politics: Black Political Behavior* (Albany: State University of New York Press, 1985); Ronald V. Dellums, "For Change or for Status Quo?" *Black Scholar* 8, no. 4 (1977): 2–5.
3. William Julius Wilson and Loic J. D. Wacquant, "The Cost of Racial and Class Exclusion in the Inner City," *Annals* 501, no. 22 (1989): 8–25; Christopher Jencks and Paul Peterson, *The Urban Underclass* (Washington, D.C.: Brookings Institution, 1991); Norman Fainstein, "Black Ghettorization and Social Mobility," in *The Bubbling Cauldron,* ed. Michael Peter Smith and Joe R. Feagin (Minneapolis: University of Minnesota Press, 1995), 123–141; Douglass S. Massey and Nancy A. Denton, *American Apartheid* (Cambridge, Mass.: Harvard University Press, 1993); Yvette Alex-Assensoh, *Neighborhoods, Family, and Political Behavior in Urban America* (New York: Garland, 1998).

4. Jonathan Kozol, *Savage Inequalities: Children in America's Schools* (New York: Harper, 1992); Gary Orfield and Carole Ashkinaze, *The Closing Door: Conservative Policy and Black Opportunity* (Chicago: University of Chicago Press, 1991).

5. Franklin and Moss, *From Slavery to Freedom*, 453.

6. Linda Williams, "Black Political Progress in the 1980s: The Electoral Arena," in *The New Black Politics*, ed. Michael B. Preston, Lenneal J. Henderson Jr., and Paul L. Puryear (New York: Longman, 1987).

7. Robert C. Smith, *We Have No Leaders: African-Americans in the Post–Civil Rights Era* (Albany: State University of New York Press, 1996).

8. Peter K. Eisenger, "Black Mayors and the Politics of Racial Economic Advancement," *Culture, Ethnicity and Identity: Current Issues in Research*, ed. William McCready (New York: Academic Press, 1985); Hacker, *Two Nations;* Lucius Barker and Jesse J. McCorry, *Black Americans and the Political System* (Cambridge, U.K.: Winthrop Publishers, 1980); Marguerite Ross Barnett, "The Congressional Black Caucus: Symbol, Myth and Reality," *Black Scholar* 8, no. 4 (1977): 17–26; Clinton B. Jones, "The Impact of Local Election Systems on Black Political Representation," *Urban Affairs Quarterly* 11, no. 3 (1990): 345–356.

9. Smith, *We Have No Leaders.*

10. Adolph Reed, "Demobilization in the New Black Political Regime: Ideological Capitulation and Radical Failure in the Postsegregation Era," in *The Bubbling Cauldron*, ed. Michael Peter Smith and Joe Feagin (Minneapolis: University of Minnesota Press, 1995).

11. Chandler Davidson, *Quiet Revolution in the South: The Impact of the Voting Right Act of 1965* (Princeton, N.J.: Princeton University Press, 1990).

12. Rufus Browning, Dale R. Marshall, and David Tabb, eds., *Racial Politics in American Cities* (New York: Longman, 1990); Betty Woody, *Managing Crisis Cities* (Westport, Conn.: Greenwood Press, 1982); Manning Marable, *Beyond Black and White: Transforming African-American Politics* (New York: Verso, 1995).

13. Barker and McCorry, *Black Americans and the Political System;* Walton, *Invisible Politics.*

14. Robert Starks and Michael B. Preston, "Harold Washington and the Politics of Reform in Chicago: 1983–1987," in Browning, Marshall, and Tabb, *Racial Politics in American Cities,* 1–243.

15. Smith, *We Have No Leaders.*

16. David R. Mayhew, *Congress: The Electoral Connection* (New Haven, Conn.: Yale University Press, 1974).

17. Reed, "Demobilization in the New Black Political Regime."

18. Browning, Marshall, and Tabb, *Racial Politics in American Cities,* 1–243.

19. Franklin and Moss, *From Slavery to Freedom.*

20. Michael Dawson, *Behind the Mule: Race and Class in African American Politics* (Princeton, N.J.: Princeton University Press, 1994).

21. Akwasi B. Assensoh, "Conflict or Cooperation? Africans and African Americans in Multiracial America," in *Black and Multiracial Politics in America,* ed. Yvette Alex-Assensoh and Lawrence Hanks (New York: New York University Press, 2000).

22. Adam Nossiter, "A Convert Goes Home to Minister as a Minister," *New York Times,* March 3, 1997, A13.

23. David Garrow, *Bearing the Cross: Martin Luther King, Jr. and the Southern Christian Leadership Conference* (New York: Random House, 1988).

24. William J. Wilson, *The Declining Significance of Race* (Chicago: University of Chicago Press, 1980); Hacker, *Two Nations;* Dawson, *Behind the Mule.*

25. Eisenger, "Black Mayors and the Politics of Racial Economic Advancement."

26. Hacker, *Two Nations;* William J. Wilson, *The Truly Disadvantaged* (Chicago: University of Chicago Press, 1987); Dennis Judd and Paul Kantor, *Enduring Tensions in Urban Politics* (New York: Macmillan, 1993); Brett Williams, *Human Organizations* 51, no. 2 (1992): 164–174.

27. Paula D. McClain and Joseph Stewart Jr., *Can We All Get Along? Racial and Ethnic Minorities in American Politics* (Boulder, Colo.: Westview Press, 1995).

28. *Jet,* February 1997.

Eleven   Where Do We Go from Here?

Epigraph: Johnson's words appear in the *Cleveland Policy Planning Report,* vol. 1 (1975): 1, quoted in William W. Goldsmith, "Taking Back the Inner City: A Review of Recent Proposals," in *The Inner City: Urban Poverty and Economic Development in the Next Century,* ed. Thomas D. Boston and Catherine L. Ross (New Brunswick, N.J.: Transaction, 1997).

1. See Manning Marable, "The Gary Black Political Convention of 1972," in *Civil Rights since 1787: A Reader on the Black Struggle,* ed. Jonathan Birnbaum and Clarence Taylor (New York: New York University Press, 2000), 638.

2. See "The Gary Declaration: Black Politics at the Crossroads," in *Let Nobody Turn Us Around: Voices of Resistance, Reform, and Renewal,* ed. Manning Marable and Leith Mullings (New York: Rowman and Littlefield, 2000).

3. Marable, "Gary Black Political Convention," 638.

4. Lucius Barker, Mack H. Jones, and Katherine Tate, *African Americans and the American Political System* (Upper Saddle River, N.J.: Prentice-Hall, 1999), 94–96.

5. Note that COINTELPRO and other counterintelligence measures contributed to the demobilization of Black nationalist and radical organizations and leaders.

6. Marable, "Gary Black Political Convention," 639.

7. Peggy Peterman, "A Decade of Pain and Gain: African Americans Suffered Setbacks, Enjoyed New Heights," *St. Petersburg Times,* December 29, 1989, 1D.

8. Adolph Reed, "Sources of Demobilization in the New Black Political Regime," in *Stirrings in the Jug: Black Politics in the Post-Segregation Era,* ed. Adolph Reed Jr. (Minneapolis: University of Minnesota Press, 1999), 128.

9. Manning Marable and Leith Mullings, "Principles of Unity" of the Black Radical Congress, in Marable and Mullings, *Let Nobody Turn Us Around,* 625.

10. Ibid., 626.

11. Ibid., 625–26.

12. Walter Williams, "Reparations Clangor," *Washington Times,* June 14, 2001, A16.

13. Reed, "Sources of Demobilization," 15.

14. See Ronald Walters, "The Black Radical Congress," *Washington Informer,* July 1, 1998, 15.

15. Salim Muwakkil, "Black Radicals Regroup," *In These Times,* September 4, 2000, 18.

16. National Count of Black Elected Officials (Washington, DC.: Joint Center for Political and Economic Studies, 1998).

17. Ibid.

18. Douglas S. Massey and Nancy A. Denton, "Hyper-Segregation in U.S. Metropolitan Areas: Blacks and Hispanic Segregation along Four Dimensions," *Demography* 26, no. 3 (August 1989): 373–391.

19. See U.S. Department of Housing and Urban Development, "The State of the Cities," report (Washington, D.C., June 1997).

20. See Gary Orfield, "Schools More Separate: Consequences of a Decade of Resegregation," Civil Rights Project, Harvard University, Cambridge, Mass., July 2001.

21. Salim Muwakkil, "The Hardest Sell in the Black Community," *Chicago Tribune,* July 6, 1998, 11 Zone, N.

22. "Measuring 50 Years of Economic Change," report, U.S. Census Bureau, September 1998, 19–20.

23. "Detailed Occupation by Race, and Hispanic Origin and Sex," report, U.S. Census Bureau, 1990.

24. "Black Owned Businesses," report, U.S. Census Bureau Statistical Brief, March 2001.

25. Barker, Jones, and Tate, *African Americans,* 217–221.

Contributors

AKWASI B. ASSENSOH received his Ph.D. degree in history from New York University. He is Associate Professor in the Department of Afro-American Studies at Indiana University, Bloomington. Among his many publications are *Rev. Dr. Martin Luther King, Jr., and America's Quest for Racial Integration* (1986) and *African Political Leadership* (1998).

YVETTE ALEX-ASSENSOH is Assistant Professor of Political Science at Indiana University. Her research and teaching interests include urban politics, minority politics, and political behavior. She is the author of *Neighborhoods, Family, and Political Behavior in Urban America* (1998) as well as several articles and book chapters. Her research has been supported by grants from the Social Science Research Council, the Ford Foundation, the National Academy of Education, and the National Science Foundation.

ALLISON CALHOUN-BROWN is Associate Professor of Political Science at Georgia State University. Her research and teaching interests include public opinion, religion and politics, and African American politics. She is particularly interested in the influence of churches and ministers on political behavior in the Black community. Calhoun-Brown's essay "Upon This Rock: The Black Church, Nonviolence, and the Civil Rights Movement" appeared in the June 2000 issue of *PS: Political Science and Politics.*

CLAUDE A. CLEGG III. earned a Ph.D. degree in history from the University of Michigan and is currently an Associate Professor of History at Indiana University at Bloomington. He specializes in modern U.S. history and the

African diaspora. He is the author of *An Original Man: The Life and Times of Elijah Muhammad* (1997).

ERIKA L. GORDON is a native of Pittsburgh, Pennsylvania, and a proud graduate of Spelman College. She received a Master's degree in American Politics from the University of Maryland in 1997 and has earned a graduate certificate in Women's Studies. She is currently a doctoral candidate at the University of Maryland, with research interests in women and politics, political economy, and political culture.

OLLIE A. JOHNSON III, Professor of Political Science at the Universidad San Francisco de Quito in Quito, Ecuador, received his Ph.D. degree in Political Science from the University of California at Berkeley. His most recent work is *Brazilian Party Politics and the Coup of 1964* (2001). He has written numerous other articles and book chapters on the Black Panther Party, the National Association for the Advancement of Colored People, race relations in the Americas, and regime change in cross-national perspective. He has lectured on African American politics and American race relations in the United States, Brazil, Colombia, Ecuador, and Japan.

VALERIE C. JOHNSON is Assistant Professor of Political Science at the University of Illinois at Chicago. She is the author of *Black Power in the Suburbs: The Myth or Reality of African American Suburban Political Incorporation* (2002), and for four years she conducted research and education policy analysis for Rev. Jesse L. Jackson Sr. and the Rainbow/PUSH Coalition. Her research interests include urban politics, U.S. government, African American politics, and education policy with a particular emphasis on the politics of urban education.

CHARLES E. JONES is the founding Chair and Associate Professor of African-American Studies at Georgia State University. He is the editor of *The Black Panther Party Reconsidered* (1998). His teaching and research interests center on African American politics. A well-known lecturer and essayist, his articles and essays have appeared in numerous publications including the *Journal of Black Studies, National Political Science Review,* and *Phylon.*

TODD C. SHAW is an Assistant Professor of Political Science at the University of Illinois at Urbana-Champaign. Specializing in African American politics, urban politics, social movements, and public policy, he is completing a book manuscript entitled *"Now Is the Time!" Detroit Black Politics and Opportuni-*

ties for Grassroots Activism. Shaw has coauthored an essay that appeared in the *Journal of Politics.*

ROBERT C. SMITH is a professor of Political Science at San Francisco State University. He is the author of *We Have No Leaders: African Americans in the Post–Civil Rights Era* (1996) and coauthor (with Ronald Walters) of *African American Leadership* (1999) as well as numerous other books, articles, and reviews on African American politics. He is currently compiling an encyclopedia of African American politics.

KARIN L. STANFORD is a former Assistant Professor of Political Science and African American Studies at the University of Georgia. She also served as bureau chief of the Washington, D.C., Office of the Rainbow/PUSH Coalition between 1997 and 1999. Her research and teaching interests include African American politics, African Americans and international affairs, and gender and politics. She is the author of *Beyond the Boundaries: Reverend Jesse Jackson in International Affairs* (1997). She has received numerous awards, including the National Conference of Black Political Scientists Outstanding Book Award (1998), a Congressional Black Caucus Fellowship, and a postdoctoral fellowship from the University of North Carolina, Chapel Hill.

JENNIFER A. WADE is an Assistant Professor of Nonprofit and Public Management at the University of Colorado at Denver's Graduate School of Public Affairs. Her teaching emphasis is nonprofit and public management, fund raising, social change, and ethics. Her research interests include alternative funding sources for nonprofit organizations and sports philanthropy.

F. CARL WALTON is an Assistant Professor of Political Science and Director of the Edmonds Leadership Program at Morris Brown College in Atlanta, Georgia. He has also taught at the University of Georgia in Athens. His research interests include Blacks in legislatures and political organizations.

BRIAN N. WILLIAMS serves as Assistant Dean for Student Affairs at the Vanderbilt University School of Engineering, while on leave from his faculty appointment at the Askew School of Public Administration and Policy at Florida State University. His areas of research include community-oriented governance, facilitative government, community policing, community building, and the impact of racial profiling on citizen-police agency integration in the coproduction of public safety and order. Recently, he was appointed Coeditor of the *Journal of the Black Professoriate.*

Index